CREATIVE COLLABORATION

CREATIVE COLLABORATION

Vera John-Steiner

OXFORD
UNIVERSITY PRESS

2000

OXFORD
UNIVERSITY PRESS

Oxford   New York
Athens   Auckland   Bangkok   Bogotá   Buenos Aires   Calcutta
Cape Town   Chennai   Dar es Salaam   Delhi   Florence   Hong Kong   Istanbul
Karachi   Kuala Lumpur   Madrid   Melbourne   Mexico City   Mumbai
Nairobi   Paris   São Paulo   Shanghai   Singapore   Taipei   Tokyo   Toronto   Warsaw

and associated companies in
Berlin   Ibadan

Copyright © 2000 by Vera John-Steiner

Published by Oxford University Press, Inc.
198 Madison Avenue, New York, New York 10016

Oxford is a registered trademark of Oxford University Press.

Library of Congress Cataloging-in-Publication Data
John-Steiner, Vera, 1930–
Creative collaboration / Vera John-Steiner.
    p. cm.
Includes bibliographical references and index.
ISBN 0-19-506794-0
1. Creative thinking.   2. Creation (Literary, artistic, etc.)
3. Artistic collaboration.   4. Authorship—Collaboration.   I. Title.
BF408 .J48 2000
153.3'5—dc21   99-053187

9 8 7 6 5 4 3 2 1

Printed in the United States of America
on acid-free paper

To dia

To my magic circle of family, friends, collaborators, and students.

who is part of my magic circle

Vera
Nov. 2011

ACKNOWLEDGMENTS

Collaboration is not only the topic of this book but also, in large part, the context in which it was created. While writing it, I was also deeply involved in research on large-scale interdisciplinary groups with several collaborative partners: Michele Minnis, Holbrook Mahn, Teresa Meehan, Kathryn Miller, and Bob Weber. *Creative Collaboration*, with its focus on dyads and small groups, is a close-up look at collaboration. It is part of, but distinguishable from, the larger ongoing project.

My work was inspired by my research partners, enriched by our diverse experiences, and sustained by our shared vision. Ideas traveled between us in the research and writing and were inextricable, one from the other. We lectured in many places on the emerging results of our work and also spent endless hours writing research grants. Our own interactions throughout these endeavors provided insights into the frequently hidden dynamics of collaboration. The prevalent cultural model of the solitary creator is challenged throughout this book. Our thinking together made breaking away from received wisdom possible. While writing, I hear my partners' voices, I cherish what they taught me, I build on what we taught each other.

My partner in life, Reuben Hersh, loves the written word. He read this manuscript as it was developed, questioned the meanings, and made steady, wonderful improvements to the text. Teresa Meehan's unfailing caring and willingness to address both necessary details and large issues were critical to the crafting of this book. I was helped by Carolyn Kennedy at both the beginning and the end of this project, by Mera Wolf's keen ear for language and dazzling computer skills, and by Seana Moran's unwavering commitment and brilliant editing of the final draft.

My daughter Suki John's choreography is profoundly collaborative, and her commitment to this work is by word and example. My sons, Sandor and Paul, and my granddaughter Laura gave me moral and practical support.

Friends were vital to keep this project alive and growing. I thank, in particular, Courtney Cazden, Susan Ervin-Tripp, Lily Wong Fillmore,

Joe Glick, Shirley Brice Heath, Enid Howarth, Ruth and Paul Kovnat, Marcia Landau, Jay Lemke, Charlotte Marzani, Carolyn Panofsky, Barbara Rogoff, Dan Slobin, and Constance Sutton for their sustained trust, support, and wisdom.

I belong to a "virtual thought" community, the computer network "Mind, Culture and Activity" (xmca for short). The participants forge connections while respecting disciplined disagreement. From them I learned a new way to shape knowledge jointly. One member, Yrjo Engestrom, used his deep knowledge of teamwork and Activity Theory to make kind and thoughtful suggestions to improve this manuscript.

I started this work in the spring of 1990 at the Center for Advanced Study in the Behavioral Sciences in Palo Alto. That magic hill is a model for exchanging ideas, for learning from friendly Fellows about interesting developments in their disciplines, and for finding new directions to one's thought. I am grateful to the staff at the center, and to the Spencer Foundation, which helped support my stay.

Grants from the National Science Foundation and the University of New Mexico (UNM) contributed to developing the theoretical framework my partners and I rely on. These funds assisted with travel and with the transcription of the many interviews central to this book. The interdisciplinary focus of the work was recognized by colleagues and administrators at UNM. Their solicitude and cheer helped to complete this endeavor.

My students at the University of New Mexico helped me see how this research is linked to collaborative innovations in teaching. They challenged, shared, and co-constructed ideas, and enriched my academic life. I spent a wonderful year (1993–94) at the Graduate Center of the City University of New York, where I enjoyed thoughtful conversations with colleagues and students. Invitations to Holland, Finland, Brazil, Denmark, and Hungary provided additional opportunities to explore collaborative thought.

My editors, Joan Bossert and Philip Laughlin, nurtured the work with encouragement, careful attention, and delightful conversations. I am most grateful to both of them.

I t seems certain that the twentieth century will be seen by history as the century of the individual, at least in mainstream western cultures if not everywhere. For better and sometimes for worse, the right of each individual to chart a course without constraint reached its apotheosis a decade or two before the twenty-first century arrived. In U.S. culture, the social and cultural experiments of the 1960s, which put freedom of expression above all other values, gave way to the remarkable self-absorption of the 1970s and the culturally admired greed and self-promotion of the 1980s, perhaps best expressed in Tom Wolfe's book (and film based on the book) *The Bonfire of the Vanities*. Finally, at century's end, a sense of increased social and cultural awareness along with a greater valuing of family, community, and national and global harmony has begun to emerge.

Although it is not widely known, the greatest developmental theorist of the twentieth century played an important role in bringing about the revolution that placed the individual self as the highest and most valuable element in western society. Jean Piaget, born in 1896, fashioned a theory of intellectual development that placed a lone seeker of knowledge (an "epistemic subject" as he called it) at the center of the developmental process. Each individual, according to Piaget, must *construct* or create increasingly sophisticated instruments for knowing and understanding the world. Although others might play a support role in this effort, each person must accomplish the goals of cognitive development largely alone.

Because Piaget's theory is usually interpreted as about *universal* qualities of mind over time, that is, qualities shared by all individuals in all cultures across all periods of history, it is not hard to understand why the role of Piaget's theory in promoting the single individual might be missed. But essential to Piaget's epistemology is the idea that *each person* has control of his or her own development, is *individually* responsible for creating more powerful structures for perceiving and interpreting the world, and arrives at the pinnacle of mind's power under *one's own command*. Piaget gave form to a twentieth-century version of free will that provided each person ownership over and responsibility for the development of structures for achieving knowledge and understanding.

Versions of Piaget's claims about individual development entered the conversation as early as the 1920s, but it was not until the 1950s (at least in North America) that they really "took." In the postwar preoccupations with rebuilding and preparing for a nuclear confrontation with new collectivist adversaries, the so-called cognitive revolution took firm root in the West, with Piaget as its champion, inspiration, and guide. During the sixties, seventies, and well into the eighties, Piaget and the Genevan establishment dominated the academic field of cognitive development. And so, perhaps paradoxically, the theory that asserted the universality of mind and its development among all peoples in all societies, also gave voice to the distinctively twentieth-century belief that individuals are responsible for themselves and have the right to become whatever kind of person they choose to be.

As in all broad portraits important details are missing. The picture, however generally accurate it may be, is never as clear and focused as it seems. When history is written, it inevitably chooses certain themes to highlight and others to subdue. Few, I believe, would question the general accuracy of the claim that the century just ended marked the moment in history when preoccupations with individual freedom and expression reached their peak. On the other hand, and especially in the latter half of the century, cross- and countercurrents gathered force, especially in North America, that began to prepare us for what is to come as we enter the twenty-first century (as reckoned, of course, by the standard Western calendar; marking time is a cultural artifact, to be sure).

In the United States, the civil rights movement made its presence felt at midcentury, and this movement to address centuries-long discrimination against black peoples catalyzed other organized efforts to gain greater acceptance of differences in gender, sexual orientation, and condition. The feminist movement (which has a prominent role in the book you are about to read), gay and lesbian rights, and demands to provide access, resources, and accommodations to those with various limitations and challenges (e.g., wheelchair ramps, interpreters for the hearing impaired) were actively and productively pursued. There is a sense in which each of these political movements could be seen as additional expressions of individual preoccupations, but they required group identification and transcended individual purposes.

As the wider society became increasingly aware of and willing to accommodate greater diversity, the scholarly world was rediscovering a contemporary of Piaget whose work had been long suppressed in his native Russia. As the Cold War between the former Soviet Union and the United States moved toward melt instead of the dreaded meltdown, works of Lev Vygotsky began to appear in the West. As

Jerome Bruner has written in "The Inspiration of Vygotsky", Piaget's star in the capitalist, individualist Western sky began to fade as the star of the collectivist, social, relationship-oriented Vygotsky rose dramatically in the East."

And what a rise it has been! With its fundamental commitment to relationship as the central ingredient in human development, Vygotsky showed how the young are brought into the thought community by caring and attentive others. Although he did not deny Piaget's claim that individuals strive on their own to achieve an understanding of their world, he argued that a uniquely human reliance on the gifts that can be conveyed only by other members of one's society and culture is the hallmark of our species' development. With speech as the example of this process par excellence, Vygotsky described how children are shown how to enter, acquire the forms of, and fully participate in the speech community. To be human, for Vygotsky, means to achieve full membership and full access to the most prized intellectual and cultural resources that one's society has to offer, with speech and language as utterly central to these purposes.

Finally, a theory had emerged (or reemerged, properly speaking) to help restore balance to the excesses of a century-long preoccupation with individual development. Ironic, perhaps, that it took a Marxist-inspired, collectivist, Russian revolutionary theory of development to provide a counterweight to Piaget's extreme individualism, but that is what Vygotsky's work has begun to do. It would be difficult to overestimate the influence on the present book of Vygotsky and those who have tried to follow his lead, an influence that Vera John-Steiner acknowledges at many points and in many ways in *Creative Collaboration*.

The central theme of this book is exquisitely Vygotskian: working together productively toward shared goals is a human activity unique and valuable in its contributions to individual and social well-being. Even when considering achievements typically believed to be individually created such as Einstein's theory of relativity or Darwin's theory of evolution, John-Steiner shows the unmistakable signs of collaboration, joint effort, and social support necessary to worthwhile human endeavors. The individual is not lost in John-Steiner's account (as is the case, for example, in some of the more extreme "contextualist" explanations of human activity); the individual is, rather, put into appropriate context as part of a uniquely human set of processes for productive, satisfying, successful contributions to knowing and understanding ourselves and our world.

One of the great merits of this book is that it provides a kind of map of the territory of collaborative activity. As is appropriate when first exploring a new place, John-Steiner wants to first bring back from the field observations and best guesses about the nature of the terrain she has discovered. What are its likely conceptual dimensions? What are the main distinctive features that strike the observer on first encounter? How large an area of theoretical, conceptual, empirical, and practical activity are we likely to find? Although it may seem hard to believe, the work presented in the pages to follow is one of the first efforts to study adult collaboration and group activity from the perspective of a cognitive developmental psychologist. Befitting the work's pioneer status, the methods used are largely informal case studies and interviews. Based on these initial forays, John-Steiner lays out before us a set of guides and landmarks to help us find our way within the almost untouched territory she has discovered.

We are provided revealing glimpses into a number of different forms of collaboration: scientific partnerships such as that of Watson and Crick, forged to crack the genetic code; artistic collaborations of great value, including that of Georgia O'Keeffe and Alfred Stieglitz; feminist collaborations such as the group led by Carol Gilligan, the results of which have helped inspire new methods and new values in scholarship; mentor relationships; collaborations across generations; partnerships between lovers, and mates; and "thought communities" that are formed to jointly accomplish what an unyoked mind cannot.

With the light touch that only a gifted writer can provide, John-Steiner takes the reader from place to place almost as if we are with her when she visits, interviews, travels, and reflects on what she has found. The author seems to want to model collaboration even as she does her work, making sure we know that what we are reading came about through long-standing joint efforts with her students, her life partner, her colleagues in various fields, her teachers, her contemporaries, and her predecessors. She is especially mindful of the efforts of the cadre of scholars (of which she is a prominent one herself) who have helped bring the perspective of Vygotsky into the mainstream of developmental theory and research: Michael Cole, Sylvia Scribner, Barbara Rogoff, Jaan Valsiner, James Wertsch, and others who are part of John-Steiner's own loosely connected "thought community."

It is of course always hazardous to predict what impact a particular work will have, as looking backward is so much easier than trying to look forward. I believe that *Creative Collaboration* will be a work of great interest to the scholarly field and to the wider community as well. The book seems to speak to what will be the central theme of the coming century, namely how to strike a balance between individuality and social connectedness. We have pushed the theme of individuality to (some might say beyond) its limits, and have recently discovered a framework that helps us see the essential role that relationship, participation, reciprocity, membership, and collaboration must play in any theory of human development that aspires to guide us through the challenges ahead.

Creative Collaboration may well be seen in the future as the opening few bars of an opera that gives voice to an age, that captures the deepest and most significant themes of an era and propels it forward to the next act. In keeping with the theme of the book you are about to enjoy, it will, of course, take many composers and others in the troupe, as well as sophisticated audiences and a wider public to support the creation of this story as it unfolds.

As we move from the Age of the Individual to the Era of Community, this book helps lead the way, with care, tact, vision, and sophistication. As John-Steiner reminds us, "Together we create our future." She is right about this, of course, but we nonetheless tend to look for guidance from those whose vision gives shape to that future and who possess the wisdom and courage and determination to lead us in the right direction. Vera John-Steiner exemplifies just these qualities in this book, and you are about to meet her.

David Henry Feldman
Tufts University

CONTENTS

CREATIVE COLLABORATION

INTRODUCTION

We have come to a new understanding of the life of the mind. The notion of the solitary thinker still appeals to those molded by the Western belief in individualism. However, a careful scrutiny of how knowledge is constructed and artistic forms are shaped reveals a different reality. Generative ideas emerge from joint thinking, from significant conversations, and from sustained, shared struggles to achieve new insights by partners in thought.

In this book, I address intellectual and artistic collaboration—the interdependence of thinkers in the co-construction of knowledge[1]—among partners and in small groups. This exploration is sustained by a growing community of scholars who view learning and thinking as social processes. This large "thought community" of interactive scholars committed to transformation has a diverse membership; it includes social scientists, philosophers, literary critics, educators, organization theorists, and media specialists. We share a recognition that in our changing world, traditional concepts are overturned at an increasing rate, habitual modes of work are transformed, and new organizational forms are established in offices and factories. These changes are usually painful for the participants, who often cannot make these adjustments by themselves. We live in a period of "necessary interdependence," wrote educator Kenneth Bruffee.[2] It is through joint activities and partnerships that we confront our shifting realities and search for new solutions. This historical and technological context promotes collaboration in science, artistic endeavors, universities, industrial settings, and schools.

The examples of partnerships in this book are drawn primarily from the joint activities of creative individuals. These are people who have chosen to pursue discovery and the co-construction of new knowledge within specific domains such as art, physics, psychology, or music. They face many hardships and reap many joyous rewards. Their lives reveal some interesting *dynamics of mutuality, which are not restricted to artists and scientists, but are relevant to people in every walk of life.* In collaborative work we learn from each other by teaching what we know; we engage in mutual appropriation. Solo prac-

3

tices are insufficient to meet the challenges and the new complexities of classrooms, parenting, and the changing workplace. These widespread developments have resulted in a large, growing body of research literature.[3] There is a shared interest in collaborative dynamics among interdisciplinary scholars who study large and small groups. My own focus is on creative partnerships, many which last a decade or more, as opposed to the shorter duration of cooperative teams. My choice of smaller groups and dyads is motivated by the desire to understand the psychological nature of collaborations. Creative collaborators provide important insights for ways to build joint projects, and their practices challenge mainstream theories focused on the individual.

Recently, powerful statements about interdependence have been made by members of diverse disciplines. The importance of cooperative work in film, musical performance, and the theater is clear to casual observers. Sociologist of art Howard Becker wrote that, even in painting and poetry, "the artist . . . works in the center of a network of cooperating people whose work is essential to the final outcome." [4] Collaboration has been widely recognized in the sciences, from the founding of quantum mechanics by Bohr and Heisenberg to the joint discovery of DNA structure by Crick and Watson, to the work of an increasingly long list of researchers in the physical and biological sciences. Even among writers, the role of the individual creator is questioned. Tony Kushner, author of *Angels in America* and *Perestroika*, told of his artistic interdependence with his friends and partners: "The fiction that artistic labor happens in isolation, and that artistic accomplishment is exclusively the provenance of individual talents, is politically charged, and in my case at least repudiated by the facts. . . . Had I written these plays without the participation of my collaborators, they would be entirely different—would in fact never have come to be."[5]

My book has three interrelated objectives: to develop theoretical approaches and models for collaboration; to identify collaborative dynamics that contribute to or undermine long-term success; and to document how experienced thinkers engage in joint efforts as they struggle against society's pull toward individual achievement.

Artistic partnerships are richly documented by humanities scholars Whitney Chadwick and Isabelle de Courtivron. In their edited volume of case studies, *Significant Others: Creativity and Intimate Partnerships*, they explored the myths and realities encountered in shared lives.[6] In this engrossing book of artistic collaborations between couples, they provided a dialogic view of creativity. The contributors to this volume examined "the real social and material conditions which enable, or inhibit, the creative life"[7] while relying upon the analytical tools of art history and criticism.

Documenting increasing prevalence and acceptance of collaboration between spouses in the sciences, Pycior, Slack and Abir-Am wrote, in their introduction to *Creative Couples in the Sciences*:

> In explaining synergistic couples, many authors emphasize the complementarity—drawn along the lines of disciplinary commitment, socially constructed gender, personality, or scientific style —that seems to have permitted some couples to do scientific work that surpassed what either the husband or wife alone would have been able to accomplish or the wife alone would have been able to pursue.[8]

Like *Creative Couples in the Sciences*, my book also explores artistic and scientific partnerships. Unlike *Creative Couples in the Sciences*, my accounts of these collaborations are integrated with theoretical approaches drawn from cultural-historical and feminist theories.

I rely on L. S. Vygotsky's cultural-historical ideas that creative activities are social, that thinking is not confined to the individual brain/ mind, and that construction of knowledge is embedded in the cultural and historical milieu in which it arises. His work focused on the dynamic interdependence of social and individual processes, especially language in thought, that leads to co-construction of knowledge, tools, and artifacts.

Vygotsky realized that works of art, mathematical systems, maps, and drawings all contribute to representational activity, to the multiple ways in which self and other are built and connected. An individual learns, creates, and achieves mastery in and through his or her relationships with other individuals. Ideas, tools, and processes that emerge from joint activity are appropriated, or internalized, by the individual and become the basis of the individual's subsequent development.[9] Vygotsky's contemporary, Russian literary critic Mikhail Bakhtin, elaborated on similar notions of experiencing the self through the eyes of the other: "I cannot do without the other; I cannot become myself without the other; I must find myself in the other, finding the other in me."[10] Vygotsky, in his own work, thrived on such interdependence with his collaborators.

This book is part of the broader cultural-historical project in the human sciences. The participants in this project share assumptions about the roles of culture, context, and history in development throughout the lifespan. We stress the dynamic interdependence of social and individual processes as conceptualized by Vygotsky. His work is both applied to and expanded in this treatment of collaborative, creative partnerships.

Feminist theories further echo the idea of the interrelationship of self and other. They challenge our current cultural and professional socialization in which the emphasis on individuation and autonomy prevails. They propose alternative relational/cultural theories that emphasize mutuality and interdependence. For example, I rely upon the voices of Carol Gilligan, Jean Baker Miller, the authors of *Women's Ways of Knowing*, and many other thinkers who have written about development as a process of growth and transformation within communities of care. Communities of care, with their ethic of responsibility, contrast with the individualistic, autonomous viewpoints, with their ethic of rights and impartiality, that are measured by most traditional psychological tests.[11] In addition, I draw on the perspective of "constructed knowing," which emphasizes situated, contextual, and integrated modes of thinking over the more traditional and prevalent separate mode of knowing.

Such feminist relational theories can be linked to other approaches concerned with the social origins of personhood, such as those of philosophers Ludwig Wittgenstein, Karl Marx, and Michel Foucault. Their notion of "social selves" examines how identities are socially constructed and shaped by participation in the communities and cultures in which the individual lives. [12]

Both cultural-historical theory and feminist theory share the belief that it is important to go beyond the popular narratives of individualism when studying human activity. There are important philosophical affinities between these traditions, such as the social sources of development, the importance of culturally patterned practices and power relations, issues of language and self, and the mutually constituting roles of self and community.[13] The contributions of scholars in these two theoretical thought communities, or groups of experienced thinkers who engage in intense interaction with each other while promoting a perspective shift in their disciplines, are critical to this study of collaboration.

By studying long-term collaborations in detail, this book weaves together theory and accounts of collaborative experience. Although my original interests focused on the intellectual dynamics of joint efforts, additional themes emerged as I interviewed dozens of working partners and members of small collaborative groups. As the stories unfolded, they revealed themes of connection, fusion, transformation, conflict, and separation, which animate joint connections. Collaboration thrives on diversity of perspectives and on constructive dialogues between individuals negotiating their differences while creating their shared voice and vision. In addition, I identify cognitive and emotional dynamics of collaboration, which are more implied than explored in the existing literature on partnerships.

To investigate these issues, my colleague, Kathryn Miller, and I conducted focused interviews with experienced thinkers in the physical sciences, mathematics, philosophy, the social sciences, and the arts.

Following these interviews and an immersion in the growing literature on collaborative partnerships, we developed a "collaborative Q-sort." This measure is composed of 50 statements which deal with motivation for collaboration, styles of work, collaborative environments, and complementarity of roles. Each participant was asked to sort these statements into a bell-shaped distribution, ranging from the item that is most characteristic to the item that is least characteristic of the person's collaboration. During sorting, participants often shifted their cards until they were satisfied with the distribution. Some participants grouped their cards so they did not follow a strict bell curve. Others eliminated some cards as irrelevant to their experience. While we administered the sort, participants' comments were tape recorded. Each member of a collaboration completed the Q-sort independently. Then they were brought together to discuss the similarities and differences of their approaches as revealed by the placement of the Q-sort items and by their commentaries. (See the appendix for a copy of the Q-sort instrument.)

The chapters in this book integrate information gathered from interviews, Q-sort commentaries, and biographical information.

One of my central claims is that *the construction of a new mode of thought relies on and thrives with collaboration.* When scientists or artists reexamine old theories that conflict with new discoveries, insights, and perspectives, they find thinking together particularly productive. Complementarity is one of the driving forces of creative partnerships.

I start with narratives of joined lives and shared work in Chapter 1. When combining family life and creative work, couples face the challenge of overcoming traditional gender roles. Establishing equality between partners who are successful in meeting this challenge is a demanding process. In charting their trajectory, I introduce some of the collaborative dynamics central to this work.

In Chapter 2, I focus on scientists—their disciplinary, stylistic, and temperamental differences, and their productive interdependence. There are interesting modality differences among collaborating thinkers—visual, kinesthetic, or verbal—which are often expressed in scientific partnerships. Complementarity provides for the diversity and growth of science, but it can also provoke intense dialogues and principled disagreements, which can, at times, be daunting. Through the partners' unity of purpose, joint efforts prevail. I explore supportive as well as oppositional complementarity, connections that contribute to addressing and resolving paradoxes in facts and theories.

Chapter 3 focuses on artists. The partnerships of two painters, Picasso and Braque, and a composer-choreographer team, Stravinsky and Balanchine, are well documented. Their collaborations highlight the power of jointly constructed creative syntheses. At the height of a transformative partnership, as in the case of the originators of Cubism, individual identities and vanities are banished. The resulting work leads to the transformation of both the domain and the participants. Artists often face loneliness, poverty, and doubts about their ability, particularly in the early stages of their careers. Creative work requires a trust in oneself that is virtually impossible to sustain alone. Support is critical, as the very acts of imaginative daring contribute to self-doubt. Mentors, family members, friends, lovers, working partners, all may contribute to the forming of a resilient self. The "literate passion" of Anaïs Nin and Henry Miller, disclosed in their letters to each other, evokes the sustaining possibilities of artistic interdependence. Their relationship also illustrates the complex demands of intense connections. For this couple, as for many collaborators, their letters show that their changing rhythms of interaction—shifts between periods of interdependence and independence—were critical to their survival.

The impact of gender on collaboration is the topic I address in Chapter 4. Do men and women feel differently about the ownership of their ideas? How does the concept of "we" emerge in creative work? Feminist theories of relational dynamics and ways of knowing offer insight into the study of joined lives and shared work. I rely on the metaphor of "a chorus of voices which was to sing the story we wanted to tell; there were to be no solos."[14] This is how the authors of *Women's Ways of Knowing* characterized their construction of a joint authorship. Both the interest in and the practice of collaboration reflect changing cultural-historical realities. Some of the broader implications of these realities are discussed.

In Chapter 5, I discuss how patterns of collaboration vary in their cognitive and emotional dynamics. The norm for complementary partnerships is a caring, respectful relationship. In other collaboratives governed by a powerful transformative vision, emotional relationships are more intense. The title of the chapter, "Felt Knowledge," is borrowed from playwright Arthur Miller. It highlights the unity of thought and motive. Some of the motivational sources for collaboration include shared, passionate engagement with knowledge in dyads and groups devoted to groundbreaking endeavors. Emotional scaffolding creates a safety zone in which support and criticism are practiced. It also contributes to human plasticity, an opportunity for growth through mutual appropriation of complementary skills, attitudes, working methods, and beliefs. But lives in which work and love are intertwined require great sensitivity. In the marriage of Sylvia Plath and Ted Hughes, for example, their emotional interdependence became excessive, and the marriage ended in tragedy. In other cases, the struggles for equality, intimacy, and mutual support are smoothly negotiated.

In Chapter 6, I discuss mentoring with a special focus on the social sciences. Experienced thinkers value the commitment, talent, and curiosity of their younger partners, while the mentors, in turn, are renewed and rewarded in the process. At its best, collaboration across generations is a process of mutual appropriation rather than a simple transmission of knowledge. It can be a shared flight into the future.

In Chapter 7, I bring together theoretical concepts embedded in the many collaborative narratives presented in this book, including both cognitive and affective dynamics. I claim that partnered endeavors contribute to stretching the self while bringing changes to the domain in which the collaborators work. The extent to which collaboration results in transformative contributions depends on many factors: the shared vision and purpose of the partners, their talent and perseverance, and their timing. The confluence of diverse fields of endeavor can bring to the fore contributions that were neglected at the time of their production. As Vygotsky and biologist Ludwik Fleck proposed: historical and social forces contribute to the relevance or invisibility of newly forged ideas. In this book, historical, cultural, and institutional conditions, which shape the nature and meaning of collaboration, are not treated in depth. While I affirm their critical roles, I rely on the growing and rich literature authored by my colleagues to complement these studies of intimate and small-group collaborations.

In every phase of this work, my partners in thought and deed have helped to realize a durable "we"-ness, built on a shared vision, patience and time, careful planning, and a chance to be playful as well as critical with each other. I can but echo the words of playwright Tony Kushner: "Had I written this book without the participation of my collaborators and my family, it would be entirely different. In fact, it would have never come to be."

1
JOINED LIVES AND SHARED WORK

The varied ways in which we share and realize our intentions are powerfully embodied in collaborative endeavors. What are the dynamics of collaboration among intimates, between partners who share their work as well as their lives? Simone de Beauvoir's description of thinking together with Jean-Paul Sartre, her lifelong collaborator, captured many features of intimate partnerships:

> A woman friend has said that each of us listens to the other with great attention. Yet so assiduously have we always criticized, corrected and ratified each other's thoughts that we might almost be said to think in common. We have a common store of memories, knowledge and images behind us; our attempts to grasp the world are undertaken with the same tools, set within the same framework, guided by the same touchstones. Very often one of us begins a sentence and the other finishes it; if someone asks us a question, we have been known to produce identical answers. The stimulus of a word, a sensation, a shadow, sends us traveling along the same inner path, and we arrive simultaneously at a conclusion, a memory, an association completely inexplicable to a third person.[1]

Joint endeavors between intimates reveal a variety of patterns. In the pages that follow, I examine variations in mutual support, roles and responsibilities, shared values and objectives, and overt and covert forms of rivalry among partners and family members. These analyses are based on interviews as well as on published biographical accounts.

CREATIVE COUPLES AT WORK

Philosopher Will Durant met his wife when she was his student at a libertarian high school in New York. The young Ariel was raised in a family of Russian Jewish immigrants. Will was of Canadian Catholic background. His family had hoped that he would become a priest. Although he studied and later taught in a seminary, he eventually shifted to philosophy and became an enormously successful writer and lecturer. The Durants differed in age by thirteen years, and they had different educational experiences and temperaments. Ariel was a lively urban creature who loved the Bohemian life of Greenwich Village. Her husband, a more contemplative person, preferred the quiet beauty of the country.

Through the first twenty years of their marriage, Will Durant did most of the writing and lecturing. Slowly his wife became interested in some of his activities. At first she lectured on women's issues and Jewish themes, but after a joint trip to Russia in 1932, they both began lecturing on their experiences. In *Dual Autobiography*, they quoted their letters (mostly Will's) and reconstructed their shared lives.[2] In 1933, Ariel wrote:

> Wherever he [Will] went, in these years, he continued to prepare *The Story of Civilization*. I did not take part in providing material for the early volumes, but, so far as my duties and my few amusements allowed, I shared gladly in classifying the heaps of notes that Will had been gathering for *Our Oriental Heritage* and the *Life of Greece*. I gave up my Greenwich Village diversions and obligations. . . . I learned to love my home and my work. . . . It took me some time to realize how important a role was played in a book by the organization of material, and how the same contents less wisely arranged might have led to repetition, confusion, and failure. The mere organization (as distinct from gathering) of the material was the most back-breaking part of the total operation. Will undertook the original part.[3]

She further described how her husband divided his books into chapters and how he marked "each of the thirty thousand slips that had been gathered for Volume 1, according to the chapter that it belonged. . . . Our task was to read each slip and to number it according to the heading under which we judged it to belong."[4]

Thus, in the early stages of their joint work, Ariel, together with their daughter, helped with the organizational work. But more important, she presented him with alternative ideas and challenged some of his formulations or concepts. As he continued to travel and write, he occasionally asked her to take a more active role. At this stage, the pattern of their interactions can be thought of as *cooperative*. The participants in cooperative endeavors each make specific contributions to a shared task. However, their level of involvement may differ, as well as their sense of intellectual ownership of the resulting product. In the case of the Durants, at this early stage of their joint work, Will had the primary control over the text, and he made most of the basic decisions concerning the first volumes of *The Story of Civilization*. There can be a more fully realized equality in roles and responsibilities in collaborative activities in which the participants see themselves engaged in a joint task. I rely upon this distinction between cooperative and collaborative activities, developed by psychologists Damon and Phelps,[5] in analyzing different stages of joint endeavors and different dynamics in intellectual and artistic partnerships.

With each new volume of *The Story of Civilization*, Ariel's role grew and changed. She described her approach while working on Volume 4:

> Back in Los Angeles [in 1946–47] I went to work, five hours a day, classifying some thirty thousand slips of material gathered for *The Age of Faith*. As I proceeded, my interest in the Middle Ages grew. I, who had not had the slightest preparation, in heritage, schooling, or character, for understanding medieval Christianity, which I knew chiefly as the theory and practice of anti-Semitism, I discovered a dozen bright faces in those centuries of groping through darkness to dawn. . . . Will approached this task almost in a mood of dislike and despair. I, the neophyte, finding gems in that pile of clips, reminded him that those centuries included the wandering scholars, the love-warbling troubadours, the Gothic cathedrals, the story of Abelard and Heloise, the *Divine Comedy*, and the beginnings of Parliament; and I pleaded with him to do justice to the medieval Jews. Gradually his antipathy to the subject faded, his interest grew. . . .[6]

Preparing their next volume on the Renaissance, Will acknowledged a growing division of labor when he wrote in 1951:

> In some measure Ariel and I divided the European Renaissance between us. I buried myself in Petrarch, Boccacio, Alexander VI, Leonardo, Leo X, Raphael, Julius II, Michelangelo, and Machievelli, while she consumed with delight every extant word of Montaigne, and spread her love to that gourmet of women, Henry of Navarre and IV [*sic*] of France.[7]

Having taken a greater role in researching *The Renaissance* than in the previous four volumes, Ariel also became a stronger critical voice in her responses to the written product. Her husband wrote in 1953:

> Ariel, however, was not content with the book, and submitted certain criticisms that had much basis and force. It began well enough, she said, with an interesting chapter on Petrarch and Boccacio . . . but then I wandered from city to city, like another Baedeker, describing picture after picture until the result was a blur in the

reader's memory; and like an unregenerate Catholic, I whitewashed those scandalous Renaissance popes; this, Ariel felt, was a let-down from *The Age of Faith*. I mourned, but such dissent kept me from quite forgetting my place in the perspective of astronomic and literary galaxies. [8]

These recollections are interesting because they highlight the role of multiple perspectives in approaching these large themes. They also reveal a slowly shifting balance between the two partners. The Durants were able to productively use their differences in age and education. They were not stymied by their unequal status at the start of their relationship. Ariel, as the younger, less educated female partner, could have remained frozen in a subservient role throughout their long marriage. The position of an unpaid secretary or a devoted editor is quite common in the family lives of male writers, philosophers, and social scientists. One can only speculate as to why Will responded positively to his wife's growing intellectual maturity and wisdom, and was willing to establish a more mutual and equal partnership. Possibly, it is because both husband and wife were somewhat alienated from their communities of origin due to their unconventional marriage. Thus, they were emotionally dependent upon each other to a greater extent than are many married partners. When their interdependence was threatened by Will's frequent absences during his long, arduous lecture tours, Ariel was at first rebellious and resentful. But with the passage of time and their move to California from their native East Coast, she realized that she could assume a fuller role in their lives if she shared his work and "gave up [her] Greenwich Village diversions and obligations." She decided to assist her husband as a way to reconnect with him, and Will was grateful.

They continued to argue about the relative importance of certain historical figures (for instance, Luther versus Erasmus). These dialogues were important to the man who held the pen. In 1956, Will wrote: "*The Reformation* will be too long for the reader, but it will be as good a job as any I have done; and as you and I have fought over every page . . . you shared mightily in producing it."[9] And later that same year, Will continued, "My hand moves the pen in [the first few volumes of] *The Story of Civilization*, but the spirit is ours, and the work is a life-long collaboration."[10] At this stage of the Durants's shared efforts, their relationship shifted from cooperation to full collaboration. The change in Ariel's roles from helpmate and occasional commentator to a fully engaged partner, with responsibility for the central ideas in the latter volumes, illustrates this shift. Even more important was Will's decision in 1957 to coauthor the series:

As *The Age of Reason Begins* progressed, I saw that it was a cooperative labor, and that simple justice required that the title page should bear both of our names. Ariel has never asked for this. When she learned of it, she vowed to dedicate herself to the work. Now we proceeded hand in hand, topic by topic, volume by volume, united as we had never been before. It was as if our marriage had received a second consummation.[11]

Thus the Durants moved from being partners in dialogue who cooperated with each other to full-fledged collaborators. Their shared autobiography provides an important documentation of these changes. While they depended primarily on each other, their daughter assisted them in editorial work. Other family members also shared a variety of daily responsibilities with them. For stimulation, they relied on travel and books rather than on intense conversation with others, although they treasured personal friendships. In this they differed from other twentieth-century intellectuals who, particularly before the onset of the Second World War, were nourished by "conversational communities" (the term is borrowed from Lisa Tickner as cited in Chadwick and de Courtivron).[12]

Few accounts of spousal collaboration are as complete as that of the Durants. Most of them are reconstructions by biographers rather than ongoing records by the participants. The partnership of Jean-Paul Sartre and Simone de Beauvoir is recounted in her autobiographical volumes, in their letters, and in the interviews she conducted with Sartre at the end of his life when he started to lose his sight. Between periods of reading to him, de Beauvoir taped his comments on a variety of subjects. Some of these comments provide important insights into their relationship. Axel Madsen's book, *Hearts and Minds: The Common Journey of Simone de Beauvoir and Jean-Paul Sartre*, is another important document of these celebrated partners.[13]

Sartre and de Beauvoir never coauthored any books. They jointly established a philosophy that governed their writings (which included fiction, nonfiction, and drama). They first met at the Ecole Normale in Paris, where she joined him and his friends who were cramming for their final exams. De Beauvoir was invited as the expert on philosopher-scientist Gottlab Leibnitz. Thus they start their relationship at a more equal level than did the Durants—sharing a similar education and an equal commitment to the life of the mind.

They treasured their equality as well as their freedom. Although each of them had other intimate relationships, they did not allow any of these to threaten their primary commitment to each other. Sartre remarked during one of his interviews with de Beauvoir: "I had one special reader and that was you. When you said to me, 'I agree; it is all right,' then it was all right. I published the book and I didn't give a damn for the critics. You did me a great service. You gave me a confidence in myself that I shouldn't have had alone."[14]

De Beauvoir's description of their joint thinking reveals that their perceptions of the importance of the "other" was quite similar. Her account of finishing each other's sentences and of arriving at the same conclusions is of particular interest in light of Vygotsky's notion of the completeness of understanding between two individuals who may communicate using condensed verbal means. The example Vygotsky chose in *Thought and Language*[15] to illustrate linguistic condensation and "living in the other's mind" is drawn from Tolstoy's *Anna Karenina*: the declaration of love between Kitty and Levin where they use only initial letters to convey their thoughts and desires to each other. De Beauvoir evoked a similar process of "thinking in common" with Sartre.

The development of a new philosophy requires not only a powerful sense of self but also an ability to step back, to view one's notions from the perspective of the critic, and to know where one develops new ground and where one is borrowing or imitating. From the very beginning of their relationship, de Beauvoir was able and willing to support Sartre when he was formulating novel ideas. She was also a consistent and thoughtful critic, one whom Sartre trusted. Some of his key ideas, such as the concepts of freedom and action, ethics and praxis, and the pursuit of meaning were developed in his philosophical essays. They were given concrete shape in their shared political activities and in fiction and drama written by each of them.

There are many more examples of close collaboration among intimates where mutual support and criticism contribute greatly to each partner's success, or to the success of a single endeavor valued by both partners. The importance of such interdependence is particularly well chronicled by the members of the famous literary and artistic group known as the Bloomsbury group. Painters Vanessa Bell and Duncan Grant were part of that community, their lives entwined with Vanessa's sister Virginia Woolf, her husband Leonard, and with many other members of this group. Their daughter described their relationship in the following way: "Where Vanessa was timid and tentative Duncan would be audacious, and when he was disoriented she would be authoritative. She would straighten out his muddles, laugh at his perplexities, and when, as so often happened, her self-confidence failed her, he would support and reassure her."[16]

A fierce belief in the work of one's "significant other" as well as a willingness to criticize it characterizes most accounts of artistic and intellectual partnerships. Whether the two people actually paint, write, or choreograph together, or are engaged in each other's work less directly, their joint commitment and the ability to sustain a generative dialogue are crucial to successful partnerships.

Interviews with collaborators are useful in providing a specific account of living-working partnerships beyond those constructed from personal documents. Psychologists Howard Gruber and Doris Wallace talked to me in their New York City apartment in 1994 about their collaboration. Gruber's case-study approach to creativity is influential in psychology and among historians of science; he and his wife have expanded this theoretical framework in their coedited volume *Creative People at Work*.[17]

Their collaborative trajectory has some features in common with the Durants as well as with Sartre and de Beauvoir. They first met when Wallace returned to graduate school after a career in editing and Gruber was one of her professors. As in the case of the Durants, there was a difference in status between the two of them when they first got to know one another, but only within the sphere of academic psychology. Both Wallace and Gruber had full lives behind them, including previous marriages and children. Their common work on *Creative People at Work* started when they were members of a larger group of individuals; all the participants were committed to the case-study approach. Gruber recalled: "For about five years, once a month we had a Sunday meeting at my house. About half the people were students doing dissertations, others included sociologists of science, psychologists interested in a variety of topics." Wallace added: "There was a woman who worked with dying children who came. So there were people who would come who were working with individuals. Maybe all of them were interested in creative processes but in very different settings, very different contexts. That was really one of the things that made the group so stimulating."

As a result of the interaction between the members of this broader discourse community, Wallace and Gruber conceived of the idea to edit a book of case studies focusing on creative individuals. By the time the idea of the book took shape, they were also planning their joint personal lives. In the contexts of their shared work and their personal relationship, they made some of the decisions about the book. One important decision had to do with the order in which the editors' names were to be listed. Gruber explained their reasoning: "We made a clear-cut agreement that Doris would be the main editor and in compensation for that she would be listed first, so it is Wallace and Gruber. And that was a very definite decision that we made. She wrote the proposal. I had input to everything, but she basically wrote it. And it was a beautiful proposal, and it worked." In talking about authorship and division of labor, some additional issues emerged. Wallace explained:

> I have edited books before, so I have quite a lot of experience as an editor. And it meant that I did an enormous amount of the scut work which appealed to him. . . . I would find a publisher. I would see the book through the process and all sorts of drudgery stuff,

and at the same time also be a contributor, as we both wanted to be. And, because of that, I asked that I go first.

Gruber interjected, "I don't think you had to ask."

Wallace continued, "Wait, wait. There is absolutely no problem about that. But you know at that time, Howard had a lot more publications out than I did. It was a very smooth, warm and easily reached decision, behind which there is something of the gender stuff."

The two of them discussed their decisions about the division of their efforts and the way in which status and gender related to these matters. The issues they touched on are of particular importance to collaboration between intimates, including the need to achieve a balance between personal commitments, concerns about the work, and each partner's individual career. Gruber reviewed some of these connections:

> Let me put it in a slightly different way. I wanted to push Doris; I wanted her . . . [Wallace interjects, "Yes, and he has always done that"] to have a chance to be the senior author on papers. . . . And I also did not want the labor involved, and I thought it was a fair exchange for her to do all that work and to be the first author. And then there was also this other feeling I had, that I had nothing to lose, because it was going to be the Gruber approach that was going to be expounded. . . . [At the same time] the fact that we were very close and there was no struggle over particular ideas we might argue about, but it was not as though you had two people with different approaches contending with each other.

Gruber likes to collaborate both with his wife and with his students. His commitment to the full professional development of those with less experience has been important to Wallace from the earliest stages of her contact with him. She also appreciates the way they share ideas now that they have achieved greater professional equality: "Everything I write, he reads, and everything he writes, I read. And in-between we are discussing things from early on."

Criticism is a central feature of good collaboration but it requires careful timing. During my interview with Wallace and Gruber, Wallace described how Gruber sometimes gave her what he had written and asked her not to edit it—"not to worry about the commas"—just to respond to the general direction. Gruber and Wallace further described areas where negotiations and compromises were helpful. Some of these were about finely tuned criticism; others involved effective division of labor and the issues of intellectual property. As they have somewhat different backgrounds in the arts and sciences, each of them focused on those chapters which best correspond to his or her interests.

Another example of their division of labor relates to work on demanding chapters: "Something that I found difficult, I would have discarded," Gruber recalled. "If she found [something] difficult, she would have discarded it. Between the two of us, we rescued difficult chapters, but that meant it was a lot more work for both of us."

Compromises have to be made in other areas as well including career decisions. But negotiations can be successful in a good partnership, because, as Gruber put it: "What a collaboration does for you is, by spreading the risk a little bit, it encourages you to take more chances."

A similar observation was made by the authors of *Rescuers: Portraits of Moral Courage in the Holocaust*,[18] whom I interviewed in their home outside Santa Fe, New Mexico. Gay Block is a photographer and her partner, Malka Drucker, is a children's story writer. They build well on their complementarity in training and temperament. Their joint project, *Rescuers*, consists of narratives by and photographs of rescuers of Jews during World War II. It was a large project initiated by Drucker who recalled: "The project took place in so many stages that each of us pushed the other one through." While they were looking for a publisher Drucker continued to work on some of her contracted children's books. They had written a prospectus and collected the interviews, and Block had taken pictures of the rescuers and started to show them. Block recalled this time as difficult: "When the rejections started coming in, I just started doing the exhibition. While showing some slides one night in Los Angeles, somebody asked if they could show this work [as an exhibition]. It was not yet in any kind of form to show, but I figured out the form to show it and did it. And it was by working on the exhibition that the form of the book came to us."

The visual format of their highly praised book combines the past and the present. It includes black-and-white pictures of the rescuers and the people whom they rescued dating back to the forties. These images are placed next to the rescuers' first-person narratives. In addition, the book contains large, full-color portraits of each rescuer taken at the time of the interview. "The latter," Block wrote in the book, is "to represent the rescuers with as much reality as possible."[19] Drucker did the interviews, and she developed a strong relationship with each of the individuals in the book. She explained, "If I am asking people, especially in the case of this subject, to open their hearts to me, the only way I know how to do that is to do the same to them. . . . With all these rescuers we became friends." The writing of the book's introduction was an example of how these two partners supported and expanded each other's work. The publishers wanted a comprehensive introduction, which was a new form of writing for Drucker since her previous work consisted of children's books. She started by writing eight pages, but the editor wanted it expanded. Drucker did not know how to do that; one of the reasons that she had difficulty in writing this text was that she usually did not read introductions: "Why read the introduction? I'll read the book." Block responded: "Because you know that you can read a book and understand what they are trying to say, but a lot of people need the introduction. Like me. I need to know what I am getting ready to read so I'll pay attention when I am supposed to."

Block's familiarity with introductions helped them in tackling this task. She suggested that they start with an outline—an effective strategy to give Drucker a clearer sense of where she needed to expand the material. Block understood what the editor wanted, but it was Drucker's imagination and writing skills that were needed to construct and write the introduction. Block commented, "I am not that kind of an idea person." Drucker, while at first resistant, wrote a clear and elegant text benefiting from their joint planning and conversations.

Rescuers is going into its fourth printing. The authors have made many presentations, and their vision of the importance of this subject is still growing. Block is trying to get Drucker to write an epilogue to the book based on her constantly developing ideas of the implications of the rescuers' moral courage for contemporary life: "Every time we do a lecture, she comes up with new ideas that were not there before. I write them down to be sure that we include them the next time. She does not always know that she said them; she just has the ideas." Their account illustrates Gruber's observation that part of the power of a collaboration lies in sharing the risks, which allows the participants to take more chances. As Drucker reiterated during the interview: "This is a project that I would have never undertaken by myself. I could not have done it myself. The sheer organization of it would have driven me crazy." And Block responded: "But that is the point. I could not have done it myself, either. That is the point of collaborating."

The public and private consequences of collaboration between intimates are not easy to assess. The willingness of Wallace and Gruber and Block and Drucker to talk about complex and, at times, troubling concerns impresses me. They each referred to issues of visibility and recognition, including the order in which their names were listed in their publications. These collaborations, while demanding, also provided the participants with new insights into their individual strengths and new directions for their solo work.

These couples have been able to deal with their differences, but not all collaborations between intimate partners are successful. The marriage of Sylvia Plath and Ted Hughes ended tragically, although in their early years they depended very much on each other for encouragement and inspiration. (A fuller account of their lives is presented in Chapter 5.) Less is known about Albert Einstein's first marriage to and collaboration with Mileva Maric. Einstein and Maric were students together at the Swiss Polytechnic Institute. In their love letters they share a dream of common interests and scientific collaboration.[20] Maric, who was the only female student in their class, and who showed promise as a scientist in 1896, eventually failed an important examination. At the beginning of their marriage, she was self-confident and had interests in subjects that were also intriguing to her future husband. But as their relationship developed further, and after the birth of three children (one of whom was given up for adoption), Maric's scientific voice became less clear. Until recently, she was usually dismissed by Einstein's biographers[21] as being a minor episode in his life. At present, there is a growing controversy concerning her contributions; some researchers have suggested that she was very helpful to Einstein with the mathematical aspects of his work. This claim is supported by some of Einstein's letters written to Mileva Maric during their frequent separations. In addition to their joint activities, Maric also gave Einstein a lot of personal support at a critical time in his development as a physicist.[22] But with the increasing curtailment of Maric's own scholarly activities, their marriage deteriorated and ended painfully. Maric lived a much diminished existence once her life with Einstein was over.

It is usually easier to document successful lives and successful collaborations than those which have failed. Consequently, our understanding of working partnerships is uneven. Although the information tends to be limited, I will attempt to present evidence concerning problems and conflicts in collaborative endeavors together with the successes.

ACHIEVING BALANCE

Before Ivan's recent death, Nan and Ivan Lyons were successful authors who started their writing careers in midlife and wrote several books together. At the beginning of their marriage, Ivan wanted to write; he tried his hand at drama, short stories, even a novel, but his agent discouraged him. For twenty years, as he worked in the advertising industry, he wrote no fiction. But during that time, his job required a lot of travel. To prepare to write their own books, "Nan and I," he recalled during my interview with them, "would be off three months at a time from Oslo to Naples, visiting every bookseller, library, and publisher in various European cities. It is basically how we became sophisticated about all aspects of travel." His wife continued: "We became interested in all aspects of travel, all aspects of restaurant and hotel life. And the closest we could come to that experience back home was to entertain by cooking extraordinary meals."

The many experiences shared abroad were only part of the Lyonses' special closeness. They enjoyed doing everything together. In fact, it took them more than a decade to prepare to have a child—to open their intimacy to welcome a third family member:

> Wherever she was, or wherever I was, we spent most of the day on the telephone. We never ran out of things to talk about, wonder about, truly, we are very best friends. Why interrupt this terrific relationship by having a child? And so we waited thirteen years to have a child until we were really sure, until we got a lot of garbage out of the way, including the legacy of our unhappy childhoods. We were terrified to recreate the kind of atmosphere we grew up in. We wanted to be sure that we had enough love for a child. We wanted her to be a joy but not a sacrifice.

In the summer of 1974, when their daughter was four years old, they were having a financially difficult time. While they were sweltering in New York City, their friends were out in the Hamptons. Their free time was spent next to a sandbox with their daughter, Samantha. Ivan was on his twenty-fifth diet, but "nothing was working." One day, he turned to his wife and said, "The thing to do is to get rid of all the chefs; that is the ultimate diet." Nan immediately saw the possibilities for a book. She suggested that they create a character who was a sort of young and beautiful Julia Child and, at the same time, a female sleuth involved in murder and sex.

Although Nan had never done any writing, she and Ivan embarked on a collaborative project in early summer. They planned a careful schedule to complete the first draft in three months. They worked three days a week and wrote eight pages each day. They also decided to keep their activity a secret. Their plan was to finish by Labor Day, which they did. The book, *Someone Is Killing the Great Chefs of Europe*—about a young New York food critic who, on her way to cook for the Queen of England, stumbles into a recipe of wit, murder, and the hilarious eccentricities of European haute cuisine—became a great success.

Before doing much writing, Ivan and Nan spent a lot of time talking, and Ivan took notes. They visualized and described all of the characters. Then, they took down the pictures in their bedroom and put up three-by-five cards summarizing scenes. They thought through the scenes carefully—plotting motivation, direction, and action. They proceeded chronologically and believed in the project. Although they were naive about the craft of writing and story construction, they knew that they could talk to each other well and exhaustively. Ivan's long years in the advertising industry were helpful in the construction of a working method, while Nan's fluency of ideas, excellent literary judgment, and sense of humor contributed to the collaboration. They developed an effective routine: they discussed a scene at breakfast, pinning down what they were trying to accomplish using their knowledge of the characters. Then Ivan sat down at the typewriter and wrote the daily eight pages. Nan provided careful critical feedback; she changed lines and suggested improvements. At this early stage of their collaboration, Ivan found it hard to accept the criticism. With considerable feeling, he remembered: "I hated it, I absolutely hated it. It was very difficult as I [had] spent a great deal of time building Nan up, and here I was facing a severe critic." But they also laughed a lot. At times, Ivan hid ideas and passages from Nan's critical eyes. At other times, he was gratified by her approval. Overall, this first collaboration was very difficult, as they were both new at it. The tension was so high that occasionally they stopped talking to each other. But what kept them going was a belief in the project, and, more important, a belief in each other.

They complemented each other well. Nan is a widely read woman with an excellent literary sensibility. Ivan, an orderly, well-organized, and disciplined man, provided the skills that Nan was lacking. They finished the manuscript on time and found an agent through personal contacts. The book was sold within two months with a movie contract following. Suddenly they were in a new world. Ivan and Nan did not discuss the book with friends until they were finished, and, like many writers when at work on a book, they read only newspapers and magazines, materials that had little to do with their project. Ivan recalled: "The basic thing is you don't want to be influenced, you don't want to be jealous, you cannot get close to anybody else's writing."

In the beginning, Ivan was the stronger partner; he was not daunted by the magnitude of their undertaking. He assured his wife that the book was going to work. But as they proceeded to books two and three and faced the usual hurdles of writer's block and related problems, Nan emerged as an equal partner, now comfortable in her role. They saw their collaboration as a powerful one as they ironed out their, at times, very strong disagreements before submitting a manuscript. They agreed that by the time they were finished, they did not know which of them was responsible for a particular idea. When they came together, sorting the collaborative Q-sort cards describing various motivational, stylistic, and organizational aspects of collaboration (see the full Q-sort in the appendix), they found that they both ranked highly the item: "My collaborator is able to make observations which makes a situation immediately clear." It is not surprising that they placed the card, "I expect my collaborator to be a critic of my work," at the high end of their distribution. Indeed, one of the most interesting aspects of the Lyonses' collaboration was the way in which they dealt openly with the issue of criticism. Over the years, they moved past their early painful confrontations to a reasoned and mutually respectful approach.

As the Lyonses' experience shows, mutuality and equality in roles are considered important defining characteristics of effective collaboration. For instance, dyads described as high on mutuality are seen by Sarah J. McCarthey and Susan McMahon as having participants who are equal contributors to a joint task.[23] In collaborative writing tasks, participants who may start with somewhat different interests frequently develop a shared intellectual "space" in which, while working together, they achieve something new. Psychological studies of collaborative interactions offer many useful concepts for the analysis of partnerships. But these concepts by themselves are but broad frames. It is through the detailed accounts of shared lives and shared work that we can access the much-needed specifics of collaboration. The Lyonses' generously shared collaborative trajectory—their description of how they chose a project, and how they faced their uncertainties and honed their skills, and how they achieved a relationship of equality which required humor and trust—exemplifies specific dynamics in collaboration.

One important issue in collaboration between spouses is that of gender roles. The Lyonses had few problems concerning traditional divisions of labor. In their lives, the main issue was who should prepare lunch. Before they became collaborators, Ivan was used to his wife cooking all of his meals for him. He clearly admired her great skills in the kitchen. But as a hard-working collaborator, Nan found it difficult to interrupt her work and think about preparing food in the middle of the work day. She quipped, "Did Rogers cook lunch for Hammerstein?" They revealed other gender differences through their discussions and Q-sort comparison. Ivan paid close attention to details, to the careful researching of facts, while Nan was more involved with character and story line. In this, they hewed to some other mixed-sex collaborators in which the men tend to be more detail oriented, preferring a very orderly environment, while the women rely more heavily on their strong literary imagination.

A difference in dealing with expectations also emerged in the interview while the Lyonses discussed their Q-sorts. They compared items dealing with the pacing of their work. "You always tell me that I expect to get too much done," Ivan commented. But Nan saw this as his own battle with deadlines rather than a problem between the two of them. The construction of a working environment was important for Ivan. He was very orderly, but the maintenance of the household as a backdrop to their working space fell on Nan's shoulders. Nan preferred to have a place to work away from their home, while Ivan loved working at home. It was his "cocoon."

In a related vein, Nan raised the issue of working couples who are together all the time: how do they deal with their need to be alone? Nan needed outside stimulation to a much greater extent than her husband did. It was the way in which she recharged. She used to enjoy having to repark their car as a way to have an hour in another environment. Nan commented further that they got their best ideas when they were away from their regular place of work—their desks. In this she confirmed what I have noted in my previous work with "experienced thinkers," many of whom reported on the generative role of walking, jogging, and having conversations with friends.[24]

The Lyonses' working environment was constructed to protect their daily efforts of problem solving and expansion. They saw as one of the greatest advantages of collaboration the fact that when one of them was stuck, the other could come up with a solution. But for new projects and beginnings, they relied on travel and interactions with the outside world. Such strategies and mutual adjustments are crucial to successful and insightful partners in work and life.

The smoothness with which couples, such as the Lyonses and the Durants, collaborate is not always the case among husband and wife teams. I have encountered a somewhat different pattern among some academic couples who work in the same field. Whereas the Lyonses developed such strong ties before they started to work together, frequently, for these academic couples, intellectual collaboration was the basis of a relationship which eventually resulted in marriage. The usually higher status of the male creates some unresolved problems concerning decision-making processes. Men are socialized to be decisive; consultation and negotiation can be difficult for some. As a result, unlike the Lyonses, they are not as able to weather the strains of gender socialization as they move slowly and steadily toward a partnership of equals.

FAMILY PARTNERSHIPS

Collaboration between marriage and sexual partners has been of special interest to literary critics and social scientists. A less frequent pattern of partnership is that between siblings and parents and children. In the case of siblings, the sharing of childhood experiences can provide an important bond for adult family members engaged in related endeavors. The practice of writing and the frequent exchange of family news has been quite common among literary British families. Jessica Mitford recalled her frequent correspondence with her sisters, and how the experience of letter writing has contributed to her ease with language.[25] Margaret Drabble described a similar childhood practice in her family—they wrote plays together and published a family magazine. This talented British novelist considered these family activities as the beginning of her writing career.[26] The vivid imaginary world of the Brontë sisters, as expressed in their shared writings as children, is thought by many to have contributed to their later work as novelists.

British nineteenth-century essayist Charles Lamb termed his powerful emotional and artistic interdependence with his sister Mary as a "sort of double singleness." Their biographer, Jane Aaron, wrote of their intense sibling bond—how they lived and worked together "writing on one table"—in a book bearing the title *A Double Singleness.*[27] Mary was ten years older than her brother, and during their childhood she was his primary caregiver and nurturer. Aaron suggested that some of Charles's beliefs and personality may have been the result of being raised by a sibling. Charles and Mary jointly authored the book *Mrs. Leicester's School*, published in 1808. In addition to this work, many of Charles's writings revealed a very unusual approach to gender roles, which Aaron attributed, in part, to his lifelong, mutually nurturing relationship with his sister:

> The reciprocity of the Lambs' relationship, and their perpetual interchange of mother/child, or leader/follower, roles, promoted an awareness of the dual, if not multiple aspects of the apparently single subject. . . . Through the formation of their lives of "double singleness" the Lambs had established an alternative pattern of gender relations, one which was not dependent upon the artificial segregation of rigidly polarized masculine and feminine roles. The vantage point of this lived experience afforded them a view of the flexible nature of subject identity: in themselves, as well as in relation to the other, each was aware of at least a double singleness. At times their writings disclose the pain and confusion entailed by such an acknowledgment of the plurality of being, when it is at odds with prevailing ideologies; but at other times their work celebrates the liberations which such a recognition brings, and extends them to the reader.[28]

In his fiction as well as in his essays, Charles depicted characters who resembled him in their willingness to offer nurturing care and to be self-sacrificing. In addition, his writing also expressed his commitment to the alleviation of suffering caused by a rigid class system and traditional gender roles, beliefs he and his sister shared.

There is increasing interest in sibling relationships among social scientists. Bank and Kahn suggested that parental unavailability, as in the Hansel and Gretel fairy tale, frequently fosters intense sibling loyalty.[29] In the relationships that emerge under these circumstances, the siblings are devoted to each other, identify with each other, and are often willing to be self-sacrificing.

In their analyses, Bank and Kahn relied on studies of children raised in large families, on Anna Freud and Sophie Dann's study of orphans whose parents were murdered in concentration camps, and on studies of twins whose parents were unable to provide them with adequate attention. In addition, they drew from interviews with adults raised by parents who were unavailable to their children due to illness or death. They identified the qualities that emerge in sibling relationships under these circumstances as cooperation, sympathy and mutual helpfulness, and the sharing of common values. Many twins also develop a common system of communication. The relationship between Mary and Charles Lamb illustrates some of these characteristics of intense sibling loyalty.

Anthropological studies of sibling-reared individuals show that this socialization practice is common in many preindustrial societies.[30] For instance, Polynesian children spend most of their time in solitary activities or with other children, including younger siblings, rather than with adults. In India, the relationship between sister and brother is particularly important. In many agrarian non-Western societies, older siblings assume the role of caregiver and socializing agent with their younger siblings. They are valued in these roles. The effect of such practices is the prevalence of cooperative behaviors among siblings, the ability to shift roles with changing circumstances, and the development of effective strategies on the part of interdependent siblings to deal with conflicts in their relationships. Anthropologist Thomas Weisner further suggested that childhood relationships which develop in these communities continue, at times in altered ways, throughout the siblings' adult lives. Many of these conclusions can be applied to the intense lifelong relationship of the Lambs.

In general, the values of interdependence and intense family bonds are nurtured in these societies, in contrast to the values of independence and individual achievement which are emphasized in technological societies.[31] In spite of these general trends, there are important exceptions exemplifying interdependence in Western societies, as documented in the studies referred to above and in other biographies, case studies, and personal interviews. The lives of William and Dorothy Wordsworth have intrigued literary critics as well as psychologists. The great English poet and his sister were well known for their reliance upon each other. They were born a year apart, and, although separated during their childhoods, they chose to live with each other in the Lake District of England and to share their love for that countryside. In this setting, before William's late marriage, their relationship was particularly close. Dorothy's journals provided her brother with important material for his poetry, an influence acknowledged by a variety of critics. Stillinger wrote that "she gave him recollections, words, phrases, and images."[32]

Psychologist Doris Wallace described William and Dorothy's collaborative relationship in the following way:

Dorothy's compelling descriptions of what her sensitive eye and ear perceived were the raw material that William mined, transformed into poetry and embellished with reflective commentary. She pointed the way for him in her prose. But just as he was guided by her, her eye was also guided by him.[33] . . . William must have habitually examined his sister's journal for material for his poetry, both to add and stimulate his own memory of events experienced with her, and to search for material from her experiences.[34]

Wallace's comments on the possible psychological sources of the Wordsworths' long collaborative relationship include the loss of their parents in childhood. In contrast to some other siblings studied by psychologists, this brother and sister were separated for a long time as children. But in their case, Wallace wrote:

[T]heir long separation served to cement rather than to dilute their affection. By explicitly renewing their commitment to each other and emphasizing their emotional ties they could strengthen the family that had been driven apart. These attitudes and feelings were especially strong for Dorothy and William who had always shared the same values, especially a love of nature.[35]

One of the most important aspects of this sibling collaboration was William's trust in his sister's sensibility and judgment. And while they did not write together, their shared journey, their commitment to the same values, and their intellectual companionship all contributed to his poetic achievements.

The impact of emotional bonds forged in childhood on adult intellectual collaboration also characterized the relationship between philosopher Hubert Dreyfus and engineer Stuart Dreyfus. They co-authored the very influential book *Mind over Machine*.[36] While they referred to their joint and individual experiences in the book, they did not write in detail about the dynamics of their collaboration. They discussed these with me during an interview in Berkeley in the summer of 1993.

Their first joint professional effort began thirty years ago when they were both young faculty members at the Massachusetts Institute of Technology. These were the years when enthusiasm for artificial intelligence was unbridled, and public promises about its future included claims about computers that the Dreyfuses later characterized as "manic."[37] They criticized these claims first in a jointly written letter to Hubert's colleagues at the RAND Corporation, followed by a more formal report Hubert wrote to the company in 1964. Hubert faced serious opposition to his stance. Thus he required help from his brother and some of Stuart's coworkers to have his paper published.

After their first joint publication, they continued to write and talk to each other about the philosophical, psychological, and engineering implications of computers. Providing support to each other was crucial in sustaining them, as they faced a lot of criticism during this period. At the same time, their ideas also received serious international attention. The beginnings of *Mind over Machine* date back to these early controversies and to the insight they summarized in their book: "[P]roblems involving deep understanding built on the basis of vast experience will not yield as do simple, well-defined problems that exist in isolation from much of human experience to formal mathematical or computer analysis."[38] In the early seventies, the Dreyfus brothers continued to explore their interests in artificial intelligence and computers. They taught an interdisciplinary seminar together at the University of California, Berkeley on the limits of scientific decision making. "The idea was you were supposed to teach your next book, not your last book," Stuart recalled. Their collaboration also included work on a grant exploring decision making among pilots. Their empirical study of human skilled behavior contributed to the development of a model of skill acquisition that they describe in *Mind over Machine.*

Their ideas emerged during conversations. And while they preferred to talk in their offices with the tape recorder on, they found themselves engaged in talk during walks, while at airports, "or whatever." Hubert described some of their interactions: "Sometimes we type. I start a sentence and he finishes it, and then he starts a sentence and I finish it. . . . Stuart frequently thinks about the common work at night. And then, when he comes in, I listen to him, and try to sort out what he is telling me . . . and then I rephrase it." Their thinking styles varied somewhat, as Stuart was an engineer and Hubert was a philosopher. Hubert further added that the process was so dialogical that thinking and talking could not be differentiated. This conjoining of thought and speech, in his case, was particularly evident in collaboration with his brother and with those of his students with whom he has coauthored books and articles. Hubert's thinking about his work involved a sequential articulation of ideas. He also used diagrams to explain what he thought, and to find gaps in his process of argumentation. In their common work, they relied on a shared framework which they developed over the years in their many dialogic interactions.

As children, Hubert was entrusted with the well-being of his younger sibling, a caring relationship that still plays a central role in their lives. When I asked him why he thought he was committed to collaboration in contrast to most of his colleagues in philosophy, he answered:

> I always thought it is because I had a younger brother. He was sort of given to me as my student by my parents. Their idea to keep us

from fighting was to say, in effect, look what we have got here. This little brother. You can help raise him and do what you want with him. . . . I think I liked to teach him things. I always had the idea, that if you looked at good teachers, they would turn out to be older siblings.

In the Dreyfus family, the parents fostered a close, mutually caregiving relationship between Hubert and Stuart. Their early connection contributed to their lifelong productive engagement with each other. Hubert described how he would start a sentence which Stuart finished, "and then he starts a sentence I finish—we sort of think things out together." These comments are similar to de Beauvoir's description of thinking in common with Sartre, and to that of others who have enjoyed the experience of intellectual interdependence.

A very different depiction of family members' impact upon each other's creative development is given by Nigel Hamilton in his book, *The Brothers Mann*.[39] The world-famous German writers had an unusually complex and productive relationship. In contrast with the Dreyfus brothers, Thomas and Heinrich were not particularly close as children. There were periods when they even refused to speak to each other. Heinrich was jealous of his younger brother's intimate relationship to their mother. But they also shared many values; for instance, they both rejected the family's mercantile traditions. And in spite of their father's sustained objection, they both became writers.

Thomas engaged in a lot of imaginative play as a child and adolescent; he set up a puppet theater, constructed sets for performances, and studied the violin. Heinrich, as the older of the brothers, staged his rebellion more openly. Nourished by his love of literature, particularly the poet Heine, he practiced his future craft whenever possible, in spite of his father's attempts to train him for a business career. Once he started to write and after his poems were first published, Thomas expressed his great admiration for the brother who paved both of their paths.

It was their mother who supported the brothers' literary ambitions, "she who would guide both Heinrich and Thomas to their first successes, who stood behind them and between them when they fought. Without her we may well wonder whether either would have achieved what they did."[40] In their twenties, the brothers encouraged each other: they traveled together; they wrote a picture book for their younger siblings; and they provided each other with ideas for their solo work. In Rome, where they shared quarters and literary tastes, Thomas started to work on his family saga, *Buddenbrooks*, which earned him the Nobel Prize for Literature thirty years later.

Subsequently, they found themselves in frequent disagreements. Heinrich was a man of great pride, in many ways a loner. While

Thomas was more comfortable with people, he also knew how to adjust and, when necessary, to compromise. The differences between them were literary, temperamental, and political. Their greatest conflict arose before and during the First World War. This was a period when Europe's intellectuals took opposing sides as they were divided by nationalist sentiment, and many of them espoused chauvinistic positions. Heinrich rejected his compatriots' widespread support of the German army and the Kaiser. His was an anti-war "cry of conscience, of passionate humanity,"[41] while Thomas took a more conventional, patriotic pro-war stance.

As writers, their opinions were publicly expressed, and their differences became the talk of literary and intellectual circles. For a time it appeared that the bonds between the two brothers were permanently ruptured. But, Thomas's opinions changed as the war's horrendous casualties became known. After the war and a near-fatal operation suffered by Heinrich, the brothers reconciled. Hamilton wrote of these events:

> The story of Thomas Mann's development after the First World War, then, is the story not only of his relationship with Heinrich in literary and personal terms but of the gradual acknowledgment of the ideals which Thomas found initially so abhorrent. This "conversion" was perhaps unique in German literary history and the symbolic importance of their fraternal relationship was not lost on Thomas. It provided the structural tension for *The Magic Mountain,* Thomas' first major novel since *Buddenbrooks* in 1901; and the resolution of their fraternal tension became the most profound and positive impetus in his whole life.[42]

The significance of this relationship, then, lies in the complex dynamics between the brothers, starting with mutual influence, then moving to opposition, and ending in reconciliation. Hamilton suggested that their serious conflicts had to be expressed and overcome before the Mann brothers were able to reach a true mutuality and the full development of their individual talents. After their reconciliation, the brothers saw their literary relationship as a "division of labor." Thomas focused on the intellectual, musical, and artistic worlds, while Heinrich was committed to social and political concerns, striving to overcome the usual barriers between art and politics. The brothers' relationship became even stronger with the rise of Nazism, their shared opposition to it, and their consequent exile.

The full chronicle of the Mann brothers' lives is beyond the scope of this chapter. But even a brief examination of this sibling relationship, so different from the Dreyfus brothers or from Dorothy and William Wordsworth, offers important insights into human interdependence.

In the case of Heinrich and Thomas Mann, rivalry and conflict played a significant role in their "network of enterprises," in the organization of their life tasks.[43] More than most siblings, these brothers were connected emotionally and intellectually in their chosen work, and eventually in the hard ethical choices they made. Their personal conflict made them deeply thoughtful, and the resolution of their conflict freed them to see each other in complementary positions.

Psychologists have suggested that the recent interest in sibling relationships is due, in part, to the expansion of professional attention beyond parental roles to other key influences on an individual throughout the life span. This is a perspective change from the discipline's previously limited focus on events and relationships in childhood. The well-documented lives of the Mann brothers, the Wordsworths, the Brontë sisters, and other siblings who have shared creative work with each other highlight the lasting importance of early connections.

It is in family life, particularly in Western, bourgeois societies, that children first experience the complexities of social connections. These complexities often include the changing patterns of sibling loyalty and rivalry. Patricia Zukow-Goldring suggested that "sibling discord provides children with a means to explore the nuances and limits of their social world and to evaluate and calibrate emotional reactions."[44] Many writers, including the Mann brothers, have relied upon their personal experiences with siblings in exploring tangled emotional connections in their works.

Solidarity and mutual support between siblings are strengthened by childhood experiences in which siblings are primarily dependent upon each other, such as the powerful interdependence of the Wordsworths and the Lambs, or the intellectually and emotionally powerful bond of the Dreyfus brothers. It is the centrality of sibling bonds and their importance for creative work that link these varied pairs.

UNITING LOVE AND WORK

The full realization of intimacy and interdependence is achieved by those intimates who share a common vision and a devotion to shared tasks. However, it is rare to find among siblings or life partners a unity that impacts all aspects of the partners' lives. Yet such a unity characterized the "common journey" of the great scientific couple Marie and Pierre Curie, who, nearly a hundred years ago, built a life based on a "community of ideas and opinions." In her short biography of her husband, Marie wrote of the many rewards of their collaboration.[45] Their remarkable research, which included their Nobel Prize–winning research on radium, started modestly. They supported each other's extraordinary devotion to scientific research, they worked together in a laboratory with limited facilities, and they jointly published reports of their findings. In her biography of her husband, Marie remembered their early years:

> We were at this time entirely absorbed in the new field that opened before us, thanks to the discovery so little expected. And we were very happy in spite of the difficult conditions under which we worked. We passed our days in the laboratory, often eating a simple student lunch there. A great tranquillity reigned in our poor, shabby hangar; occasionally, while observing an operation, we would walk up and down, talking of our work, present and future. When we were cold, a cup of hot tea, drunk beside the stove, cheered us. We lived in a preoccupation as complete as that of a dream.[46]

Their work drew upon several fields. Historian of science Helena Pycior described their investigations as follows: "the study of radio-activity [is] a multidisciplinary phenomenon that the couple soon realized involved chemistry, physics, and medicine. Theirs was a fruitful collaboration, in which Pierre served primarily as the physicist, and Marie, although trained especially in physics and mathematics, as the chemist."[47] Both Marie and Pierre had collaborated with others in addition to their own joint endeavors. They brought to shared work their ability to place the scientific task above narrow ego considerations, and they treasured the synergy of collaboration.

A similar bond existed between Louise Erdrich and Michael Dorris, writers of American Indian descent. Journalist Vince Passaro wrote of them that "theirs is an art, as well as a life, directed towards synthesis and unity."[48] This literary couple, whose jointly written novel *The Crown of Columbus* was recently published, received a lot of critical attention. Their working partnership was a central part of their married life as it reflected shared literary passions as well as the similarity of their ethnic and class backgrounds. Both writers were of "mixed blood," raised jointly by their Indian and non-Indian relatives. For each of them, the reservation became a sort of second home.

Before Dorris's life ended in tragedy,[49] the couple described their writing methods to a variety of interviewers. One of the most striking aspects of their collaboration was the way in which they expanded the scope of each other's work. When they married, Dorris was an academic, heading Dartmouth College's Native American Studies Program, and Erdrich was a published poet. Neither of them was ready to write full-length books before their marriage. "I tended to be a person who thought in terms of stories and poems and short things," recalled Erdrich. They first started collaborating on light, romantic stories under the single pen name Milou North. Erdrich continued, "The book [*Love Medicine*] became a novel because of Michael. He came one day and said pretty much, 'Oh, this is a novel,' and you know we began to write it in that way."[50]

Similarly, Dorris stated in several interviews that he would not be writing fiction if he were not working with his wife. Most of their projects started with conversations:

> We'll start talking about something a long time in advance of it: the germ of a plot, or a story that has occurred to us, or an observation that we have seen. *A Yellow Raft in Blue Water* [Dorris's first novel] started out with the title. The title came before the book. After we talk, one of us, whoever thought of it probably, will write a draft. It might be a paragraph; it might be ten pages; it might be something in between. We then share the draft with the other person.[51]

Shortly thereafter they sat down with a pencil and made comments about what worked and what did not work, what needed expanding and what might be overwritten. Then they gave that draft with their suggestions back to the person who wrote it, who had the option of taking or leaving the suggestions, but almost always took them. The original drafter then did a new draft, gave it back to the reviewer, and the process repeated. This exchange took place five or six times. The final say clearly rested with the person who wrote the piece initially, but, as Dorris characterized, "we virtually reach consensus on all the words before they go out, on a word by word basis. There is not a thing that has gone out from either one of us that has not been through at least six rewrites, *major* rewrites."[52]

Their way of editing each other's work was not identical: Dorris was very careful about word repetitions, overwriting, and issues of structure when addressing his wife's work. Erdrich was particularly interested in issues of character when she made suggestions to her husband. Although they could identify some differences in their emphases, their work was thoroughly interdependent. Dorris recalled:

> A long time ago, when we first started out, in those very early drafts of *Tracks*, or while building *Love Medicine* [both books "authored" by Erdrich], it was much clearer where I was coming in. Over the course of the next three or four books, though, whatever each of us individually contributed was always perched on the other one's shoulder, even when we weren't physically there.[53]

The careful editing of each other's work was a necessary part of this working, literary marriage, but even more important was the joint planning of their books. These took place in many contexts, but they particularly liked to talk about the characters in their books during long car trips. Dorris described having written three chapters of *A Yel-*

low Raft in Blue Water, his first novel, and saying to Erdrich on their way to Minnesota: "You know, I am really getting bored with this character."[54] The book was becoming a story of a boy's coming of age, and that was not what he wanted to write. During their conversation, they came up with a changed idea, that of having a female main character. Suddenly it became a much more interesting book: "Once we settled into the project, I'd write some, and we would talk about it; I'd write some more, take it to Louise, she'd like it or not like it, and she would suggest where it should go next."[55]

Their choices reflected a belief in a kind of community and connectedness where the whole is larger than the sum of its parts; these choices embodied the fundamental promise of collaboration. Their ability to accomplish this demanding, elusive objective was based, in part, on their exposure as Indians to cultural practices that honor human bonds. At the heart of their work together was a commitment to egalitarian values, including that of gender equality.

The intense, dialogic interaction of Erdrich and Dorris is akin to the partnership of choreographers Art Bridgman and Myrna Packer, who described their working styles in an evening devoted to dance collaborations, when they joined two other duets.[56] This married couple started to collaborate with each other in 1978 at a relatively early stage of their careers, before they were "stamped" by the style of a major choreographer. Like many other collaborators (for instance, Nan and Ivan Lyons), they emphasized the crucial role of dialogue: "We are always talking, at the physical level, at the emotional level, and at the spiritual level." When they described their joint explorations, their words had a strong physical resonance; they bounced "ideas off each other," and it was "a physical and emotional push and pull."

Although Bridgman started in sports, Packard had danced since her childhood. While he was the physically stronger partner, she was always committed to the development and maintenance of her own strength, as their dancing involves a lot of lifts, weight shifts, and powerful physical dialogues. Some of their work was fueled by the dynamics of conflict, which they saw as part of human interdependence. But the dominant theme that made exploration possible was their deep trust in each other. They spoke of the importance of honesty and patience as necessary features of effective, long-term collaborations. Their dances continue to address political issues and, more recently, issues of intimacy and gender stereotypes. They see in their sustained, demanding work together an opportunity to experience the creative process in ways that cannot be sustained in solo endeavors.

Even a brief examination of these joined lives suggests that many couples who have successfully combined family and creative work have also succeeded in overcoming traditional gender roles. Gender equality makes the collaboration more productive as a wider array of each individual's strengths can be drawn upon. The Curies pioneered gender equality, even though that was not their major concern. Myrna Packer and Art Bridgman addressed issues of intimacy and conflict in their choreographic work, striving consciously to explore the complexities of gender relationships. Louise Erdrich and Michael Dorris shared with interviewers the dialogic, interdependent ways in which they co-constructed their writing and living.

DISCOVERING COMMON VALUES

Building an effective collaboration can be a long process, as shown in some of the accounts presented in this chapter (for instance, the Durants and the Lyonses). The transformation of a limited partnership into one of equality requires a closer meshing of values as well as working styles. Will and Ariel Durant had different backgrounds and interests at the time of their marriage, as well as traditional family and work responsibilities. But they shifted to a more equally distributed engagement and more fully shared values in the research and planning of *The Story of Civilization.*

A shared family life does not guarantee a common set of values. During their youth and their first writing decades, Heinrich and Thomas Mann had very different beliefs. Indeed, many observers thought they defined their personal identity in contrast to each other, rather than through their sibling relationship. But they were always aware of the other; arguing, comparing, appreciating, and eventually treasuring the talent and convictions that each brother offered to his sibling. Their closeness following World War I was accompanied by the increasing commonality of their anti-fascist and democratic values.

Shared opposition to a belief system that collaborators consider dangerous or faulty frequently strengthens an already important bond. Hubert and Stuart Dreyfus built upon their strong interdependence as brothers when challenging the unbounded optimism of the artificial intelligence community. They posited an alternative view, one that respects the role of computers as powerful and flexible tools while celebrating the powers of human intuition, expertise, and creativity. A similar pattern of common values characterized the loving relationship of William and Dorothy Wordsworth. They shared a love of nature and a belief in the communicative power of poetry based on observations drawn from daily life. They not only cultivated their intimacy by their common pursuits, but also they celebrated it in their writings. A somewhat different expression of family partnership was the establishment of the Hogarth Press by Virginia and Leonard Woolf. These two members of the Bloomsbury Group created one of the most influential publishing companies in the twentieth century. Their complementary talents and joint vision contributed to their success. Leonard, like many of the collaborating males mentioned in this review of intimate partnerships, was a man with a nurturing temperament. His steady care of his wife, her deep devotion to him, and their shared activities all contributed to their impact upon twentieth-century literature.

Some intimate partnerships are rooted in childhood experiences; others result from complex growth in adulthood. Some couples live and work together sharing space, conversation, and meals. Others, like Georgia O'Keeffe and Alfred Stieglitz, or Simone de Beauvoir and Jean-Paul Sartre, are selective about their times together. Partners are sustained by their interest in each other and in each other's work. Intimate partnerships demand delicate balances between interdependence and individuality, between a trust in one's own strength and the supporting power of connection.

2

PARTNERSHIPS IN SCIENCE

The intimate partnership of Pierre and Marie Curie has been well
documented by their family, friends, and biographers. They had
a shared vision and a powerful combination of disciplinary and temperamental complementarity. In this chapter, I focus on the balance
of productive differences between individuals accompanied by a unity
in purpose. In this time of rapid scientific advances and grave moral
challenges, some of the most critical problems require "unity-in-
diversity" as exemplified by the Curies.

Irene Joliot Curie, their daughter, described her parents' complementarity. Of her father, she wrote: "He was an excellent experimenter
. . . [and] also a thinker . . . The thought of my mother was more
often directed toward immediate action, even in the scientific domain."[1] Helen Pycior elaborated: "Marie appreciated Pierre's need for
an active, complementary partner."[2] In her biography of Pierre, written after his untimely death, Marie described how he and his brother
Jacques worked together: "[T]he vivacity and energy of Jacques were
of precious aid to Pierre, always more easily absorbed by his thoughts."[3]
Her role as "thinker-doer" (Pycior's term) complemented that of "a
thinker-dreamer who reveled in broad reflection on nature."[4] Marie
assumed a large part of the organizational work in the laboratory, directing discussions, while Pierre provided some conceptual scaffolding. Secondly, as mentioned in Chapter 1, they complemented each
other in scientific training: Marie's background was in chemistry and
Pierre's in physics. Thirdly, they were complementary in temperament. This also contributed to the success of their collaboration.
Pierre was somewhat retiring and cautious; he was reluctant to publish until completely satisfied with the accuracy of his findings. Marie
was quick, determined, and more willing to work with institutions
that required negotiations and at times compromise. Their partnership was fueled by their love for each other and their shared passion
for scientific work.

Not all the partnerships about which I write have the qualities for
which the Curies were so widely honored. But the inclusiveness of
their work together illustrates the major aspects of complementarity,

including disciplinary training, work styles, roles, and temperament. The following examination of complementarity among scientists supports my claim that the potential of human talent is powerfully revealed in partnered endeavors. Rather than viewing individual possibilities as points on some universal "bell curve," in these varied partnerships a different possibility is revealed—the complementarity of equals.

Complementarity is a consequence of a basic and often ignored reality. Each individual realizes only a subset of the human potential that can be achieved at a particular historical period. Individual trajectories are facilitated and constrained by subtly varied genetic, familial, and cultural resources. In Western societies we treasure our "uniqueness," but we are also wary of its limitations before society's increasingly demanding and critical tasks. In partnerships, starting from the youngest age, we broaden, refine, change, and rediscover our individual possibilities. In partnerships, we strive toward the equality of dignified interdependence. Some collaborations collapse under the weight of individualistic habits. Others flourish. In this chapter, I examine the dynamics of complementarity between individuals who bring different disciplinary and personal resources to their partnership. I also discuss conceptual complementarity—the dynamic and productive tension between ideas.

COMPLEMENTARITY IN SCIENTIFIC TRAINING AND DISCIPLINE

Physicists and their collaborators provide intriguing examples of complementarity. The young Albert Einstein, while a student at Zurich's Polytechnic Institute, befriended future mathematician Marcel Grossmann. Their friendship sustained Einstein while at school, and Grossmann's father helped Albert get a job in the patent office in Bern. This job left him time for physics. While there (1902–09), he wrote his papers on special relativity. In working on these papers, Einstein received help from his friend Michele Besso (who also worked in the patent office), from his wife, Mileva Maric, and through correspondence with Marcel Grossmann.

Einstein's thinking was visual and kinesthetic. He relied on "thought experiments" and responded to space "by being sympathetically in touch with experience." In describing his mode of thought, he claimed: "The physical entities which seem to serve as elements in thought are certain signs and more or less clear images which can be 'voluntarily' reproduced or combined."[5] As a child, Einstein built complicated structures from blocks and cards. His uncle Jacob, an engineer, stimulated him in science and geometry. He also enjoyed popular science books given to him by a medical student, Max Talmey. Most likely, he visualized what he read, as his memory for words was limited. On the other hand, his ability to solve scientific and engineering problems was recognized early by his uncle Jacob.[6]

Historian of science Gerald Holton wrote extensively about Einstein. He was fascinated with the physicist's mode of thought and attempted to reconstruct how it developed. He quoted Albert's sister Maja Einstein, who recalled that her brother was slow in developing language, and that the family was concerned. But Holton suggested that this lack was accompanied by "an extraordinary visual imagery that penetrated Einstein's very thought processes."[7] Holton quoted Einstein's depiction of thinking from his *Autobiographical Notes* in which he evoked the play of patterned pictures/images, which to him were basic in the construction of concepts. Holton commented on these recollections: "The objects of the imagination were to him evidently persuasively real, visual materials, which he voluntarily and playfully could reproduce and combine, analogous perhaps to the play with shapes in a jigsaw puzzle."[8]

One of Einstein's earliest visual thought experiments occurred as a student when he read Maxwell's theorems about light waves: "He imagined himself riding through space, so to speak, astride a light wave and looking back at the wave next to him."[9] His sister recalled how, as a young man, "he loved to observe the smoke clouds' wonderful shapes, and to study the motions of the individual particles of smoke and the relationships among them."[10] Einstein visualized the jostling agitation of motional energy, the relationship between a light beam and a field. He was able to reverse physical relationships (for instance, between a magnet and a stationary conductor) in his imagination, and to pose and eventually overcome conceptual polarities.

These characteristics of his ways of thinking played a particularly important role in his development of general relativity theory. His insights were linked to "a tactile coexistence with natural phenomena" wrote Holton.[11] "Sometimes the mind seems to move into the problem of nature as if it were a hand slipping into a glove. Another element may be . . . the simplicity and ingenuity of his *Gedankenexperimente* — experiments carried out in thought in just the idealized milieu that turns out to be needed."[12]

In 1907, while working on a comprehensive paper on the special theory of relativity, Einstein wrote:

> . . . then there occurred to me the happiest thought of my life, in the following form. The gravitational field has only a relative existence in a way similar to the electric field generated by magnetoelectrical induction. Because for an observer falling freely from the roof of the house there exists — at least in his immediate

surrounding—*no gravitational field* [his italics]. Indeed, if the observer drops some bodies then these remain relative to him in a state of rest or of uniform motion, independent of their particular chemical or physical nature. The observer therefore has the right to interpret his state as "at rest."[13]

This insight was the bridge between Einstein's special and general theories of relativity. But of course, despite its visual and kinesthetic power, it was just the starting point for a long process of physical and mathematical problem solving. Between 1905 and 1912, Einstein published a number of papers, some of them more tentative than his earlier work. He had "embarked on one of the hardest problems of the century: to find the new gravitational dynamics."[14] He had to develop new concepts, including a nonlinear theory of the gravitational field, and he needed mathematical tools that were new to him. Einstein described his own strengths and weaknesses: "My power, my particular ability, lies in *visualizing the effects, consequences, and possibilities*, and the bearings on present thought of the discoveries of others. I grasp things in a broad way easily. I cannot do mathematical calculations easily. I do them not willingly and not readily."[15] Einstein's relationship with mathematics is crucial to this discussion of disciplinary complementarity.

Einstein turned to his friend Grossmann for help in choosing mathematical models for his emergent understanding of general relativity.[16] Grossmann suggested an approach drawn from the nonlinear geometry of Bernhard Riemann. The two men coauthored a paper in 1913 and again in 1915. With Grossmann's help, Einstein expanded his mathematical understanding to appropriate a mode of thought which, until the time of their collaboration, he had used in a very limited way.

The relationship between experience, visualization of physical relationships, and formal representations of physical forces interested Einstein all his life. In 1921, in a lecture entitled "Geometry and Experience," he asked: "Can we visualize a three-dimensional universe which is finite yet unbounded?" He answered that such a theory cannot be directly pictured: it is a system of concepts, "but these concepts serve the purpose of bringing to mind a multiplicity of real or imaginary sensory experiences connected in the mind. To 'visualize' a theory, therefore, means to bring to mind that abundance of sensory experiences for which the theory supplies the schematic arrangement."[17]

While Einstein was able to synthesize his strong visual orientation with new conceptual and mathematical approaches, such a synthesis became difficult for physicists exploring subatomic phenomena. In 1925, Danish physicist Niels Bohr wrote of "the limitations of our usual means of visualization."[18] His German colleague, Werner Heisenberg, commented that their new theories labored under "the disadvantage that there could be no directly intuitive geometrical interpretation because the motion of electrons cannot be described in terms of the familiar concepts of space and time."[19] Their attempts to develop alternative ways to visualize physical phenomena were documented by Arthur I. Miller in *Imagery in Scientific Thinking*.

Early in the century, French mathematician-physicist Henri Poincaré wrote of sensual imagery that he saw as guided by aesthetic sensibility and an awareness of patterns (for instance, the patterns of lines resulting from the pull of a magnet on iron filings). These types of patterns became increasingly removed from direct perception as physicists explored subatomic phenomena. Consequently, scientists needed to develop new forms of imagery. While intuition—the seeing and feeling of relationships—remained an important part of their thinking, it was insufficient for explaining quantum jumps and the transition states of electrons. To develop more effective ways of describing nuclear phenomena, physicists started to rely on abstract diagrams that were supported by mathematical calculations.

This move from visual images to diagrams—linked with complex mathematical formulations and abstract mental imagery—was part of a broad process of conceptual change. The physicists working on atomic theory in the 1920s were faced with the limitations of existing representational concepts based on classical physics. "While classical concepts are certainly good enough for dealing with macroscopic objects, they are only of limited use for atomic or molecular dimensions" wrote Victor Weisskopf.[20] But rejecting these concepts produced doubt and painful confusion among these scientists. To address these concerns, the participants in this new framework of subatomic physics engaged in sustained, exhausting debates (for instance, Bohr and Schrodinger's lengthy talks in Copenhagen in 1926). Heisenberg said that in 1924–25 the participants were like mountain climbers surrounded by fog, "where the fog was thick but where some light had filtered through and held out the promise of exciting new vistas."[21]

Heisenberg's own work at that time was primarily mathematical, and he shared some of his calculations with colleagues in Gottingen, Copenhagen, and Cambridge. While these young physicists were making progress in mathematically specifying some characteristics of electron orbits, they were facing many difficulties. These included the wave-particle duality of light and matter, and related concerns with continuity and discontinuity in subatomical physical processes.

The challenges posed by the construction of a new paradigm, and the attending uncertainties and theoretical contradictions, were shared by a dozen theoretical physicists. The participants in this construction of a radically new way of viewing physical phenomena frequently criticized each other's notions. But they also knew that no individual could develop a whole new system of concepts on his or her own. Some, for instance, Erwin Schrodinger, preferred models of continuity. He described his findings in analytical terms. Others, including Heisenberg, emphasized phenomena that revealed discontinuities and used more algebraic modes of thought.

In 1927, Niels Bohr proposed a theory of complementarity, suggesting "that we should not reconcile the dichotomies, but rather to recognize the complementarity of representation of events in these two quite different languages. . . . Unlike the situation in earlier periods, clarity does not reside in simplification and reduction to a single, directly comprehensible model, but in the exhaustive overlay of different descriptions that incorporate apparently contradictory notions."[22] Another description of this principle is offered by Weisskopf, who was Bohr's student in 1932. He wrote in *The Joy of Insight*: "An electron is neither a wave nor a particle, but it exhibits one or the other set of properties under certain well-defined conditions. The systematics of these dual roles represent the essence of quantum mechanics. Bohr used the term *complementarity* for the apparent contradiction between the two mutually exclusive properties."[23]

Even before his formulation of the complementarity principle in quantum mechanics, Bohr emphasized conceptual conflict as a necessary preparation for conflict resolution. Holton thought Bohr was strongly influenced in his concept of complementarity by the psychologist William James. In his chapter on "The Stream of Consciousness," James contrasted the flights and resting places of thought. Flights are "changes, from one moment to another in the quality of consciousness," and the resting places correspond to the sustained continuity of awareness.[24]

Holton quoted other sources for "the roots of complementarity" in Bohr's thinking; these included philosophers Kierkegaard and Hoeffding. Kierkegaard used a qualitative dialectic, where thesis and antithesis coexist without proceeding to a higher stage in which the tension is resolved in a synthesis. This is similar to Bohr's approach to complementarity. Bohr was a dialectical thinker; Holton wrote: "[He] looked for and fastened with greatest energy on a contradiction, heating it to its utmost before he could crystallize the pure metal out of the dispute. Bohr's method of argument shared with the complementarity principle itself the ability to exploit the clash between antithetical positions."[25] Bohr's concepts have important implications for a view of complementarity that go beyond the challenge presented by classical and quantum descriptions of physical phenomena. They prepare us for contemporary approaches to social phenomena in which we represent our experience as an "exhaustive overlay of different descriptions that incorporate apparently contradictory phenomena."[26]

Bohr's mode of thought is what I call *dialogue thinking*—thinking that is fashioned, refined, and elaborated in the course of intense exchanges. Weisskopf says: "Bohr, in his Socratic way, always asked the relevant questions and pointed to the depth of the problems and the plenitude of the phenomena. . . . he was always active—talking, creating, living, and working as an equal in a group of active, optimistic, jocular, enthusiastic people."[27] Bohr's scientific method consisted of thinking aloud. "It was the 'victim's' [the junior person asked to assist Bohr] job to speak up when he couldn't understand what Bohr was saying or didn't think it was clearly formulated. . . . He [the victim] was witness to the mind of Niels Bohr in action. It was a chance to learn how Bohr thought and how he constructed the solutions to the problems he posed."[28] While Bohr's thinking was geometric and visual, it was also verbal. In contrast with some physicists, he consciously relied upon spoken dialogue and letters as part of his theory construction.

Bohr's intellectual breadth was nurtured in his childhood by his father, a distinguished physiologist, by his mother, a highly educated, warm, and cultured woman, and by a lifelong close relationship with his brother, the mathematician Harald Bohr. "For Niels, . . . Harald was indispensable not only as a mathematician and brother, but also as a debater. Niels thought best when he had someone on whom to try out his ideas. He loved to be contradicted in order to get deeper into the subject, but he progressed best when the person with whom he thrashed out the problem had the same attitude as himself, not only in approaching the problem but also in needing to penetrate its depth to the uttermost."[29] These qualities and his experience with Harald may have contributed to his ability to collaborate with so many different individuals.

Heisenberg was one of the young physicists who spent time in Bohr's Institute. His famous uncertainty principle—based, in part, on some of Bohr's notions—deals with the limitations imposed by physical measurements upon experimental information. Bohr approached these notions verbally, but Heisenberg expressed them mathematically. According to Miller, Heisenberg succeeded in overcoming the limitations of visual representational modes of thinking. In contrast to the more intuitive ways of Einstein and Bohr, he developed the fundamental notions of nuclear physics in complex diagrams linked to mathematical formulations.

The diverse modes of thought physicists relied on during this period reveal personal preferences as well as the need for multiple representational modes when faced with a paradigm shift. No single method sufficed. Visualization, common among physicists in earlier periods, was insufficient. While constructing new theoretical models, these scientists resorted to a combination of verbal metaphors, mathematical formalisms, and abstract visual modes. Some, like Heisenberg, linked mathematical formalisms with abstract representations. Others, like Bohr, combined verbal dialogues, geometric intuitions, and mathematics.

The modes of thought involved in *generating* explanatory principles are not necessarily the ones used in *communicating* scientific discoveries. Historians of science, such as Gerald Holton, Frederick Holmes, and Arthur Miller, rely on "private" documents—correspondence, autobiographies, conversations, and laboratory notebooks—to reconstruct scientists' working methods. They focus on what mathematician Reuben Hersh has called "the backstage" of discovery—a notion he adopted from the writings of sociologist Erving Goffman. The "front" is mathematics in its finished form—lectures, textbooks, and journals. The "back" is mathematics among working mathematicians discussed in offices or at cafe tables. Mathematics in back is fragmentary, informal, intuitive, and tentative. "We try this or that. We say 'maybe' or 'it looks like. . . .' "[30] In attempting to analyze the way scientific advances are co-constructed, it would be helpful to rely on both the "front" and the "back" of creative practices. Some scientists share only their finished products. Others, like the physicist Richard Feynman, reveal some aspects of their modes of thought.

In interviews with Christopher Sykes (1995) and in his own books, Feynman described some ways he met scientific challenges. From childhood on, he loved to tinker, and he was proud of his versatility with machines.[31] He visualized problems. His notebooks are full of sketches, diagrams, formulas. Feynman's curiosity, energy, and passionate engagement in physics were legendary. He learned with people as well as on his own. Throughout his undergraduate years at MIT in the late 1930s, when quantum physics was not yet fully integrated into the curriculum, he studied the writings of Einstein, Dirac, Bohr, and others. He shared these readings with a friend, T.A. Walton. They took classes together. During the summers they used a single notebook, which they mailed back and forth to each other. They also challenged each other to try to solve increasingly more difficult problems. Feynman kept probing at the edge of what was known, looking for important new problems, some of which he could visualize.[32]

He believed in the importance of desire: "Not so much the ability but the desire to play around and notice . . . I've always played around . . . I would make radios, or try to make a photocell work. I had a spark plug from an old Ford car that I would set up and use to burn holes in paper, or see what would happen when I tried to put a spark through a vacuum tube."[33]

Some of these activities and skills are usual in the development of an experimental physicist. But Feynman was a theoretician. He commanded diverse modes of thought. He experienced the physical world intensely with all his senses. He visualized physical relationships. He liked to talk about his ideas, and he was a vivid lecturer. He used mathematics, although his thinking was more intuitive than formal. His mind worked hard, at times at an astonishing pace. The originality of his thinking, according to many of his colleagues and collaborators, consisted of his ability to represent physical laws graphically. Hans Bethe commented that "Feynman's great secret in solving the problem of quantum electrodynamics was that he developed this way to do it graphically, rather than by writing down formulae. . . . [T]his led to the famous Feynman diagrams."[34]

As a young man, when Feynman first worked with microscopic processes in his graphical way, his thoughts did not communicate easily. In later years, he was articulate about the challenge of translating the inner imagery of phenomena at the atomic level into a mode that can be shared with others. But when he first developed his notions about quantum electrodynamics, he had difficulty communicating them to his colleagues. Freeman Dyson, a young mathematician at Cornell University at the same time as Feynman, became interested in the man and his ideas.[35] Dyson was a patient and careful listener. The two spent hours together on long car trips, and Dyson became familiar with Feynman's way of thinking. At first Feynman's ideas didn't make sense to him. He worked with them over time and contrasted them to those of another young physicist, Julian Schwinger, who used more formal, classical methods. Feynman and Schwinger were competing, approaching the dynamics of their field in two different ways. Dyson's mathematical skill provided a bridge between Feynman and Schwinger, and he achieved an insight that was crucial to the development of quantum electrodynamics. He was able to reconcile the two different approaches and to publish the theory.[36]

Dyson recalled, "I had to translate Feynman back into the language that other people could understand."[37] Feynman himself enjoyed solving problems, not writing up the solutions. On the other hand, he loved to talk physics across the whole range of the subject. The complementarity between Feynman and Dyson includes more than just their different scientific specialties. It also includes differences in temperament and working style.

Thus, complementarity has several aspects. In one meaning, used throughout this chapter, it means productive interdependence—the ways that people with different backgrounds, training, and modalities of thought complement each other in joint endeavors. Through collaboration they address a problem and find new solutions that they haven't been able to find as individuals. In this context, as I emphasize early in this chapter, we include the broadening of a collaborative partner's intellectual and artistic possibilities.

Collaborations benefit from complementarity in skills, experience, perspective, and the use of diverse methodologies honed within a discipline. Commitment to shared objectives, or a joint "passionate interest" in the subject matter, is crucial to joint endeavors. Sustained thinking and writing together, then, are not solely a cognitive activity. They involve relinquishing some aspects of individual autonomy, a possible temporary strain. But they can result in a broadening of the participants' talents and resources, an appropriation of strategies, or modes of thought, that contributes to growth, even among mature thinkers. Sustained, mutually beneficial collaboration provides a mirror to an individual, broadening his or her self-knowledge, which is crucial to creativity.

A second form of complementarity is linked to differences in temperament and working style, to which I turn next.

COMPLEMENTARITY IN WORKING STYLES

The success of some of the closest collaborations in the physical and social sciences is achieved by a combination of sustained sharing and of specialization between the partners. Nobel prize–winning biochemists Carl and Gerty Radnitz Cori formed an unusually close partnership: "The Coris conferred with each other constantly. When one started a sentence, the other finished it. Listening to them talk, friends had the impression that two voices were expressing their impressions from the same brain."[38]

The Coris' work on carbohydrate metabolism and specific enzymes was very influential in biochemistry and in medicine. They were prolific writers, and most of their publications were co-authored. As partners, they accomplished more than either of them could have achieved singly. Their strengths consisted of their shared vision, their common passion for their pioneering work, and the ways in which they complemented each other.[39] Biochemist William Daughaday, who had worked in their lab, describes their complementarity: "Carl was not the lab genius. . . . Carl was the visionary. Gerty was the lab genius, omnivorous in her interests, gobbling up new issues. They discussed everything together. Gerty read enormously widely and deeply. She was his initial processor, and he got many of his ideas from her outreach . . . he set the information into concepts."[40]

Some of their responsibilities reflected their complementary skills. Carl did administrative work and teaching in addition to their joint research, while Gerty trained their research collaborators. She was exacting, as one of their graduate students, Jane H. Park, recalled: "Nothing less than perfection, and every experiment was a burning and exciting event."[41]

There were interesting temperamental differences between the two. Mildred Cohen, who spent fourteen years in Carl's department at Washington University, wrote:

> Gerty was vivacious and outgoing; her mind was quick and sharp. Her enthusiasm for and dedication to science were infectious, and she supplied enough motivation for both of them. She was a tireless worker in the laboratory, arriving with Carl promptly at nine in the morning, beginning her experiments immediately, and continuing until six in the evening, totally involved in her research every moment. . . . Carl generally appeared somewhat aloof and austere but never pompous and frequently displayed an engaging gaiety and wit. His intellectual and personal impact was so compelling that he rarely failed to influence those who interacted with him. The economy and rigor of his writing style are quite in character. When one reads their joint Nobel address, part written and delivered by each of them, there is no difficulty in discerning where Carl ended and Gerty began. His section reads like a proposition in Euclidean geometry.[42]

The collaboration of two mathematicians, Philip J. Davis and Reuben Hersh, also reveals a complementarity in the way they approached their jointly authored books. While working on *The Mathematical Experience*[43] (for which they received the American Book Award), they found that their shared philosophy sustained them in a collaboration that required long-distance exchanges. Although mathematics is so specialized a field that communicating to people outside the field is an intriguing challenge, they shared the desire to meet that challenge. Their complementarity in writing styles—Davis more expansive, Hersh more concise—contributed to the success of their book: it combined diversity and expansiveness with a stylistic control that fit the subject matter. In my interview with them in March 1991, Davis also spoke of complementarity in another sense: "I feel very often when I don't understand something, the collaborator does. . . . I am more than myself. . . . I think in every single case of collaboration, the project required a contribution that each collaborator could only make. . . . Complementarity was the basis [of the project] in the first place. . . . It is almost as though I have two brains!" Hersh elaborated further:

> There have been some research projects where I and my collaborator actually would meet with each other over a period of time and struggle with the problem. And of course, each of our thoughts was necessary to finally get the solution. But even there, the reason for doing this was that the problem involved both his

and my area of expertise, so our thinking together consisted of each bringing our competence to bear on the problem. Ultimately, we would each write part of the piece separately and put it together. A collaborative partner can also perform the very useful role of being the external critic who relieves the writer from applying too much criticism to him or herself.

Davis commented: "One can block oneself terribly by being too critical of one's own writing. And I expect my collaborator to criticize me. . . . I like the quote from James Thurber: 'Don't get it right, get it written.' Then I use the collaborator to get it right."

In addition to the clarifying and magnifying effects of collaboration, they emphasize the role of trust and mutual regard as central to their partnership. It makes accepting each other's corrections a comfortable process. Davis recalled: "My trust in him was that if he said something was right I believed he would get it right. . . . He is very good at working with text. Of course there are plenty of times when you change something around—it can be that way, it can be this way. If he changed something around that I thought was valid the other way, I said, 'Well, what difference does it make, let it go his way.'" The willingness to compromise, not to "fall in love" with one's own text or words, is important for collaboration. Some efforts at writing together flounder on a partner's unwillingness to relax the tight hold on his or her stylistic preferences. But when the collaborators enjoy each other, and when "you like that person, you want to join with that person in some way . . . and your personalities click," explained Hersh, "it's easier to make adjustments."

Psychologists Harold Stevenson and James Stigler expressed the same idea in an interview at Stanford. They were working on their book after a decade of research collaboration in cross-cultural studies of mathematical education. Stigler was a student at the University of Michigan when he met Stevenson, already a well-known professor there. The difference in their age and status mattered little once they discovered their complementarity both in training and in some of their interests. Stigler's knowledge of Chinese was an important asset in this cross-cultural study. The two wanted to present their findings and the implications of those findings in a book accessible to an American audience.[44] Both hard workers and good listeners, they talked about such a book for years before they were able to devote sustained, shared time to writing it. While emphasizing the critical role of complementarity in a working relationship, they also pointed out the willingness to look at the written material as text rather than claiming, "that is his or my idea." Stigler explained:

One of the things we do when we write chapters is we [frequently] rewrite what the other person has written. Then we have a kind of a rule, you are not allowed to compare [the new chapter] to the one you have written. You have to look at it on its own merits. And if something is glaringly missing when you read it, then put it back in. But don't just go back through and try to find all the things that were changed. . . . You have to be willing to give up your own words. When we get done with these chapters, you can't say I wrote that sentence. . . . it is more, this is the product.

Frequently, in jointly authored books, each partner chooses the topic he or she is most familiar with and then writes that part of the first draft. This is the way Stevenson and Stigler constructed their book. Stevenson focused on the cultural background of the study and a description of the participating families, while Stigler wrote about classroom practices in the United States, China, and Japan. They spent a lot of time talking, but also knew when they needed to shift from talking to writing. Like many effective collaborators, they developed a successful rhythm between planning, writing, criticism, and mutual encouragement. Davis and Hersh also remembered one of the great benefits of collaboration: mutual confirmation. Davis recalled, "He [Reuben] confirmed that this material that I had been writing was interesting, and that the philosophy that it expressed, either implicitly or explicitly, was fairly consistent with his own." Hersh added, "I think both have to be stimulated by the same idea, the same goal, really want the same goal. I can conceive of a situation [in which] people are just pulling themselves apart; one person wants to go this way, the other to go that way, and it adds up to zero."

Stigler and Stevenson made a similar observation. They contrasted collaboration with the widespread academic practice of looking for holes in one's argument. Stigler explained:

What you get in a collaboration is the assumption that there must be something interesting there. You are able to work on a generative rather than evaluative level. I know a lot of people who are good critics. If I want to know what is wrong with my idea, they will tell me. But not very many—it is much more special—to have someone who is going to try to take your idea and help to develop it.

Stevenson added:

I think one of the most frustrating things of working with someone is that they are not tolerant of your lack of clarity. You can't be perfectly clear in every utterance. And you can't be perfectly sequential in every utterance. . . . If you are referring to old things, fine. But if you are coming up with new things, you do go here and there, and that is one of the important things of being able to collaborate with someone.

Davis and Hersh described another collaboration that was less comfortable. Mathematicians Richard Courant and Kurt Friedrichs, co-authors of *Supersonic Flow and Shock Waves*,[45] had different notions of what constituted an acceptable presentation of their ideas. Friedrichs' then graduate student, Cathleen S. Morawetz, presented some of Courant's writing to Friedrichs, who said, "No, no, that is much too vague and sloppy," and he rewrote it. Subsequently, after she worked with the text further, she presented it to Courant, who looked at it and said, "Oh no, that is much too complicated. No one could read that." And he redid it. Each chapter went that way until they both got sick of it and stopped, settling for the latest version. They worked through Morawetz rather than confronting each other and their differences.

These different patterns of complementarity are aptly captured by Stevenson's metaphor of collaboration as a Chinese family: "You give up some of your freedom, in a sense. On the other hand, you expand your reach by such a great amount."

COMPLEMENTARITY AND OPPOSING PERSPECTIVES

In creative work, opposition and dynamic tension often yield new understanding. Holton saw continuity and discreteness as opposing "themata" in the study of nature. This chapter has dealt with such oppositions, especially the wave-particle paradox that was central in the transition from classical physics to quantum mechanics.

The new physics had to deal with this paradox. Different scientists have done so in different ways. Einstein in his early years proposed a new integrative theory of light "that can be interpreted as a kind of fusion of the wave and emission theory."[46] But twenty years later, when a more complete fusion of theory was developed in the form of quantum mechanics, Einstein could not fully accept it. Although his own results forced him to include chance as part of an account of spontaneous processes, he hoped that a final theory would be deterministic: "That business about causality causes me a lot of trouble, too. Can the quantum absorption and emission of light ever be understood in the sense of complete causality requirement, or would a statistical residue remain? I must admit that there I lack the courage of conviction. However, I would be very unhappy to renounce complete causality."[47]

Einstein's work became tangential as quantum mechanics developed further, but he continued to write on the topic, hoping that the paradoxes could be overcome and an integrated physical picture of nature could be constructed. (Interestingly, in the late 1990s, some of his theories were supported by new empirical data.)

Einstein cherished his friendship with Bohr, but they had deep differences on this topic. The two met in Berlin in 1920 after paying close attention to each other's work. At that time they had considerable agreement about the wave-particle paradox. But as new developments came, their views diverged. Einstein proposed an experiment to overcome the uncertainty principle of Bohr and Heisenberg. At first Bohr was troubled by Einstein's proposed experiment, which gave a possible counterexample to the statistical aspect of quantum physics. But in 1927, he developed an effective answer to Einstein, which sustained the uncertainty principle.

Bohr's answer, as characterized by his biographer, Abraham Pais, proposed the notion of complementarity:

> The question whether an electron is a particle or a wave is a sensible question in the classical context where the relation between object of study and detector either needs no specification or else is a controllable relation. In quantum mechanics that question is meaningless, however. There one should rather ask: Does the electron (or any other object) *behave* like a particle or like a wave? That question is answerable, but only if one specifies the experimental arrangement by means of which one looks at the electron.[48]

Bohr dealt with the duality of particles and waves by means of complementary descriptions of phenomena, contextualized in the modes of measurement. Einstein could not reconcile himself to all the implications of complementarity and in 1935 proposed a countertheory. His arguments were not accepted by his colleagues. But to Bohr, Einstein's objections were important. They motivated him to formulate his complementarity principle more and more precisely.

The debate between Einstein and Bohr illustrates a widespread phenomenon in science. The tension of sharp opposition can engage individuals in principled disagreement, which can contribute to the advancement of knowledge. The role of opposition in science can be further illustrated with the ongoing debates about the biological basis of language. At issue are basic questions about the modularity of language structures and the universality of cognitive processes. In Noam Chomsky's generative grammar, first presented in full in his book, *Aspects of the Theory of Syntax*,[49] language is an independent, self-contained system. He conceptualized it as a separate organ in the brain. As such, syntax is inborn, hard-wired, and universal.[50] His analysis of the human language capacity focused on a universal grammar; the specific features of a given language are determined by parameters (rules) which speakers acquire through exposure to their speech community. This has been a very influential theory during the last thirty years, with many linguists contributing formal studies to support Chomsky's claims. This nativist position has been further popularized by Steven Pinker, whose highly popular books, including *The Language Instinct*,[51] have contributed to a debate that some have referred to as the language wars.

But Chomsky's theory also has strong opponents. These include researchers whose empirical studies focus on language acquisition. They have described the development of language as a process in which meaning, sounds, grammar, and communicative strategies are interwoven (e.g., studies by Halliday, Bates, Slobin, and Berko-Gleason).[52] Some of these developmental scholars rely on cognitive linguistics as an alternative to Chomskian theory. In this newer approach, syntax is seen as part of a broader system in which meaning is linked to phonological (sound) expression.[53] Coevolution of language and brain is yet another theory that represents an alternative to Chomsky's nativism.[54] Students of language variations in differing social contexts have also opposed nativist theories.

Scholars who study language as an evolving system are growing in number. They see language as socially, cognitively, and physiologically situated between and within human beings, and are strongly motivated to present arguments and data that challenge the powerful, formal logic of Chomsky. This ongoing linguistic debate is contributing to the exploding study of cognition and neuroscience.

Generative tensions between competing positions are found in many disciplines. The Einstein-Bohr debate was remarkable because the protagonists were able to maintain a caring and deeply respectful personal relationship. This is not always the case when scholars oppose each other's position.

Most of this chapter has been devoted to scientific partnerships in which thinkers work with each other supportively. I must add *oppositional complementarity* to these accounts. Effective debate requires deep familiarity with the thinking of the opponent—an immersion into a thought structure that can sharpen one's own. That familiarity happened to Bohr as he defended his complementarity from Einstein's criticism. Scientists who attack each other's approaches are in conflict, but they are also partners, just as opponents in chess or tennis are partners. They form a connection that is important in constructing knowledge and confronting paradoxes in their field.

COMPLEMENTARITY IN THOUGHT AND ANALYSIS

Bohr's development of complementarity, as described above, addresses difficult and recurrent problems in intellectual history. In the introduction to this chapter, I emphasize complementarity between individuals as "the pluralism of human possibilities powerfully realized in partnered endeavors." Many of the scientific partnerships described above show mutual support based on training, working style, temperament, and mode of thought. Bohr's ideas go beyond complementary relations between individuals to complementary relations between ideas — *conceptual complementarity.*

In some other efforts involving traditional polarities, scholars develop a new synthesis. A recent example is neurologist Antonio Damasio. He reformulated the longstanding dichotomy between reason and emotion in an integrated theory of "somatic-markers."[55] His work is based on examination of brain-damaged patients as well as on analyses of experimental studies. He situated a system of neural connections between rational and emotional behavior in the prefrontal area of the brain, a region he called an "eavesdropping post": "The prefrontal cortices thus contain some of the few brain regions to be privy to signals about virtually any activity taking place in our beings' mind or body at any given time."[56] In this area of the brain, categorizing behavior takes place, connections to motor areas of the brain are made, and "[the] prefrontal cortices send signals to autonomic nervous system effectors and can promote chemical responses associated with emotions."[57]

Damasio argued that feelings contribute in significant ways to decision making and rationality. At times they inhibit effective choice, but frequently they enhance it. He did not link emotions to the body and thought to the mind as so many dualists have done in the past. Instead, he integrated the body, the brain/mind, and emotions when he wrote: "The organism has some reasons that reason must utilize."[58] In titling his book *Descartes' Error*, Damasio aimed to replace Cartesian dualism with a theory that includes a passion for reasoning —what playwright Arthur Miller called "felt knowledge."

A third way to deal with polarities in conceptual systems was suggested by Bohr. He did not absorb one member of an oppositional pair into another, as did Pinker, nor did he aim at a synthesis between previously polarized concepts, as did Damasio. Instead, he wrote of complementarity as the *acceptance* of two contradictory phenomena, neither reducible to the other, and not forming the components of a new synthesis. To him, the coexistence of waves and particles meant that a researcher focuses on one or another plane of analysis depending on the physical question being asked. Bohr recognized the study of "phenomena," which includes both the objects of study and the modes of observation. Simplification and theories that rely on a single cause are effective in classical physics, but Bohr argued that in quantum physics a different epistemological stance was necessary. As quoted above, Holton described Bohr's stance as follows: "Unlike the situation in earlier periods, clarity does not reside in simplification and reduction to a single, directly comprehensible model, but in the exhaustive overlay of different descriptions that incorporate apparently contradictory notions."[59] Bohr believed that this concept of complementarity is also relevant to psychological phenomena. I share that belief.

A recurrent dichotomy in the study of human beings occurs between the focus on social activities and socially mediated action, on the one hand, and individual processes, including brain activities, on the other. The nature/nurture controversy is an example of such a theoretical tension, as are recent discussions of mental representations. In my theoretical framework, cultural-historical theory based on Vygotsky's thinking, some dichotomies are resolved in syntheses, such as the broad unification of nature and culture in the course of socialization and development. In this theory, cognitive development is seen as occurring first in the shared activities of individuals, followed by internalization of the consequences of such interaction. For instance, verbal discourse between individuals, particularly between young and mature speakers, is transformed into inner speech and further into verbal thinking. Young speakers appropriate socially elaborated symbol systems which form the basis of their own representational systems. Individual and social processes are unified through a dialectical synthesis, frequently referred to as the *zone of proximal development.*[60]

At the same time, to fully explore the ways in which social processes are transformed and unified with individual development, we cannot always make a synthesis. Some aspects of our analyses require a different way of dealing with traditional polarities. It is not always possible to unify dichotomies by weaving them together into a new resolution or synthesis. Some analyses reveal an irreducible tension between two aspects of a complex situation; Vygotskian scholar James Wertsch wrote of these irresolute analyses.[61] He conceived of people (or agents) as engaged in mediated action by using socially constructed tools. Wertsch suggested that thinking, communicating, and acting constitute a complex system. He viewed some individual and social processes in dynamic tension with each other, and this tension produces important and, frequently, useful changes. Wertsch's stance is akin to Bohr's analysis of subject/object relationships: he conceives of two poles characterized by an irreducible tension that I call *conceptual complementarity.*

In trying to explain the construction of knowledge, Vygotskian theorists speak of representational activity, or the way experience is generalized and mediated through jointly crafted symbols. These representational activities include complementary processes: on the one hand, neurochemical action in the brain that cannot be explained through social analysis; on the other hand, social interactive processes of symbol development that cannot be explained through neurophysiology. Yet these individual and social processes are profoundly linked. They are examples of conceptual complementarity.

When individuals join together and build upon their complementarity in scientific disciplines, they expand their reach. The strength of these partnerships is as much in their common vision as in their complementary abilities. Collaboration offers partners an opportunity to transcend their individuality and to overcome the limitations of habit, and of biological and temporal constraints. The unity in diversity of complementary relationships is further strengthened when partners create an amplification of individual vision and purpose. In generative scientific partnerships, collaborators redefine their own personal boundaries as they strive toward mutuality and deep understanding.

Simone de Beauvoir and Jean-Paul Sartre. Photograph by Loomis Dean, Life Magazine. Copyright © Time Inc.

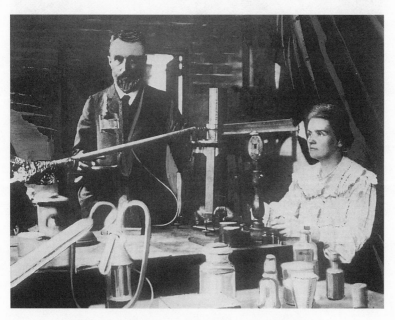

Pierre and Marie Curie in Laboratory. © Bettmann/CORBIS.

Georgia O'Keeffe and Alfred Stieglitz, Lake George, as published in *Stieglitz: A Memoir/Biography*, page 297, by Sue Davidson Lowe. New York: Farrar, Straus & Giroux, and United Kingdom: Quartet Books, 1983. Photograph courtesy of Sue Davidson Lowe.

Frida Kahlo and Diego Rivera. Photograph courtesy of George Eastman House.

The authors of *Women's Ways of Knowing* (clockwise from top left): Mary Belenky, Blythe Clinchy, Jill Tarule and Nancy Goldberger. Photograph courtesy of Barbara Viniar.

Gerty and Carl Cori, circa 1946. Photo courtesy of Washington University School of Medicine, Becker Library.

3

PATTERNS OF COLLABORATION AMONG ARTISTS

Accounts of creative partnerships are increasingly featured in the media and in the professional literature. Many articles tell how partners complement each other in style, temperament, disciplinary training, and their specific vision. Some accounts report insiders' views of complementarity and interdependence, such as that given by choreographer Murray Louis about his four-decade partnership with Alwin Nikolais.

In private life, they "somehow merged into a single identity,"[1] but as choreographers they had different approaches:

> In our creative work we were very different individuals, a difference that was easily perceptible on stage. Without that difference any collaboration between us would not have been possible. He approached his work from the outside, painting the stage with light and color while I worked from the interior, with much concern for choreographic detail. . . . In our work together, neither of us was interested in narrative plot line or specific meanings; instead we aimed to create imagery that would encourage audiences to be involved with what they were seeing and experiencing. His canvas was broad and large; mine was more intimate, poetic and detailed. From early on, I could sense what he was after, just as he recognized my choreographic intent.[2]

In contrasting their styles, Louis described the complementarity in their partnership. Two different artistic styles, when closely observed and respected, can provide revealing mirrors for each partner. These mirrors add a third dimension, a deeper view, to their knowledge of themselves. They enrich the partners' options in solo and joint work.

Some writers acknowledge the joint thought and understanding required for large writing projects, even though that profession has traditionally been considered solitary. Tony Kushner, the author of *Angels in America* and *Pereistroika*, credited a wide range of contributors to his plays.

> While the primary labor on *Angels* had been mine, over two dozen
> people have contributed words, ideas and structures to these plays
> . . . Two in particular, my closest friend, Kimberly T. Flynn
> (*Pereistroika* is dedicated to her), and the man who commissioned
> *Angels* and helped shape it, Oskar Eustis, have had profound, de-
> cisive influences. [3]

Kushner said the belief that a writer alone is the wellspring of his or
her creativity is a debilitating myth. But he understands its wide cur-
rency and the way it challenges many artists. In his essay, he mentioned that German revolutionary playwright Bertold Brecht was ide-
ologically committed to collectivity, yet also hungered for personal
recognition; indeed, the tension between connectedness and his individual ego fueled some of Brecht's work. That same theme threads
through much of the dialogue of the collaborators I have studied.

By sharing a vision with Flynn, Kushner drew on her qualities as a
teacher and her range of "rhetorical strategies and effects," which he
has transformed into his own. His tribute to Flynn and to others
who shared his thinking about *Angels in America* is moving:

> I have been blessed with remarkable comrades and collabora-
> tors: Together we organize the world for ourselves, or at least
> we organize our understanding of it; we reflect it, refract it, crit-
> icize it, grieve over its savagery and help each other to discern,
> amidst the gathering dark, paths of resistance, pockets of peace
> and places whence hope may plausibly be expected. Marx was
> right: The smallest indivisible unit is two people, not one.
> From such nets of souls societies, the social world, human life
> springs. And also plays.[4]

Shared vision, as exemplified by Kushner and Flynn, is crucial to
successful collaboration, but is not always sufficient. For a partnership
to be truly creative—to change a discipline and transform a paradigm
—multiple perspectives, complementarity in skills and training, and
fascination with one's partner's contributions are also essential. Illustrating these themes was the particularly well-documented collaboration of Picasso and Braque. They were the creators of Cubism, a new,
twentieth-century approach to painting that focused on the interrelation of objects. Their painterly vision of our understanding is akin, to
some extent, to Bohr's notion of complementarity described in the
previous chapter. Art critic John Berger wrote: "The Cubists created a
system by which they could reveal visually the interlocking of phenomena. And thus they created the possibility in art of revealing
processes instead of static states of being."[5] The transformation of understanding, and the use of new forms and materials, requires collaboration. Interactions that helped shape Cubist thought also involved

Fernand Leger, Juan Gris, and other painters, as well as poets such as Guillaume Apollinaire. Their relationship illustrates one of the major themes of this book: that *the juxtaposition and joint exploration of ideas are crucial for constructing a new paradigm in art or science.*

But while collaboration is empowering, it can be fragile. Once a new mode of thought is established, it can be implemented in many divergent ways. Picasso and Braque's partnership reveals this dynamic. It also raises the emotional aspect of significant partnership, including financial and artistic interdependence and the dynamics of long-term collaborative groups in the arts.

PICASSO AND BRAQUE: JOINING, TRANSFORMING,
AND PARTING

As a child, Picasso drew incessantly. He was the son of an academic painter in Malaga and was encouraged by a loving, devoted family. Although Picasso's childhood was happy in many ways, it was overshadowed by tragedies. An earthquake shook his hometown when he was three. His younger sister, Cochita, died when he was fourteen. And the family had to move many times as his father chased work opportunities. When Picasso was eleven, a year after moving to Corunna, he started art school. At the same time, he studied Latin, French, and Castilian grammar at a regular school. Picasso was not a brilliant student, but his self-description as seriously limited in academic subjects may have been exaggerated—one of many myths about himself that Picasso enjoyed perpetuating. Picasso's biographer, John Richardson, traced many of the painter's themes and personal traits to these early events. He was deeply indulged, particularly by many female relatives. He started to draw early. According to family legend, his first word was "piz," for *lapiz*, Spanish for "drawing pencil."

From an early age, Picasso did *papiers decoupes*—cutouts of animals, flowers, and figures. His graphic vision was inspired by both his aunts' embroidery and his father's drawing and painting. His early work expressed his and his father's interest in pigeons and bullfights. A painting of a picador, and a drawing of a torero tossed by a bull, are the first pictorial records of Picasso's lifelong *aficion*— "a legacy from his father, who had such a passion for corridas that he started taking his son to the bullring as soon as he could walk."[6] In *Creating Minds*, Howard Gardner wrote of Picasso's breadth in observing and depicting what he saw: "Part of Picasso's prodigiousness stems from the fact that he was gifted across the range of relevant skills and could draw on them synergistically."[7] Gardner argued that Picasso's willingness to experiment with graphic forms, even before he began formal art school, contributed to his extraordinary range throughout his career.

We have few records of Picasso's work before the age of ten, but by his early teens, his artistic gifts were evident. In 1895, at age fourteen, portraits he exhibited in store windows in Corunna were reviewed in a local newspaper: "We do not doubt that he has a glorious and brilliant future ahead of him. . . . the execution denotes real courage as if the brushes had been handled by an artist of considerable experience instead of a neophyte."[8] While Picasso went to art school in Corunna, Barcelona, and Madrid, his most important apprenticeships were to "distant teachers"—artists from the past who provided powerful models.[9] These included Goya, Velasquez, and El Greco. He also learned from friends, many of whom were artists. Starting in adolescence, Picasso was surrounded by companions—poets, painters, sculptors, newspapermen. Gardner suggested that the admiration of his friends contributed to Picasso's confidence that "there were no limits on what he could accomplish."[10]

The first time Picasso went to Paris he was not quite nineteen. It was the beginning of the new century. He sold a few paintings and started to make a place for himself in this center of the arts. But his life was difficult. He was short of money, a close friend committed suicide, and he knew little French. For several years he shuttled between Paris, Barcelona, and Madrid. At last in 1904, he settled in Paris, in a building full of artists. Here he painted his "Blue period" works and developed one of his many groups of companions, calling themselves "*the bande a Picasso.*" An enduring strength was his ability to engage friends and admirers into sharing his own activities."[11]

This ability exemplified what Howard Gruber termed network of enterprises. Gruber wrote of creativity as a complex human activity, within which a group of related projects and activities form an *enterprise.* This dynamic concept includes not only productive projects but also disruption, strategies for dealing with obstacles, and the possibilities of new, related projects when a current project comes to an end. A network of enterprises constitutes a creative individual's life tasks. Gruber suggested that "people with different networks of enterprises can and must collaborate."[12]

Picasso usually traveled with a friend. He shared many early experiences in Paris with fellow painters from Spain. His group included poets as well. When the great French poet Apollinaire joined the "*bande,*" his impact was considerable: "Until he died, fourteen years after they met, Apollinaire would be a constant solace, a constant goad to Picasso. He opened up his imagination to vast new ranges of intellectual stimuli: to new concepts of black humor, to the pagan past, and the wilder shores of sex."[13] At one point, both were preoccupied with harlequins. Dealing with this joint subject matter revealed a remarkable symbiosis. Richardson wrote: "So similar is their imagery that sometimes it seems as if the painter and the poet had access to the same imagination."[14]

In these years Picasso absorbed the work of Cezanne, Manet, Gauguin, Degas, and particularly Matisse. Some critics have found these diverse influences in his important painting, *Les Demoiselles d'Avignon*. Richardson called this work "the first unequivocally twentieth-century masterpiece, a principal detonator of the modern movement."[15] It was an important transition between Picasso's earlier Fauvist paintings and his move toward Cubism.

Les Demoiselles is a savage, angular painting of prostitutes. Their forms are flat. Some of the figures recall African masks. In his notebooks preparing for this painting, Picasso experimented with simplifications and distortions of the nude.[16] To art critic Berger, this painting was "concerned with challenging civilization. The dislocations in this picture are the result of aggression not aesthetics; it is the nearest you can get in a painting to outrage."[17] Berger saw *Les Demoiselles* as the work that provoked Cubism. It was an artistic insurrection that foretold the sustained, collaborative construction of a revolution.

Picasso met Braque in 1907, the year of *Les Demoiselles*. They were introduced by Apollinaire. Braque had been raised in Le Havre, the son of a house painter with interests in modern art. He was different from Picasso—tall, athletic, deeply attracted to music. As a child and an adolescent, he enjoyed looking at the sea, drawing caricatures, and sketching on weekend expeditions with his father. He took art classes in a local Ecole des Beaux Arts, but official art did not stimulate him. His experience in house painting and decorating nourished his interest in the physical materials of painting. Braque visited museums in Paris, and in 1902 he moved there to become a painter. His father helped him financially.

His early work was influenced by the Fauvists (for instance, Matisse and Dufy). Some of his finest paintings during those years were of seaport scenes. Braque was driven beyond these works, mostly by the influence of Cezanne, whose impact was also considerable on Picasso.[18] When Braque saw *Les Demoiselles*, it had a shock effect on him. It stimulated him to experiment with figures, and one notable result was his *Large Nude*, painted in 1908. The next year, he worked to reverse the approach to visual perspective that painters had practiced since the Renaissance. He developed a new idea of bringing shapes forward on the pictorial surface toward the viewer. In critiquing an exhibition of Braque's work in 1908, reviewers reached beyond the existing language, and the term "Cubism" was coined.

Picasso sensed that their movement would get heavy criticism. He gladly let Braque take the public role of exhibitor. (His reluctance was due partly to insecurity as a foreigner.) The two painters saw their innovations leading to work that was tactile, palpable, hefty. The central theme of the first—analytical—phase of Cubism was representing objects from several points of view on a single surface.[19] Their technique was to dissect and dismantle objects. In this way they brought a new modernism to painting. They chose objects and scenes that were at hand, including manufactured objects. By reducing forms to geometrical structures, they were able to paint the interaction between solids and the space around them,[20] or, to use Picasso's description, "to shatter the enclosed form."[21] The two painters frequently chose similar scenes: following Braque's *Harbor Scenes* painted in 1909, Picasso painted *Harbor at Hadaques* in the summer of 1910. Techniques such as a visual grid appeared in the work of both. They used similar devices to avoid traditional perspectives; they relied on the size of objects to construct a tactile space. In this phase of their most rigorous experimentation, their color spectrum was limited. They focused on shapes and edges.

Many years later, Picasso told Francoise Gilot: "Almost every evening I went to Braque's studio or Braque came to mine. Each of us *had* to see what the other had done during the day. We criticized each other's work. A canvas was not finished until both of us felt it was."[22] These were the days of their most intense visual dialogues (powerfully reconstructed by the Museum of Modern Art's joint exhibit of their work from 1908 to 1914). They resonated to each other's themes and techniques, which emphasized movements within the surface, and they made steady innovations. They spent the summer of 1911 together in Ceret, in French Catalonia, and actually succeeded in exchanging artistic personalities. Richardson wrote: "Braque comes up with an image that has the incisiveness and sharp focus we associate with Picasso, while Picasso paints the rooftops with the soft sensuousness we usually associate with Braque[23] . . . It is no coincidence that Braque's best drawings were done when he was closest to Picasso."[24]

Braque described their closeness during these prewar years by comparing it to mountain climbing. Picasso thought of it as a marriage. When they were separated, he wrote to Braque: "What has happened to our walks and our exchanges of feelings? I can't write about our discussions of art."[25]

As we've seen in other joined lives, this partnership vividly illustrates how the act of constructing a new mode of thought in art or science thrives on collaboration. With Picasso and Braque, the partnership provided new visual possibilities through each other's eyes, and through verbal and visual dialogues. Occasionally they achieved such complete fusion of styles that it was impossible to distinguish the work of one from the other. At one point in their collaboration, each signed his own name, not in front, but on the back of the canvas: in this way the painter's identity remained in the background. "We were inclined to efface our personalities in order to find originality," Braque wrote.[26] And Picasso recollected: "So you see how closely we worked together. At that time our work was a kind of laboratory research from which every pretension or individual vanity was excluded."[27]

At first they constructed an analytical version of Cubism, where objects are decomposed and flattened using only one color. In 1912 they changed to more inclusive methods. Their palettes became richer in colors and materials. They mixed paint with sand; they used oilcloths and stenciled letters. Braque's experience with diverse materials in his father's house-painting business helped them in these appropriations. Picasso enjoyed pushing these innovations, which led to further discoveries. The most important were their collages, or *papiers colles*:

> An object could now be presented by some foreign element that was an equivalent, as opposed to an image, of itself. A piece of newspaper, for instance, could stand for a newspaper; it could also signify anything else the artist wanted to signify. Drawing could function simultaneously and independently to indicate volume and integrate the real element (the piece of newspaper or wallpaper) into the composition. Furthermore, by enabling color to function independently of form, papier colle made it easier for Picasso and Braque to introduce positive color into a Cubist composition.[28]

During these productive years of 1912–14, Picasso started to experiment with three-dimensional cardboard constructions. They allowed him to represent objects from multiple perspectives. He even connected different parts with his mistresses' dressmaker's pins. In 1914 he continued to work in three dimensions, using sheet metal and wire. These new constructions helped change the course of modern sculpture.[29]

This second period of innovation is called synthetic Cubism. The breadth of materials the painters used, the new forms with which they experimented, and their growing reputations made 1912–14 particularly significant. Their close partnership remained the center of Cubism, but the style was spreading. Younger painters such as Juan Gris and Fernand Leger carried out some aspects of the Picasso-Braque conceptual and artistic transformations. Their contemporary, Henri Matisse, with a different approach made a mutually beneficial alliance with Picasso.

The influence of Cubism continues to this day in the way we experience space, graphic forms, and the relationship between the many facets of immediate reality. Berger described the significance of this artistic revolution as follows:

> Cubism is an art entirely concerned with interaction: the interaction between different aspects; the interaction between structure and movement; the interaction between solids and the space: the interaction between the unambiguous signs made on the surface of the picture and the changing reality which they

stand for . . . It is to Cubism that the next serious innovators are bound to return.[30]

The daily, heady collaboration of Braque and Picasso ended with the French mobilization at the start of World War I. Braque left for the war. Picasso, a foreign national and a pacifist, did not participate. Braque was wounded in 1915 and went through a long convalescence. This injury changed Braque's personality, his relationship with Picasso, and eventually his style of work. After they had achieved their fundamental, transformative task, each partner carried the legacy of their common work in different directions.

This famous partnership of Braque and Picasso is an *integrative collaboration*, which transforms both the field and the participants. In such a collaboration partners frequently suspend their differences in style. While creating a new vision, they can experience a profound sense of bonding. This pattern contrasts with the *complementary* mode of collaboration, in which differences in training, skill, and temperament support a joint outcome through division of labor. The complementary pattern is common in universities, research laboratories, and commercial workplaces. Complementarity in science in its varied forms is described in the previous chapter. There I also note the role of specialized disciplinary knowledge and contrasting modes of thinking (visualization versus mathematical representations).

It is difficult to draw a definite line between the integrative and the complementary patterns of joint activities in creative work. Integrative or generative thinking is rapid, condensed, and embedded in the cognitive processes of individual(s) who challenge the known. It requires expansion, challenge, and translation into external, communicative forms. It relies on dialogue. Complementarity is well illustrated in Dyson's rethinking of Feynman's diagrams (see previous chapter) and his translation of them into verbal and mathematical forms accessible to an entire discipline. The collaboration between these two scientists, while illustrating complementarity, also embraces moments in thought when they approached integrative collaboration, which requires a long process of committed activity. It is motivated by the desire to *transform* existing knowledge and paradigms into new visions. This task is so formidable that it is better accomplished in collaboration than in solitude.

VISUAL PARTNERSHIPS AND COMMUNITIES

In current accounts, collaborations of two individuals or of small groups are well documented. At the same time, literature about larger groups is increasing. For instance, the recent book, *Organizing*

Genius, by Warren Bennis and Patricia Ward Biederman,[31] about large, mixed groups such as "Troupe Disney" describes the need for collaboration in innovative, labor-intensive endeavors. (In order to create the first feature-length animated movie, *Snow White and the Seven Dwarfs*, Disney assembled 300 artists and architects from all over the country.) In large collaboratives, members vary in their closeness to each other, disciplinary training, and skill. In many artistic fields, such groups or communities have been influential during periods of stylistic and conceptual transformations. But other collective activities involved in the construction of paintings and murals, collages, and monuments have frequently been ignored. Sociologist of art Howard Becker asked: Shouldn't we understand painting as embodying division of labor, akin to that in the making of films? He answered:

> The division of labor does not require that all the people involved in producing the art object be under the same roof like assembly-line workers, or even that they be alive at the same time. It only requires that the work of making the object or performance rely on that person performing that activity at the appropriate time. Painters thus depend on manufacturers for canvas, stretchers, paint and brushes; on dealers, collectors, and museum curators for exhibition of space and financial support; on critics and aestheticians for the rationale for what they do; on the state for the patronage or even the advantageous tax laws which persuade collectors to buy works and donate them to the public; on members of the public to respond to the work emotionally; and on the painters, contemporary and past, who created the tradition which makes the backdrop against which their work makes sense.[32]

In a similar vein, psychologist Mihaly Csikszentmihalyi argued that creative work is situated and supported in a complex network of institutions that constitute the "fields" of creativity. He illustrated his idea with fifteenth-century Florence:

> When the Florentine bankers, churchmen, and heads of great guilds decided to make their city intimidatingly beautiful, they did not just throw money at artists and wait to see what happened. They became intensely involved in the process of encouraging, evaluating, and selecting the works they wanted to see completed. It was because the leading citizens, as well as the common people, were so seriously concerned with the outcome of their work that the artists were pushed to perform beyond their previous limits.[33]

Increasingly, scholars acknowledge the many social facets of art-making. These include the social forces and institutions of which Becker and Csikszentmihalyi wrote and the common trajectory of artists who encourage each other while learning and transforming their craft. Even when artists do not meet face to face, their connections to each other and the broader world are complex. "Fragment joins fragment to make humanity," wrote art critic Ernst Fischer.[34] The artist "wants to refer to something that is more than the 'I,' something outside of himself and yet essential to himself. He longs to absorb the surrounding world and make it his own; . . . to unite his limited 'I' in art with a communal existence; to make his individuality *social*. . . . Art is the indispensable means for this merging of the individual with the whole."[35] Artists broaden their sense of "I" in many ways. The Impressionist painters of the late nineteenth and early twentieth centuries sought to do so by identifying with nature and by maintaining close collaboration with each other. Their idea was to transmit their immediate perceptions onto canvas *without any interpretation*. They used pure colors and paid close attention to the effects of light. In the early years, Manet and Cezanne shifted the understanding of how painters should approach the painterly surface. Their experiments with trying to paint exactly what they saw on the canvas, without any cognitive or representational mediation, greated affected their contemporaries (primarily the Impressionists) and later the Cubists.

Some Impressionists met as students. Renoir, Monet, and Sisley attended the atelier de Gleyre. In the evenings at the Cafe Guerbois, they were joined by Manet, Pissarro, and Guillaumin. They discussed their emerging ideas and fashioned an art philosophy of direct perception. They were a "persevering confraternity that was distrustful of the Academy and the art schools that emphasized hackneyed traditions at the expense of sincere, untaught ways of looking at the world and inventing new ways to express a personal vision."[36]

Their difficulty in winning public recognition only strengthened their comradery. They shared an interest in landscape "motifs," which they identified during expeditions to Chailly. Monet was particularly good at choosing creative settings, which attracted his fellow painters to his village of Argenteuil on the Seine and, in his later years, to Giverny. Painting side by side, these Impressionists would sometimes get so immersed in their work that they forgot each other's presence. Their work linked in theme and approach, with many obvious ties: they shared a deep reverence for nature as the source of their paintings; exhibited together when excluded from the official salons; helped each other with money; often traveled together, and stayed in each other's homes.

The relationship between Monet and Renoir in particular illustrated this interdependence. As very young men, they shared quarters and meager funds. They helped each other and their friends to arrange the first exhibit of Impressionists in 1876. They often chose the same scene to paint, and served as mirrors to each other for making self-discoveries and developing artistic identities. Monet wrote of their formative years in Paris, where Renoir and other friends, Sisley, Bazille, Cezanne, and Degas, as well as some writers, met and argued:

> Nothing could be more interesting than these causeries with their perpetual clash of opinions. They kept our wits sharpened, they encouraged us in sincere and disinterested research, they provided us with stores of enthusiasm that for weeks and weeks kept us up, until the final shaping of an idea was accomplished. From them we emerged tempered more highly, with a firmer will, with our thoughts clearer and more distinct.[37]

These partnerships among the Impressionists were less intense than the visual dialogues and transformative connection between Picasso and Braque. But they illustrated, in some ways parallel to the bonding of nuclear scientists in the 1920s, the strength of companionships based on intellectual and artistic mutuality. This was a structure within which new and difficult visual concepts could be forged.

Partnership among scientists, whose sharing of large-scale equipment creates a special kind of interdependence, is somewhat different from that among artists. In both cases, transformations of thinking styles and novel understandings of the physical and humanly crafted world are best achieved when supported by an engaged thought community.

The difference between mutuality in the arts and the sciences stems from the artist's greater emphasis upon individuality, his or her need for a recognizable style. But such an individual style is embedded in a broader framework of shared understandings of visual conventions; these are shaped and transformed by thought communities of artists who interactively and significantly change the domain of art during different historical periods.

The contemporary Western emphasis on an individual artistic identity connected to a distinctive individual style arose in the Renaissance. In earlier times, the building and decorating of churches by anonymous artists expressed their deeply shared religion. During the Renaissance, individual artists started to compete for major commissioned works. But the execution of their work was still accomplished in groups: the best-known example, Michelangelo's Sistine Chapel, required the joint labor of thirteen workers.[38]

Still there are several forms of co-construction in the visual arts: one of these is the shared activity of many artists engaged in large works, such as churches, frescoes, and, in modern times, large-scale murals. In such works, there is a shared vision, along with a division of labor according to skill and experience, further examples of the widespread pattern of complementary collaboration.

Another form of partnership occurs when friends choose to render the same motif in different ways (sometimes, in ways hard to distinguish from each other). In such spatially and conceptually close collaboration, artists heighten their own understanding of their purpose and evaluate its execution by examining the work of their partners. The novice immerses him/herself in more mature work as, for example, the Impressionists studied Delacroix and Japanese painters. The young artist frequently copies masterworks. Atelier students working with the same model watch, criticize, and appropriate each other's visual understanding. The impact of distant teachers, mentors, and peers on developing artists is well documented in art history.

SUPPORTIVE PARTNERSHIPS

Many of the examples of collaboration described in this book deal with the co-construction of knowledge and art forms among individuals trained in the same or complementary fields. The assistance they give each other is discipline based and intellectual. But there are many partnerships where interdependence requires also meeting each other's *emotional* needs. Creative people often face loneliness, poverty, and recurring doubts about their abilities.

The relationship between Vincent Van Gogh and his brother Theo was a partnership of an artist and an art dealer. They shared the travails of a painter whose life was fiercely committed to creativity. Vincent, the oldest child of a Dutch pastor, did not start drawing and painting until his twenties. His family included art dealers, and he worked for a short time in galleries himself. This profession did not suit his retiring personality. His brother Theo was more comfortable buying and selling art work. As the older brother, Vincent advised and encouraged Theo in developing his taste and judgment and in achieving a breadth of culture. But once Vincent decided to devote himself totally to painting, he became the dependent member of the pair. He was financially supported by Theo, and he relied on his brother's emotional availability and artistic judgment. In hundreds of letters, Vincent confided all aspects of his life to Theo: his choice of mentors, their criticisms, his relationship with the rest of their family, his loneliness, and the difficulties of life with his model, with whom he lived in his late twenties. Once Theo assumed financial responsibility for Vincent, he became an all-around advisor to his brother, dealing with most aspects of Vincent's life. The painter cared deeply about Theo's judgment of his work. Vincent shipped much of his work to him to Paris, hoping that it would sell.

Vincent painted his world with words as well as with paint. His letters to Theo evoked the settings where he worked and captured his love of nature and the people who worked in the fields:

And on that muddy road a rough figure—the shepherd—a heap of oval asses, half wool, half mud, jostling each other—the flock. You see them coming—you find yourself in the midst of them—you turn around and follow them. Slowly and reluctantly they trudge along the muddy path. However, the farm looms in the distance—a few mossy roofs and piles of straw and peat between the poplars. The sheepfold, too, is a dark triangular silhouette. The door is wide open like the entrance to a dark cave. Through the chinks of the board behind it gleams the light of the sky. The whole caravan of masses of wool and mud disappear into the cave—the shepherd and a woman with a lantern shut the doors behind them.[39]

As with many intense bonds, the relationship between the two brothers was not always peaceful. Vincent's total financial dependence, while necessary for his survival as a painter, was a burden for both of them. Vincent also craved Theo's approval of his work and wanted him to fight for the paintings. This need was difficult to meet, as Theo worked for a rather conservative art dealer. Also, as Vincent started late as a painter, it took a while for him to master certain existing conventions and to develop his great talent. He was a fanatical worker and needed response to his canvases. Theo was his primary source for response, but for more than a decade his praise was cautious. It was only when Theo moved to Paris in 1886 that he was under the influence of painters he respected that he began to believe fully in his brother's genius.

Both brothers were shy in social relationships, and in their connection they expressed a lot of their individual conflicts and depressions. When sharing an apartment in Paris, they felt pride as well as despair toward each other. Their bond was complex but essential to both of them. Regardless of the way they felt about each other at certain times, Theo steadfastly supported Vincent's work. His support made it possible for a penniless painter to become one of the major artists of the twentieth century. While collaboration traditionally has been thought of in relation to work, it also provides many personal benefits. Theo's emotional and financial support profoundly shaped the extraordinary chances Vincent took (and could take) in this work.

The literature on collaboration focuses primarily on the cognitive aspects of mutuality. Emotional aspects of collaboration are most likely to emerge among intimates: brothers, sisters, lovers, marriage partners, parents and their collaborating children, and close friends.

But students of creative partnerships have not yet provided a theoretical framework to account for the significance of emotion in partnership. The challenge of effectively integrating intellectual, aesthetic, and emotional aspects of creativity is of increasing concern to many scholars, including those working within the cultural-historical, or Vygotskian, framework. In this chapter and Chapter 5, I identify some recurrent emotional themes in existing accounts and from the interviews among collaborators I have conducted. These include care and conflict, fusion and separation, trust, individual artistic identity, and partners' negotiations about the ownership of ideas. These themes are relevant to collaborative interdependence and also to the ways a partnership changes over time.

The artistic and sexual liaison of writers Anaïs Nin and Henry Miller tumultuously and interestingly exemplified some of these themes. They both were imbued with the nineteenth-century Romantic view of the rebellious lives of artists when they first met in Paris in 1931 through an acquaintance. Nin, married to American banker Hugo Guiler, lived in Louveciennes, a suburb of Paris, in a house the couple shared with Nin's mother and brother. Miller was an impoverished bohemian American writer. Nin characterized Miller's artistic stance in 1937: "He has a human love of writing, of words, and takes a sensuous pleasure in writing. It is flesh and life and food."[40] Nin was a self-taught writer who penned *D. H. Lawrence: An Unprofessional Study* in 1931. This small book, first published in 1932,[41] was inspired by her belief that Lawrence "opened a new world in modern literature."[42] Although she never met Lawrence, he provided for her the distant teacher or model that she needed. Nin had no formal literary education or affiliation with an artistic community, so her connection to Lawrence's work was crucial in guiding her in her first attempts at writing. Lawrence remained a major influence on her work for the rest of her life.

Miller, though living at the margin of society, was an enthusiastic, often exuberant man. He appreciated the fine meals in the Guiler-Nin household, Nin's admiration, and her husband's frequent although reluctant financial help. Nin and Miller became lovers, and their relationship lasted for a decade. Her husband could not ignore their liaison, but still he tried hard to stay close to his wife, whom he adored. Nin's attraction to Miller was based on his artistic vision, which was similar to that of Lawrence. She also appreciated the openness and forcefulness with which he wrote about sexual experience, his personal directness, and his verbal power. He opened a new world to her in sharing his sexual, intellectual, and fantasy experiences: "Occasionally they went out for lunch; more often they prepared *dejeuner a deux*. . . . After lunch with Anaïs he'd push the dishes to one side and read from his manuscript, show her his watercolors, or explain a wall chart that might interpret world history through a color wheel."[43] From the very beginning of their relationship, Nin considered Miller a true modernist. His many needs for her help and his admiration filled her life in a new and exciting way. Miller praised her study of Lawrence and encouraged her to develop her female sensitivity as a writer. A collection of their letters from 1932 to 1953 entitled *A Literate Passion* fully documented their mutual support of each other as writers, lovers, and friends. Miller had great confidence in the literary and emotional power of Nin's journals; they vividly described a young woman's struggle against the odds to become an artist. He fought to get them published, and in retrospect his judgment about their literary worth was correct. Nin wrote: "You came when I had nothing to live for, and gave me life and strength, and inspiration, Henry. All the joys. And then your letter comes to confirm this faith of yours, this life-giving enthusiasm, this sustenance. . . . So definite you are, and illuminating for me."[44]

Miller had a complicated, tortured relationship with his wife, June. He tried to capture her character in *The Tropic of Cancer*, based on an earlier novel about his wife, which Nin had previously tried to resurrect after he had abandoned the attempt. Nin also helped him find literary agents to place *The Tropic of Cancer*, which he had written during the early stages of their liaison. Her belief in his talent, her help in cooking for him and his friends, and their talks about what they had read contributed to the emergence of Miller as a self-confident writer. In one of his most passionate passages, he praised Nin: "*You* have been the teacher, not Rank, nor even Nietzsche nor Spengler. All these, unfortunately, receive the acknowledgment, but in them lies the dead skeleton of an idea. In you was the vivification, the living example, the guide who conducted me through the labyrinth of self to unravel the riddle of myself, to come to the mysteries."[45] Through 1932 and 1933, Nin and Miller spent a great amount of time with each other. Miller read Nin's writing seriously; he was always willing to discuss it, word by word, line by line. No idea was too silly, too outrageous; everything was open to discussion. But, unlike Nin's husband, Miller did not give her total admiration and frequently made her angry with his critiques. She curbed her anger and listened carefully to what he said.[46]

Miller urged her to transform her personal writing into fiction, a struggle that was hard for her to resolve. Her best writings were her portraits of people, of events, and of fleeting, complex emotional states. Her difficulties were with plots. And as she believed in Miller's work with an unusual passion, she frequently put her own work aside to assist him. During these early years of their relationship, she took great pride in her role in his life:

> She believed she had guided him from unpublishable ramblings to the two successful *Tropics: Cancer and Capricorn*. She took

credit for identifying what were to become his major themes, the lives and adventures of himself and his friends and their extraordinary (i.e., for the historical time in which he wrote) sexuality. She insisted that, in a number of crucial instances (June, for example), she provide the outline of what he should write, and he merely filled in the detailed observations.[47]

Miller's criticisms helped Nin's writing style. Her first published prose-poem, *House of Incest*, was finished with Miller's stylistic help and emotional support. As the first person to be allowed to read her complete *Diary*, his unstinting praise for it contributed to Nin's sustained fight for her journals. Miller believed in the diaries' constructive role in her personal life and in their literary value.

At the same time, Nin's belief in Miller helped him to forge a self-confidence he had not been able to achieve before. Each enriched the life of the other. For a while Miller seriously considered marriage. But their financial dependence on Guiler's income, and Nin's ambivalence about Miller's ability to make a living coupled with her lasting commitment to her husband, whose loyalty she trusted and needed, eventually undermined these marital plans. At the same time, their connection to each other remained a significant aspect of their lives.

But in 1939, at the eve of World War II, after they and all the American expatriates had left France, their affair ended and their paths started to diverge. Miller traveled a lot, while Nin became established in New York and developed a new circle of friends and admirers in Greenwich Village. Nin continued to help Miller financially, frequently cutting her household expenses to give him money. When Nin decided to buy a printing press in order to publish her own work, Miller, who was by then in California, responded positively to her productions as he came across them, which helped her to summon the self-confidence necessary for promoting her publications.

Their impact on each other was lasting, both in their sense of who they were and, increasingly, in how the world saw them. As each gained fame, particularly in the 1960s, their relationship was explored in biographies, in the study of Nin's published *Diaries*, and in the film *Henry and June*.

CREATIVE GROWTH IN RELATIONSHIPS

A life devoted to creative work in the arts is insecure. In contrast to academics who can rely on an institutionally organized work environment, most artists have to mobilize personal, emotional, and financial resources in order to fulfill their objectives. Central to meeting such a challenge is belief in oneself and one's talent. Such a belief is seldom built without the support of mentors, personal partners, family, and friends.

Artistic development illustrates the feminist concept of "self-in-relation,"[48] the notion that the self develops in the context of important relationships. I suggest that interdependence and the appropriation of a new perspective through working closely with partners are not limited to the cognitive domain. The Vygotskian genetic principle, that "[a]ll higher psychological functions are internalized relationships of the social kind, and constitute the social structure of personality,"[49] is powerfully realized in partnerships. Trust between collaborators often contributes to the heightened self-confidence needed to overcome the weight of artistic traditions.

In addition to trust, partnerships can support a person's willingness to take risks in creative endeavors, a process considered critical by many researchers of creativity.[50] In speaking of his own collaboration, Howard Gruber, a leading scholar in creativity, suggested that, by "spreading the risk between partners, each participant is encouraged to take more chances."[51]

Risk taking is a particularly urgent concern for young artists who are faced with the challenge of gaining recognition while also testing their own sense of worth and promise. Two young collaborators, theater director and playwright Bill Conte and choreographer Suki John described in an interview the way they encourage each other to take chances.[52] They first met while still in their twenties. They were attending an interdisciplinary seminar in the arts at New York University, and they worked together on a vocal and choreographed rendition of T. S. Eliot's "The Love Song of J. Alfred Prufrock." During that first endeavor, they discovered their ability to complement each other. Conte thinks in broad philosophical terms and has a resonant voice and mind. John shares Conte's conceptual breadth, but she also strives to embody his theatrical ideas in rhythms and movements. Their many-sided collaboration spanned the last ten years, involving major projects, such as Dante's *Inferno*, and a dramatization of Eliot's *Waste Land*, as well as choreographed dance-drama pieces, such as "Cartas de Amor" and "Sh'ma," created by John and deepened through their interactions. When I interviewed them in a Soho loft a few years ago, they spoke of the way they were expanding their capabilities through a slow process of mutual appropriations. It was only when preparing for the third performance of "Prufrock," years after the original class exercise, that John felt she could give Conte direction as an actor. Up until that point, she saw herself as solely in charge of movements. He appreciated her added role: "As an actor I cannot see myself, I need the feedback." Conte learned much about his own body while working with John, integrating this new knowledge with his textual orientation as a writer.

These artists have little stable financial support, but in spite of that constant difficulty, they have been committed to demanding projects of philosophical and social significance. They collaborate with a variety of people. Conte has built an ensemble group of actors on Staten Island; John has worked with dancers and actors in several countries. But their interdependence continues: whether by phone or face to face, they provide hope, insight, and emotional support to each other during these rocky times for artists. Conte explained during the interview: "You think like I do!" meaning they share an inclusive view of the theater, they both reject its current limited role as commercial entertainment. In their collaborations they both are open to experimentation, prepared to face failure, and willing to take criticism and suggestions from each other and from the actors and dancers with whom they work. And in this way they share the risks so necessary for innovation.

They see their partnership as particularly successful because they jointly generate a wealth of new ideas. John commented, "Ideas create ideas, it is like ping-ponging." When issues of ownership or territoriality surfaced, they spoke bluntly about their boundaries to each other. They trust their personal fluency and know that they can increase it through their interaction.

Writing a play can be very lonely, Conte confided. But he found that being able to share his self-doubts and worries about finances, or being able to meet a deadline, helped in facing some of his solitary labor. Artists can get stuck at times when creating; Conte called it "the vacuum," when having a trusted collaborator, even if he or she is not working on a joint project, can be a support to both of them. John described such periods: "When that happens, I turn to Bill, and his confidence in me helps me out of that rut. I rely on Bill's experience of me as a choreographer and a friend to bolster me through those lean times." They think of each other as family, and as family members they not only love each other but also know how to argue and shift roles (be assertive or take the back seat).

One of their most demanding joint productions was staging Eliot's *Waste Land* on the polluted shores of Staten Island, using an abandoned industrial site as their stage. Their setting was as desolate as the view of reality that the poem implied. Their intent was to take their audience through a journey, through the emptiness of a waste land, to experience the worst possible industrial nightmare, and then move past it to experience some sense of peace. This journey depended on their ability to forge a togetherness with the actors, which formed the basis of a cathartic resolution. But much of their ensemble was inexperienced, so Conte and John had to help each other keep the company focused and together. They had to be both strong and diplomatic when facing their manifold challenges. In that process they also learned how to work with each other in more effective ways. The effort of keeping a theater group going without financial support caused the people in it to pool all of their artistic, emotional, and problem-solving resources. Such pooling required ongoing interaction and "reasoned, impassioned debate." In their commitment to a communal, serious theater with volunteer actors, it has always been very important that they know themselves, each other and the groups with which they worked.

When asked to describe their similarities and differences, John mentioned their complementarity in voice and movement. Conte reflected, "Sometimes I feel you are just a female me!" He elaborated some of the similar qualities they share: "her strength, her leadership ability, her aesthetic." In thinking further about similarities and differences, they related these qualities to gender roles and physical size. Conte's more massive presence contrasts with John's small dancer's body—and these differences result in somewhat different ways they relate to their casts.

Their actors need to be joyously engaged, as they give their time without pay; they need to gain value and pleasure from the theatrical process, to experience, in Conte's words, "love and family." The closest collaborations usually have been between playwright, composer, and choreographer. All three were part of the creative process from its beginning. Actors entered the collaboration later, and they gained their greatest rewards when performing for an audience that resonates to their work. John and Conte both recognize the difference between their motivation and rewards and those of the actors. They try to help each other create a situation where inspiration, discipline, and playfulness are shared by all members of their theater community.

Since the production of *Waste Land* in 1990, they have continued to work together. Conte has encouraged John to expand beyond her early personal dance-dramas. He suggested that she unearth new topics waiting within her, including dances with political and satiric content. And John, on her part, has helped Conte with the restaging of his major works based on Dante's *Inferno*. She continues to teach the actors movement (the discovery of their own embodied emotions), and she remains the thoughtful critic and loving, enthusiastic co-worker to her writer-director friend. Their professional and personal relationship is effectively balanced by their primary, marital partnerships, in each case, to a person who is not a professional artist.

Social psychologist Michelle Fine called collaboration "an affair of the mind." As in most intense relationships, the emotions that support the connection between partners can undergo interesting and, at times, painful transformations. In looking at particularly intense collaborations, one is led to ask: Is it possible for productive lives to mesh without arousing competitive feelings? Do some partnerships have too much interdependence, and consequently experience a painful separation after the period of fusion? One tragic example was the recent suicide of writer Michael Dorris. We do not know whether his death was linked to the intense interdependence between him and his wife and co-author Louise Erdrich. He was suffering from depression, which he had been able to keep under some control through decades of their close collaboration.

A different example of fusion and separation emerged in the artistic partnership and personal relationship of dancers and choreographers Martha Graham and Erick Hawkins. The young, ballet-trained Hawkins joined the Graham Company in 1936. He added a strong male idiom to a predominantly female group. Agnes de Mille examined his impact in *Martha*, a biography:

> Above all, he got her to think in terms of relationships to men, in terms of their way of moving, their bodies, their dynamics, their presence. He paved the way for work with other men. He immensely broadened her canvas. Besides his role as a performer, Hawkins took on many artistic and organizational responsibilities. He helped create a disciplined, well-organized ensemble. He attended to fund-raising, as well as to the physical work in setting up productions. His impact on Martha Graham was considerable. They married in 1948 in Santa Fe, New Mexico. As a consequence of the intensity of their personal relationship, Graham started to move to new themes which included powerful emotions, sexuality, and conflict. Hawkins shared with her his interest in Jungian psychology and Oriental philosophy. Their years together were artistically productive. But Graham's extraordinary gifts and achievements were hard to equal, they presented a threat to her ambitious husband. Although Graham tried hard to choreograph strong parts for him, Hawkins was not recognized at the level that he had expected. Eventually, he was unable to live with the disparity between them. He walked out of the marriage and the company. The break produced a serious depression in Graham. She never married again.[53]

Hawkins started his own school and company in 1951 with a dance technique quite independent of his early mentors and collaborators. His intent was to "find the equivalent simplicity, clarity, directness, effortlessness, strippedness, in dance movement that I knew I liked in everything else."[54] In his aesthetic and movement choices he was influenced by Indian myth, the philosophy of F.S.C. Northrop, and his belief in dance as nature inside humankind. His direction diverged significantly from Graham's. His dance aesthetic was closely studied by modern composer Lucia Dlugoszewski, who became his life companion and close collaborator. Their more balanced relationship contrasted with his emotionally demanding years with Graham.

From the Graham/Hawkins partnership, we see that some patterns of collaboration and mutuality seem time limited. This may be particularly the case with partners in the same discipline, such as Nin and Miller, Picasso and Braque, and Graham and Hawkins. Their connections are very intense; while working together they are very productive and even transform their domain.

Intensity is essential to creative work. But how it is managed within and between people has not been carefully explored. In long-term artistic partnerships, mutual commitment to shared and emergent goals is the foundation of a successful collaboration. In these well-documented partnerships one can discern several stages of the relationship. Each stage is characterized by a different mode of joint activity and emotional dynamics.

During the early stages of an integrative collaboration, mutual discovery and a certain temporary fusion of individual personalities take place. Enchantment with the partner contributes to eagerness to learn, to explore, and to engage in new work. Nin and Miller described in great detail these experiences and their productive interdependence. But as their relationship became less idealized, some ambivalent feelings emerged. They needed to deal with their own creative individuality, to focus on one's own contribution as well as on the development of the other. Nin was pleased that Miller relied on some of her verbal portraits in his writing, but she wondered about the consequences of such "borrowing" for her own growth and reputation as a writer.

In relationships where financial dependence is important, as between the Van Gogh brothers and between Nin and Miller, resentment may not be safe to express. Nin paid for the original publication of Miller's *Tropic of Cancer*, but when it gained a reputation beyond her own, she felt overshadowed. Trust is central to collaboration, particularly among dyadic partners. But it cannot be taken for granted. It needs nourishing. It may require honest confrontations of problems between the partners and a willingness to adjust a relationship that has lost its original intensity. There may be a time limit to particularly intense, transformative collaborations. Interestingly, these tempestuous relationships seem to terminate after a decade. In *Organizing Genius*, Bennis and Biederman made a similar observation about intense, creative collaborations. They suggested that "Great Groups" do not last, "if only because of their intensity they cannot be sustained indefinitely."[55]

Eventually these passionate collaborators start to attend to their own individual needs and even to compete with each other. Their emotional trajectory starts with fusion, out of which important works are produced, but it is followed by ambivalence, which can result in a painful separation.

Still, there are many artistic collaborators who manage to develop ways to protect their relationship. They are skilled in knowing how to modulate it, fine-tune it, and, at times, build some artistic distance between each other while treasuring their primary connection. Choreographers Louis Murray and Alwin Nikolais illustrate such a connection. Their bond was more balanced and cooperative than that of Miller and Nin.

Another example of a balanced, supportive partnership lasting several decades was the relationship of painter Georgia O'Keeffe and photographer Alfred Stieglitz. They met when Stieglitz exhibited O'Keeffe's work in his New York gallery. His affirmation of O'Keeffe as a promising artist (first through letters, later in person) contributed greatly to her determination to pursue her career full time. Although she was much younger than he, she was not a novice painter when they started living together. O'Keeffe's biographer, Roxana Robinson, described their relationship during the crucial decade of 1919–29 as follows: "Georgia steered quietly and serenely around his sharp and obdurate corners. . . . Most of Stieglitz's eccentricities she found beguiling, and she recognized the anxiety and vulnerability that lay behind his need to control an argument or an idea. Georgia's capacity to appreciate without judging allowed her to love the best of Alfred. He was brilliant company, charming and inventive."[56] While Stieglitz and O'Keeffe built a solid egalitarian relationship in their private lives, in public he was dominant. His championing of her work as part of the modernist movement in the arts was important in winning attention for her in a world still riddled by gender prejudice. Their personal relationship could have been damaged by their unequal standing were it not for Stieglitz's great warmth and O'Keeffe's astonishing self-reliance and independence. In the midst of the commotion of Stieglitz's life, full of family obligations and time spent with friends and admirers with whom he shared his ideas passionately and volubly, O'Keeffe managed to create stillness for her work. But increasingly, she realized that to do her artistic work justice, she needed to maintain some distance from his busy life. In 1924, she wrote: "I have to keep some of myself or I would not have anything to give."[57]

It is this insight, and O'Keeffe's ability to act on her self-knowledge, that made her such an influential figure. Although Stieglitz and O'Keeffe did, at times, experience conflict in their claims on each other, they maintained a relationship supported by what Robinson described as "a sense of vivid, overflowing, mutual tenderness." They cared for each other, even when physically apart, as during O'Keeffe's increasingly long summers in New Mexico. Stieglitz's portraits of her became his great tribute to this extraordinary woman, part of their joint legacy. Their relationship informed psychologists as an unusual resolution of the conflicting pulls of loving interdependence and creative determination, which in their case flourished both in joint and separate endeavors.

A somewhat different emotional engagement develops among groups of artists who battle existing conventions and the dominant judges and power holders in their disciplines. These relationships are also exhilarating in their early stages. (The Impressionists illustrate this kind of a connection.) But they become more complex once the major artistic and emotional challenges that the partners choose for themselves have been addressed. The community is based on a pattern of mutual respect and connection, which does not require artistic fusion of the kind Picasso and Braque enacted in the formative years of Cubism.

Creative collaborations take many forms. In some groups or dyads, the cognitive and emotional dynamics reach a certain height, after which the collaboration starts to disintegrate. In others, there is a carefully maintained balance, in which individuals who are committed to each other professionally and personally develop a variety of means to protect their partnership. Santa Fe artists Gail and Zachariah Rieke's account, and their generosity in showing me their ongoing and finished work, give immediacy to the notions of supportive collaboration discussed in this chapter.[58]

The couple first met thirty-two years ago as graduate students at the University of Florida. Gail was interested in collaborative drawings with children and adults as a way of overcoming "responding to myself." By the time she asked Zack to join her, she had a lot of experience in this activity. But with him, she discovered a "singleness of mind" that was very different from what had happened when she drew with others. Their visual conversations preceded their talking to each other verbally. Their interactions were fruitful and exciting. Eventually they married.

Artistic development is seldom a straight line, Gail suggested in my interview with them; it is like arching and twisting, where a person picks up things learned in the past from other artists or musicians and from personal experience. In their case, their paths are like a dance, where the partners may switch places while retracing, circling, and moving forward—such as when Zack worked on collages before Gail discovered that this art form was natural for her, too. They share materials—old manuscripts, feathers, stones, found materials. Their collections are carefully filed. When they examine the contents of their many, beautifully arranged drawers, they see new possibilities. They are committed to the exploration of surface texture and to the integrity of that surface. They approach that challenge with a double perspective. Zack described their collaboration: "When we work together, we play off from one another and there are quantum leaps that are made. . . . Something happens because of this stereo sort of vision that does not otherwise happen." Such importance of talk as well as a shared aesthetic is emphasized by many collaborators; as Russian artists Vitaly Komar and Alexander Melamid reported, "Our best ideas are born from talking—then the spark comes."

Gail is the collector: she brings objects and people into their environment. Zack is more contained. Their pieces frequently start as collections, which give rise to new insights once the materials are sorted. "It starts to fill the void," they observed. At times, their pieces start with a found object—one of these was a boot scraper Zack used when he was ten years old. Once the construction matures and satisfies a certain visual logic, Zack builds the frame for the work. One of the Riekes' most important collaborations was the construction of a three-dimensional box that started with a dream Gail had. By superimposing an old window frame, her husband helped her build the box, using his more formal sense of design. This frame provided the visually necessary grid that the collage lacked until that point. Another box they built started with a Victorian journal Gail found and loved. Zack took a travel trunk and built six long, flat drawers, each of which held part of the journal and their visual responses to it. They thought of this very successful piece as a three-way collaboration between the two of them and the writer of the journal.

Zack and Gail are often asked how they handle each other's suggestions or criticism. During thirty-one years of marriage they have built a shared aesthetic and a great trust. Their responses to each other are akin to an artist stepping back from his work after achieving some distance from it, and seeing it with a new pair of eyes. When Zack is in his studio working on a new painting:

> I constantly bug Gail, "Come in and see what I just did." . . . I am a very explosive kind of painter, a lot of dramatic stuff involved in it. . . . I very much value her giving a fresh, even if it is just a quick kind of spontaneous, response to what is going on. And just recently she said, "Stop right there! Don't do anything."[59]

These artists are very aware of time. In music, time is an explicit part of the work, but in visual constructions time is a hidden variable. It is part of the changes that the work undergoes as it ripens. A painting or a construction is often put aside for a while, to be completed much later. Time is also part of their relationship. Just as their constructions and paintings are organic, growing and changing, so is their connection.

When they talk of their partnership, Gail and Zack include the shared responsibility for their children. Their pattern bears some likeness to the *family pattern of collaboration*.[60] An important feature of family-type partnerships is the development and cherishing of common values. For the Riekes, their approach to their work, their love of found objects and intriguing use of these, and their contemplative attitudes reflect beliefs and values that they have jointly honed over decades.

Another interesting feature of family collaborations is fluidity of roles. At times, Gail takes the role of the critic; she knows how to make immediate, even urgent suggestions. At other times, she stays in the background and gives her reactions only when they will not interfere with her husband's artistic flow. They also know how to take over for each other as artists and parents. Central to their collaboration is their trust in each others' sensitivity and support. Their success is due partly to the internalization of that support, resulting in strengthening their solo and joint works.

FAMILY PATTERNS OF COLLABORATION

Theater, film, music, and dance require different forms of flexible partnerships. As playwright Tony Kushner reminded us, dozens of people contribute ideas and structures to a play: actors, directors, and audiences, as well as personal partners. While preparing for a theatrical production, participants form intense connections. French novelist and playwright Françoise Sagan knows the experience of theater intimately:

> [T]he magic of rehearsals, the smell of newly cut wood that hangs over the set, the last minute chaos, the excitement, the optimism, the despair. . . . Only those who had some connection with our play, our show, our achievement were admitted to our internal circle. We were fanatics, sworn to martyrdom or triumph, adherents of a religion no one else has ever heard of. Even husbands . . . had been caught up in this engulfing force, and I believe they knew the play as well as we did.[61]

For most actors and playwrights, once a play closes, the bonds established during rehearsal and performances become less intense. But there are exceptions. The desire to create and sustain a "common faith and cooperative action"[62] was what motivated one of the most collaborative ventures in the history of modern drama, the Group Theater. It was established in New York in the 1930s. The history of this brave and influential organization, told by its founder, Harold Clurman, in his book *The Fervent Years*, explicated their beliefs: "The development of playwrights, actors, repertory and the rest are important only as they lead to the tradition of common values, an active consciousness of a common way of looking at and dealing with life."[63] The members of the Group Theater fought hard to forge such a consciousness. In order to sustain their cohesiveness, "stars" often had to settle for smaller parts than their talents and experience warranted. The actors shared the economic trials of this experimental group; they performed in many challenging settings; they worked at making sound collective decisions, and they participated in articulating a common philosophy.

The group started informally. Clurman brought together actors he had known as a play reader for the Theater Guild. He found an enthusiastic partner in Cheryl Crawford, who had some managerial experience. From the beginning, their emphasis was on joint creativity that was to include playwrights, actors, stage designers, and directors. They started to work as a company in the summer of 1931. The directors were committed to maintaining a year-round organization that included summer rehearsals and teaching. Both Clurman and Lee Strasberg, one of the directors, expressed their intent to create an "artistic organism" of actors and other participants. Their concept was akin to that of psychologist David Feldman, who characterized "cultural organisms [that] are specialized social structures designed to carry out ambitious human goals; in the current context their special purpose is to nurture and direct the expression of extreme talent. [They] are constructed with humanly crafted tools, techniques, technologies, symbol systems, traditions, rules, customs and beliefs, organized around a particular human collective enterprise."[64] Feldman gave several examples of such structures, which interested him as a student of prodigies. One of these was the Aspen Music Festival, which relies upon the extensive coordination, organization, management, and interpersonal skills of a large musical and technical community to bring forth the best music they are capable of producing.[65] Thus the purpose of "cultural organisms," as Feldman saw it, was to organize existing knowledge and to provide the challenge and the context for individual and joint creativity.

The Group Theater required complex coordination between playwrights, actors, directors, and financial supporters. Their goal was to create a permanent repertory theater, "the chance to tie sporadic individual work into units of collective endeavor. This would not only strengthen them individually but would serve to make their values objectively effective, forceful, permanent," wrote Clurman.[66] Central to the success of their collective endeavor was the development and practice of a powerful acting technique, Strasberg's adaptation of the famous Stanislavsky method. His adaptation included improvisation and the use of affective memory. During early rehearsals the actors developed their parts by relying on their own words rather than reading the script.[67] They created moods relevant to their parts by remembering events from their own past. These moods animated their work. Strasberg knew how to stimulate, feed, and protect these genuine emotions.[68]

Many of the actors discovered companionship, security, work, and dreams as participants in the Group Theater. Sometimes, when the actors were having a particular hard time living on their meager salaries, they set up joint living quarters. They shared the cooking: "on special occasions a friend or a more fortunate Group member sent a chicken or meat for a pot roast."[69] When the Group brought in new members, it required them to stretch and, at times, to reluctantly reorganize themselves. In this, the Group was like a biological family that must adjust when a new relative is included. And, like families, Group members experienced rivalry, jealousies, and the loss of valued members (to Hollywood or the commercial theater). Through dealing with these challenges, they became more aware of what connected them. They shared a philosophy and a theatrical method; they staged innovative works that dealt with socially significant issues of particular importance during the Depression to help create a new, politically committed American theater.

Clurman's careful documentation of the life story of this "extended family" gave many insights into large-group collaborations. He raised such issues as leadership in an organization dedicated to democratic co-participation, hidden hierarchies and group versus individual decision making. Clurman showed different phases of this collaborative process. At the beginning, the directors provided much of the leadership of the group. But as the group developed, roles became less sharply differentiated. Directors initiated and actors participated in long discussions and criticisms of performances and theories. They started to appropriate, or internalize, these voices and created a new balance in the group. They helped to fashion a more dynamic, egalitarian organism. They were aiming to construct meaningful theatrical experiences, for actors as well as audiences, rather than limiting themselves to simply repeating nightly performances.

Understanding their challenges required collaborative problem solving akin to what social psychologist David Middleton described as "talking work":

> Team members' talk continually handles uncertainties concerning their work; for example, what should they be doing next in relation to problematic cases? are there any misunderstandings of purpose between the various professionals involved and between team members and their families? . . . Team members' talk about work therefore gives voice to contradictory and dilemmatic aspects of team practice.[70]

Like other working communities and teams, Group actors had to confront their financial and organizational problems more directly. In 1937, an Actors Committee from the Group's membership developed an analysis of the situation the theater ensemble faced: the ensemble was highly praised by the critics, but internally its members were suffering from emotional and artistic exhaustion. That state of affairs made them reflect on their history and on the balance of forces within the group. The committee declared:

> We are writing this paper so that the Group will go on . . . We are trying to find the truth regardless of personal feelings . . . We all know that six years ago the Group was wrenched out of the American theater by the sheer force of the directors' will. They, at that time, were indubitably the Group Theater. Now six years have passed and the picture is different. We are sure that today the Group is no longer the three directors . . . If any generalization should be made it is much more true to say that the actors by their dogged faith and belief in the idea of the theater (which was planted six years ago by the directors) are keeping each other and the directors together.[71]

This manifesto led to the Group's reorganization, a new joint leadership between Clurman and the actors. Interestingly, the artistic force that Strasberg provided in the first half of the Group Theater's existence became a burden as the community reshaped itself. In this period they staged some of their most successful plays. The new, stronger role of the actors, provoked by financial crises and aided by their history of mutuality in many practical situations, contributed to the Group Theater's reorganization. At the cognitive and emotional levels, these shared experiences led to expansion in the participants' personalities. They made some of their peers' strengths and perspectives their own, exemplifying the cultural-historical notion of "mutual appropriation."

The political atmosphere in America between 1937 and 1939 was sympathetic to their ideals. Their work with playwright Clifford Odets resulted in one of their greatest successes, *Golden Boy*. Besides long performances of the play in the United States and England, Group members taught theater classes and participated in events to support the civil war in Spain. Their effectiveness in this period brought forth long-hidden desires about the central role they wanted the Group Theater to play in their lives, which Clurman described:

> The desire for some center around which one might build a complete life was basic, and almost all the people in and around the Group clamored for it even more insistently. Bitter disappointment, even hate, developed within the group, when the

Group failed to furnish such a center. Though no Group manifesto had ever promised it, there was something in the Group's attitudes that made its members, and even many outside of its ranks, feel it could be, should be, the focus of a world of activity that made great actors of some, writers of others, directors, designers, teachers, organizers, producers, administrators, or a combination of several things of the rest. . . . The Group had to become a society within a society, a protected unit, a utopia, an oasis within the city, in which one could work out one's life career and salvation.[72]

While such objectives were unrealistic, they contributed to the Group's idealism and its desire to become a community, even while facing serious problems. It had no permanent funding or endowment. It had to raise money for every production while trying to preserve its artistic identity and continuity. For a decade the Group Theater survived and grew, even while facing serious contradictions between its artistic accomplishments and its financial instability. But eventually, as Clurman wrote, "my will and the collective will of my fellow workers was not sufficient to establish a Group Theater in the early forties that might endure despite the jungle life, the drought and the famine of the Broadway theater in the early forties."[73]

Creative groups and collaboratives may function for a while through determination, talent, sacrifice, and intermittent funding, but long-term survival requires stable inclusion in the larger society. According to Csikszentmihalyi's analysis of creativity, the Group made important progress in and contributions to their domain, the theater's organized set of symbols and rules, but couldn't marshal the favor of the field, the institutional and financial "gatekeepers" necessary for it to win a secure, lasting position. The theater "field" includes experts (theater critics), sources of money (producers, fund raisers, federal programs in the arts) and the broader socio-historical forces that affect the direction of cultural movements.[74] This is particularly true of theater, opera, and symphony orchestras. Early in World War II, the Group Theater ceased to exist as a repertory theater. But its legacy continues. Group members have become influential as actors and as teachers of the Stanislavsky method. Clurman's vision of a theater community inspires new generations of writers, directors, and producers. The longing for an artistic home and family continues among its former members. In 1974, Clurman wrote, "In a personal way the Group Theater has never ceased being. With its feuds, its celebrations, its cults, its legends, and its binding love, it is like a close-knit family."[75]

Like an extended family, a collaboration bears the complexity of human connectedness, strengthened by joint purpose and strained by conflicting feelings.

Another way to look at complex collaboratives, such as the Group Theater, is to conceive of them as "communities of practice."[76] This term, coined by Lave and Wenger, refers to "participation in an activity system about which participants share understandings concerning what they are doing and what that means for their lives and their communities. . . . A community of practice is an intrinsic condition for the existence of knowledge, not least because it provides the interpretive support necessary for making sense of its heritage."[77]

The powerful impact of situational and economic forces affects all communities of practice, including artistic ensembles such as the Group Theater. These tensions include long-term funding, the changing political climate regarding social plays, and the composition of the audience. These factors affected the way in which the Group conducted its affairs. As Clurman clearly demonstrated, the Group's relationship to the larger society was critical to the connection between the actors and directors and, most important, to their long-term survival.

While the artistic community of the Group Theater led a very different existence from teams engaged in industrial production, there are some important commonalities between them. They share joint activity which requires talk and what social scientists Engestrom and Middleton refer to as the "mindfulness" of human action: "remembering, reasoning, seeing, learning, inventing."[78] Studies of "communities of practice" frequently refer to the front and the backstage of situated activities. The front is visible to the outsider. It constitutes an orderly and rational sequence visible to an audience. It is in the busy backstage that the real operations, which are frequently messy or redundant, take place. This theatrical metaphor, first proposed by sociologist Erving Goffman, reveals some additional common features of communities of thought and practice.[79]

INTERDEPENDENCE AND MUTUAL APPROPRIATION

The many facets of artistic interdependence cannot be captured in a single chapter. There is, however, a growing literature on the complexities of artistic lives. These complexities include the dynamics of connection as well as "the wrenching pain of sitting alone in front of a blank page or a blank canvas."[80] These experiences are documented in individual biographies, in case studies of artists, and in volumes such as *Significant Others*, edited by Chadwick and de Courtivron. Through these narratives, a new understanding of human development is achieved: it is an understanding of the crucial, frequently neglected role of mutuality. They detail the way interdependence is fashioned, then either resisted or effectively balanced, among partners who practice the varied skills of collaboration.

Appropriation of new roles, and the possibility of empowerment by individuals with limited power or voice, is illustrated by the history of the Group Theater. The actors changed from novices and learners into a cohesive, influential collectivity. When the directors of the Theater faltered, the actors took a guiding role. Bennis and Biederman suggested that many "Great Groups" have strong leaders who can build on the participants' need to share a vision and to joyously contribute working at their highest level. Collaboration requires certain skills: the ability and willingness to take partners' questions and needs very seriously, and to hear their concerns even before they are fully articulated.

Some partnerships start within a larger group; for instance, Renoir and Monet were part of the "causeries" of the Impressionists. The Ballets Russes of Monte Carlo provided many artists with a shared stage for their talents. It was one of the most important artistic ensembles established early in this century. The participants included painters Picasso, Rouault, Utrillo, Miro, Gris, Braque, and Matisse; choreographers Fokine, Massine, and Nijinsky; and composers Stravinsky, Dukelsky, and Nabakov. One of the most important partnerships that emerged from this large group was between George Balanchine and Igor Stravinsky. The young choreographer Balanchine first worked with Stravinsky's music when he joined the Ballets Russes company. He had been deeply influenced by music as a dancer and choreographer, and was attached to Stravinsky's music while still at the Maryinsky ballet school in St. Petersberg.

In the words of his biographer, "The chief stimulant and deepest fount of inspiration for Balanchine was music."[81] He made his greatest choreographic discoveries through musical masterworks. While many other choreographers found it intimidating to work with masterworks, Balanchine relied on them. Bernard Taper quoted him as saying: "A choreographer can't invent rhythms, he only reflects them in movement. The body is his medium and, unaided, the body will improvise for short breath. But the organizing of rhythm on a grand scale is a sustained process. It is a function of the musical mind."[82]

Balanchine and Stravinsky's first full collaboration took place during the creation of *Apollo* in 1928. It was to Stravinsky's music for this ballet that Balanchine owed some of his most important technical and artistic discoveries. Previous to this crucial joint endeavor, Balanchine's choreography was a mixture of styles. In contrast, "[t]he score Stravinsky provided for *Apollo*—restrained, disciplined, yet uncommonly lyrical—taught Balanchine the most useful lesson of his career: that he, too, could clarify his art by reducing all the multitudinous possibilities to the one possibility that was inevitable, that he could, as he has since put it, 'dare not to use all my ideas.'"[83]

Stravinsky conducted his music at the premiere of *Apollo*. It was a major artistic event and the beginning of a long partnership between these two seminal figures of the twentieth century. According to psychologist Howard Gardner, the success of their partnership spanning forty years was due to their shared artistic heritage and a unique understanding of the connections between music and dance. Balanchine's reliance upon music was not mechanical. Stravinsky said that he freed himself of the tyranny of the beat, a challenge other composers did not always meet. He constructed dance pieces which "have a life of their own yet are always subtly linked with the musical phrases."[84]

After *Apollo*, they worked together in 1937 for a Stravinsky-Balanchine festival at the Metropolitan Opera in New York. The composer developed two new commissioned pieces for the festival: *Le Baisée de la Fée* and *Card Game*. Although these pieces were successful, they did not have the sustained impact of *Apollo*. It was not until the production of *Movements* in 1963 that the two again collaborated on a ballet that fully captured their joint creativity. Reflecting on this work, Stravinsky wrote, in *Themes and Episodes* coauthored with Robert Craft, of their artistic interdependence: "To see Balanchine's choreography of the *Movements* is to hear the music with one's eyes; and this visual hearing has been a greater revelation to me, I think, than to anyone else. The choreography emphasizes relationships of which I had hardly been aware—in the same way—and the performance was like a tour of a building for which I have drawn the plans but never explored the result."[85]

This expression of visual hearing articulated by Stravinsky captured the notion of mutual appropriation which is central to this cultural-historical analysis of collaboration. In seeing his music danced, Stravinsky came to appreciate his own work at a deeper level, to reexperience it and to gain new ways to expand it. Stravinsky's music remained a source of artistic expansion for Balanchine even after the composer's death. In 1972, the New York City Ballet organized a Stravinsky festival for which Balanchine choreographed new works (which included *Symphony in Three Movements*, *Danses Concertantes*, and *Violin Concerto*, among others). According to Taper, "It is probable that the weeks in which Balanchine was preparing his Stravinsky festival ballets were the most intensely creative period of his life."[86]

Artistic interdependence is a critical generator of creativity. Bach's music has been a source of discovery and inspiration to many cellists, most particularly for Pablo Casals: "It was the great revelation of my life. . . . I started playing them in a wonderful state of excitement and it was only after twelve years of practice of them that I made up my mind to play them in public."[87] Casals's discovery is a rich example of the power of connections across generations. Many artists and musicians experience a need to discover their own "teachers from the past"; they recognize that an intense and personal kinship can result when the work of another evokes a special resonance. Once such a bond is established, the learner explores those valued works with a keen absorption, the hallmark of creative individuals. In this way, creative people stretch, deepen, and refresh their craft and nourish their intelligence, not only during their early years of apprenticeship, but repeatedly throughout the many cycles of their work lives.[88]

One of the most dramatic examples of generative artistic interdependence is the collaboration between cellist Yo-Yo Ma and members of other disciplines. In the late 1990s, he created a series of six films based on Bach's *Suites for Unaccompanied Cello*. Yo-Yo Ma first played Bach's *Suites* when he was four years old when his father taught them to him:

> The Suites were the very first pieces of music I learned, and they have been with me ever since. . . . In a very real sense, they are some of my oldest friends. We all go through periods when we take old friends for granted. . . . [Recently], I felt an urge to re-examine my relationship with these suites, to deepen my understanding of them. But how do you go deeper? Do you practice more? . . . I needed an approach that would lead me in a new direction, take me somewhere new.[89]

Ma decided to work with a varied group of contemporary artists, each suite embodying a particular collaboration. The basis was in the music, but the art forms that were brought to expand its impact varied and were at times surprising. The first in the series, called "Six Gestures," featured ice dancers Jayne Torvill and Christopher Dean. Their lyrical movements highlighted the patterned intricacies of Bach's music. The changing surfaces on which they danced reflected, as did their choreography, different parts of the suite. In addition, some of the most important events in Bach's life were enacted in this first film, against the background of the music. The visual, musical, and textual modalities were used to a wonderful effect, as were the simple human moments when Ma performed on his cello in the midst of busy city traffic.

Ma brings a sense of wonder, modesty, and discovery to his collaborations with visual, architectural, and movement artists. Their joint work spans centuries. The *First Suite* (performed as the fifth installment of the televised series) is called "Music Garden." It documents the collaboration between Ma and landscape designer Julie Moir Messervy as they envisioned the joining of music and nature. Their commitment was inspiring, as were the beauty and variety of the sights they planned. They shared with viewers their battles and their disappointments. But one is left with hope at the end of this program. A music garden is going to be built in Toronto, Canada.

In this series, Ma and his collaborators succeeded in enriching the continuing legacy of Bach—their distant teacher. His music became a bridge to the twenty-first century through a program that combined modern technology, varied and complex interpretations, and a truly collaborative spirit. The cellist's search for deeper understanding of music he has lived with all his life has produced a new synthesis between different art forms. It is another example of Stravinsky's visual hearing of mutual appropriation that leads to reflexivity as well as discovery.

COLLABORATION AS TRANSFORMATION

In this chapter, I have looked at collaborations in which artists discover their complementarity, then push farther to forge a union. Such unions, which I have called *integrative collaborations,* transform both artistic work and personal life. Artists working together combine their different perspectives and their shared passion to shed the familiar. In fashioning novelty, it is often hard to overcome practiced modes of seeing and creating. The partnerships of Picasso and Braque, Stravinsky and Balanchine, and O'Keeffe and Stieglitz, among others, provide many examples of this dynamic. Transformative contributions are born from sharing risks and challenging, appropriating, and deepening each partner's contribution. Individuals in successful partnerships reach beyond their habitual ways of learning, working, and creating. In transforming what they know, they construct creative syntheses.

4

A CHORUS OF VOICES:
WOMEN IN COLLABORATION

Do women find collaboration more congenial than men? Some, particularly feminists, have argued that this indeed is the case. At the same time, as described in previous chapters, there is tremendous evidence of both male and female participation in cooperative and transformative joint efforts. In this chapter, the debate about gender differences provides useful insights into human interdependence and the shifting dynamics of the co-construction of thought.

Feminist literary critics Carey Kaplan and Ellen C. Rose, who have worked together writing grant proposals, editing books, and jointly authoring a book, described their collaboration:

> Our minds meet in the air between us and we achieve, at our best, an unfettered, creative, generous reciprocity.[1] . . . "She" and "I" metamorphose into "we," hypothetical, invisible, yet nonetheless articulate.[2] . . . As our collaboration has progressed . . . our self-confidence has grown in direct proportion to our fluency in speaking as "we." . . . We have formed a bond different from family, sometimes transcendent of family, profoundly connective but never taken for granted, never an inescapable given.[3]

They are separated in space, so their work together must be planned carefully:

> We learned first that we could sit together before a computer and write sentences that worked even better than did sentences we wrote alone. Then we learned to prepare for our time together by stimulating each other with ideas and hints in letters. Indeed, we now write diary letters to one another each week, letters that include gossip and daily-ness as well as intellectual exchange. We learned to read the same books at the same time and to exchange our different but complementary responses. We learned the pleasures of delaying our time together until we were both ready to explode or implode with new words, new ideas. We learned each other's best hours for work, for relaxation, for solitude. We learned

an accretive interplay in which one of us roughs out a chapter, then sends it to the other for expansion and clarification, and then we go back and forth until we are both satisfied.[4]

While celebrating their very successful intellectual and emotional interdependence, Kaplan and Rose asked, "Is collaboration a peculiarly female and/or feminist mode of production?" They answered, "Our experience and the statements of other feminist collaborators would seem to suggest that feminists find collaboration particularly congenial."[5]

How widespread is female commitment to collaboration? Why do some writers view collaboration as particularly linked to women's ways of working and thinking? And, more important, if this is indeed a phenomenon that reflects gender differences, *is female preference a culturally and historically patterned phenomenon, or is it a human universal*?

To answer these questions, I first deal with theoretical concerns, including contrasting modes of thought as expressed in the writings of psychologists, philosophers of science, biologists, and anthropologists. Then, I offer a novel synthesis of feminism and cultural-historical theory dealing with interdependence and mutuality.[6] In addition, I describe the practice of collaboration among women drawn from written accounts and interviews.[7] These issues are central to collaboration and also have wide implications for explorations of human nature.

MODES OF THOUGHT, MODES OF TALK

A few years ago, I interviewed Cecile DeWitt-Morette, a mathematical physicist whose work has received many honors in the United States and her native France. She revealed that her talk about her ideas is different from that of her physicist husband:

> When we say, "I understand," we don't mean the same thing at all. When I say, "I understand," I speak of an idea that I like, that seems promising, and I like it enough to make that decision. When he says, "I understand," it means he has looked at it this way and that way, looked at it in all the little corners. The way he would describe the difference between the two of us is that he says his mind is extremely focused, like a spotlight, while mine is a more diffuse floodlight.[8]

It is hard to believe that the co-author of two influential volumes of *Analysis, Manifolds, and Physics* thinks diffusely.[9] DeWitt-Morette's thinking ranges broadly; her husband's is focused sharply. Clarity of focus is effective in academic discourse. It is connected to an adversarial mode of thought, described by Peter Elbow as the "doubting game," in which "players" respond to examples by looking for counterexamples.[10] Elbow traces this mode of thought back to Socrates and Descartes: Socratic dialogue is "deflating . . . some belief [that] is shown to be silly or empty or contradictory,"[11] and Descartes' method proceeds "to the truth by doubting everything. . . . This spirit has remained the central tradition in Western civilization's notion of the rational process."[12]

Developmental psychologist Blythe Clinchy described a person explaining her adversarial approach: "I never take anything someone says for granted. I just tend to see the contrary. I like playing the devil's advocate, arguing the opposite of what somebody's thinking, thinking of exceptions, or thinking of a different train of thought."[13] This focused, confrontational view of reasoning is fostered by socialization practices aimed at developing a critical mind. The opponent's argument is examined for logical errors rather than for its power or persuasiveness.

The ability to approach ideas as decontextualized propositions is valued highly in science, mathematics, and law. Traditionally, the physical scientist is supposed to formulate consistent propositions whose truth value is determined by experiment. This discourse model searches for mistakes. It also fosters scientific and academic competition. Scholars engaged in severe competition accept, as part of the process, the public critiquing of their positions. Some are invigorated by competitive, adversarial exchanges. The pressure for speed and sharpness in this discourse helps them to focus on the point of argument. This is the dominant model into which young scholars are socialized. It is so pervasive in academia, and so deeply formative of what we consider as knowledge construction, that it cannot be considered only a male model.

Clear thinking sharpened by these exchanges has often correlated with a concept of nature in which nature obeys simple, elegant, timeless rules. Anthropologist Sharon Traweek found that high-energy physicists dwell in a culture "which longs passionately for a world without loose ends, without temperament, gender, nationalism . . . an extreme culture of objectivity."[14] But today we are witnessing changing concepts of nature and nature's laws. Physicist Victor Weisskopf wrote: "In previous periods physicists concentrated on regular, repeatable phenomena in order to get at the fundamental laws that govern nature. But complex situations do exist that are not repeatable because very small changes in the external condition produce large changes in behavior. Such situations are what one calls 'chaotic.'"[15] Philosopher of science Mary Midgley further elaborated:

> Order in the world does not consist in a single, simple, basic arrangement of indestructible balls or bricks which give the real

explanation to everything. Instead, it is a wide range of much less simple, interconnected patterns. Order as we perceive it at the level of everyday experience is not an illusion. . . . It is one set among others of these real patterns—subtle, complex, interconnected arrangements.[16]

Nevertheless, the hope for a complete, consistent, lasting description of the universe persists. It is part of our intellectual legacy and of prevalent forms of academic discourse that such a description requires a particular mode of analytical thought, untainted by intuitive or imaginative leaps. While such a longing is widely shared by men and women in the twentieth century, many conditions make its satisfaction more and more difficult. The most urgent social problems—corruption of the environment, AIDS, ethnic and religious conflicts—demand interdisciplinary effort and a combination of experimental and descriptive approaches. In contrast to "an extreme culture of objectivity," these problems are concerned with values that include conflicts between research and service commitments. In addition, contemporary research is seldom conducted by individuals or by very small groups from a single tradition; the advance of scientific work requires large-scale collaboration. Such large groups need a fine balance between independent, analytical thinking and interdependent planning and organization. Joint endeavors are also increasing in social science, environmental studies, education, business, and the arts.

In these emergent shared endeavors, the participants must reconcile conflicting styles of work, temperament, values, and role expectations. But as I argue throughout this book, socialization practices prevalent in contemporary Western society emphasize competition and the adversarial mode of self-presentation. These practices do not prepare us well for the interdependence and mutual adjustments needed in collaborative endeavors.

At the same time, members of groups who have been marginal to the power institutions of Western society—women, minorities, and economically oppressed groups—have been less trained in adversarial modes of thought. As a consequence of their marginality, many women (and some men) are more at ease with interdependent modes of work than their peers who have been socialized into the "mainstream." Today's more complex, less stable image of nature opens the way for modes of thought and discourse which encourage multiple perspectives and for what the authors of *Women's Ways of Knowing* call "constructed knowledge."[17] This is an integrative mode of thinking aimed at overcoming the Cartesian ghosts of dualism and dichotomy. Instead it offers "world pictures which balance each other and constantly need modification."[18]

People who are comfortable in the collaborative mode see debate and reasoning as part—but not all—of intellectual effort. An effective case was made by Clinchy for integrating the separate and connected modes of knowing: separate knowing is based on an epistemology of critical reasoning, while connected knowing relies on an integration of perception, insight, analogies, and empathic understanding. Such an integration of different modes of thought may be more available to those women and men whose responsibilities span the private and public spheres, and who have the ability to shift between work-related and care-related concerns. DeWitt-Morette attributes her form of reasoning, including the broad range of her attention, to both her professional training and her role as a mother. Her comments help to approach the issue of gender and modes of thinking as multifaceted, as an ensemble of activities resulting in the use of diverse modes of thought. By connecting gender, thought, and discourse to recurrent experiences, rather than universal biological "givens," our accounts become more specific.

GENDER DIFFERENCES

In recent decades, feminist scholars have focused on the complex issue of gender differences. One of the first books to address the psychological consequences of gender socialization in Western society —Jean Baker Miller's *Toward a New Psychology of Women,* published in 1976—described women's traditional identity as linked to caregiving and subject to conflicting pulls of independence and interdependence.[19] The sources of her work were clinical, but the ideas that emerged in her writing were not restricted to that domain. They have been amplified by her collaborators at the Stone Center at Wellesley College. At about the same time, Carol Gilligan of Harvard University came to similar notions studying young women facing ethical decisions. Gilligan developed a critical approach to moral development. Her book, *In A Different Voice,* identifies an ethic of responsibility and care that is important to women and different from the ethic of rights and impartiality preferred by men.[20] The importance of connectedness and the valuing of relationships are themes that join Miller, Gilligan, and other scholars who have listened to women describing their experiences.

One of the most influential books in this tradition, *Women's Ways of Knowing,* was published in 1986.[21] The authors explored different epistemological positions—how women think about themselves, authorities, and choices in their lives, and how they construct their knowledge—of the diverse urban and rural women of varying age, class, ethnicity, and educational history they interviewed. This book has become influential in social science, law, philosophy of science, and education. It raised important issues of identity, knowing, judgment, language use, and the relationship between women's historically shaped experience of oppression and their ways of exploring and representing that experience.

The authors' emphasis on gender differences has been criticized by some as "essentialism." These critics viewed the authors as giving support to biological determinism, which conceives of women "as fundamentally all alike, a homogeneous group with common life opportunities and experiences already 'known' to us before we actually see them or hear from them."[22] I believe this criticism is a misrepresentation of the authors' intent and the way they think of differences. Their focus is on women voicing their own perspectives. Such a focus is badly needed in the field of psychology, where male consciousness was exclusive during the formative years of the discipline. Psychologists who choose to overcome this serious limitation broaden psychological inquiry beyond the scope of the "fathers" (e.g., Freud and Piaget) to expand our understanding of what it is to be human.

I argue that variations in men's and women's collaborative engagement are the outcome of social, rather than biological, forces. Difference in reliance on collaboration is connected to patterned experiences not necessarily shared across gender: these consequences include women's long-time exclusion from higher education and their limited participation in public institutions. The psychological consequences of these patterned experiences are powerful, but they are open to change—both the stable and changing aspects of historically shaped modes of thought, discourse, and adaptation must be considered. To do so, new conceptual tools must allow for dynamic rather than essentialist approaches. Essentialism rejects the role of history; it views women as specified by "one or a number of inborn attributes which define across cultures and history her unchanging being."[23]

A dynamic systems approach escapes the dichotomies of essentialism and environmentalism; it is sensitive to change and open to reorganization. I rely on the notion of functional system developed by Russian psychologists Lev Vygotsky and A. R. Luria. Functional systems are dynamic; they respond to changing circumstances. They are systems of processes woven together in the course of development. In cultural-historical theory, the notion of functional systems has been used in a variety of ways, such as in studies of classroom practices and concept development. The use of functional systems enables researchers to overcome static dichotomies such as nature-nurture or individual-social. Instead, they can highlight hidden connections and changing relationships. A functional—dynamic—systems approach is gaining in influence among scholars, as shown by anthropologist Edwin Hutchins's application of this concept to his study of navigational systems.[24]

Vygotsky proposed that culture and biology are interweaving processes. Their unification is embedded in the historically specific ways men and women manage their commonalities and differences. In the last thirty years, new social practices have caused rapid shifts in women and men working together. Central to such changes are issues of collaboration and gender. I first approach these issues theoretically and then illustrate them through biographies and interviews. I include the voices of Gilligan, Miller, and the four authors of *Women's Ways of Knowing*. Each of them has given much thought to the contradictory possibilities of connectedness and independence, viewed as dynamic functional systems rather than dichotomies. I link their approaches to those of cultural-historical thinkers, including Vygotsky, Luria, and contemporary contributors Michael Cole, James Wertsch, David Feldman, and Barbara Rogoff. In the following section, I discuss mutuality, interdependence, and autonomy from the perspectives of feminist and cultural-historical theories.

MUTUALITY AND INTERDEPENDENCE:
ARE THEY GENDER SPECIFIC?

Life starts with infants totally dependent on their caregivers. As they mature, they start to participate in the vast pool of transmitted experiences of those caregivers. Both cultural-historical and feminist theorists emphasize this primary dependence as essential to the survival of the young human. In writing about "reason's femininity," Sara Ruddick evoked the earliest and simplest relationship of a parent and a child.[25] She suggested that this "fundamental 'relationality' . . . precedes both knowing and gender."[26] But the way in which early care is given is highly sensitive to the culturally patterned social arrangement where it takes place.

Even early nourishment is linked to such cultural practices as exemplified in bottle feeding (necessary for working mothers in industrial countries), wet nurses, day-care facilities, and the roles of fathers and siblings. Variations in how infants' needs are met contribute to the contextualization of their basic biological drive: sucking for nourishment. Cultural beliefs about infants influence how their appearance and behavior are interpreted and whether they are seen as agentive or helpless. These beliefs are among many forces affecting the development of mutuality, autonomy, and interdependence. Cross-cultural studies have found great variations in developmental patterns. For instance, Whiting and Whiting compared child-rearing in six societies.[27] In the Gussi of Kenya, the primary farm laborers are mothers, and children as young as three are expected to share in household tasks, including caring for younger siblings.[28] Girls have caretaking roles in most societies, but in the Gussi and many other preindustrial communities, boys also are called on to participate in nurturing. Such responsibilities contribute to children's early awareness of their social world and shape their sense of mutuality in a way different from the heavy emphasis on autonomy common in industrialized society.

The differing patterns of interdependence found by cross-cultural comparisons help us to understand gender socialization in our own society. Learning to become male or female starts early. Adult gender stereotypes are already evident hours after a child's birth. In one study in which weights and vital signs of male and female infants were carefully matched with each other and parents were asked to describe their infants soon after they were born, "the parents described their daughters as 'little,' 'beautiful,' or 'cute' and as resembling their mothers. Sons, on the other hand, were described as 'big' and as resembling their fathers. Fathers, the researchers found, were more likely to sex-type their babies than were mothers."[29]

The complete reliance of infants upon their caregivers makes them highly susceptible to the way adults interpret their behavior. The view of infant boys as big (though actually no heavier than the girls in this study) is carried further by many families who expect little boys to be more aggressive and adventurous than little girls. Miller claimed that "culturally induced beliefs about boys and girls play a role from the moment of birth."[30] Such pervasive socialization practices have many consequences. In analyzing girls' and boys' stories, Ann Dyson, a student of literacy development, found that 49 percent of writings by girls center on relationships with family and friends, and three-quarters of their narratives include specific, named emotions. Only 14 percent of the boys address such themes. Instead, their texts draw on superhero stories from the media, a theme hardly occurring among girls.[31] Dyson's findings support the claims of relational theorists, who say girls are deeply involved in the intricacies of interpersonal connections, while boys fantasize about mastery and achievement through identification with "superheroes."

The consequences of gender socialization permeate our existence. Although variations in gender roles are well documented by anthropologists and historians, there is a tendency in our society to view male/female differences as universal. Such views include the image of males as self-reliant, independent, and competent, while females are seen as dependent, enmeshed in relationships, and lacking in "healthy" aggression. But such generalizations ignore the enormous variation within each group. Age is one source of variability. Gilligan and her collaborators found interesting differences between girls, ages seven to eleven, and adolescents. Younger girls are self-confident, speak freely of anger, and can resist unfair rules, but many adolescent girls cover over the voices of their younger selves with a new socially-imposed voice. This process can cause psychological dissociation.[32] Such age-related changes document great variability among women and challenge simple biological explanations of gender differences. In spite of the oft-stated reality of such female variability—during development, and among women from different ethnic, class, and cultural backgrounds—explanations of sex differences which stress biological and essentialist explanations remain popular among sociobiologists and in the mass media.

I propose that socialization practices play a crucial explanatory role in the complex tapestry of gender, and that multidisciplinary studies focusing on women provide new, challenging information about our differences, our complementarity, and our shared humanity across the sexes. My stance is not unique. It is shared by social scientists, philosophers, and psychologists who recognize the complex, varied nature of gender-linked practices and behaviors. Nevertheless, gender stereotypes, such as the cultural icon of the strong, independent male, still persist. Autonomy and independence are still regarded as vital signs of mental health by psychiatrists and psychologists. They are seen as primarily male characteristics even by female therapists. In a classic study of "sex-role stereotypes and clinical judgments of mental health," Broverman and colleagues showed how similarly therapists view the "normal male personality" and the "healthy personality": the majority perceive women as more nurturant and more emotional.[33] It has taken the work of Miller, Gilligan and her co-workers, Nancy Chodorow, the authors of *Women's Ways of Knowing*, and many others to find alternative notions of mental health.

In the eighties, members of the Stone Center at Wellesley College joined to develop and apply Miller's work. They constructed a relational/cultural theory (formerly called a "self-in-relation" theory). This new approach differs from prevalent concepts of development that stress separation as part of healthy individuation, as Janet Surrey described:

> Our conception of the self-in-relation involves the recognition that, for women, the primary experience of self is relational, that is, the self is organized and developed in the context of important relationships. To understand this basic assumption, it is helpful to use as a contrast some current assumptions about male (often generalized to human) development.
>
> Developmental theory today still stresses the importance of separation from the mother at early stages of childhood development (Mahler, 1975), from the family at adolescence (Erikson, 1963),

and from teachers and mentors in adulthood (Levinson, 1978) in order for the individual to form a distinct, separate Fidentity. High value is still placed on autonomy, self reliance, independence, self-actualization, listening to and following one's own unique dream, destiny, and fulfillment. . . . Our theory suggests, instead, that for women a different, relational pathway is primary, although its centrality has been hidden and unacknowledged. . . . The notion of the self-in-relation involves an important shift in emphasis from separation to relationship as the basis of self-experience and development. Further, relationship is seen as the basic *goal* of development: that is, the deepening capacity for relationship and relational competence. The self-in-relation model assumes that other aspects of self (e.g., creativity, autonomy and assertion) develop within this primary context.[34]

This model analyzes the gender specialization so prevalent in our culture and suggests alternatives to such dichotomies. The authors argued that male-type autonomy itself is possible only when scaffolded by caregivers and partners—often women—who support the man's questing for fulfillment. Poet Adrienne Rich described this aspect of "woman's work":

Yet it is this activity of world-protection, world-preservation, world-repair—the million tiny stitches, the friction of the scrubbing brush, the scouring cloth, the iron across the shirt . . . the invisible weaving of a frayed and threadbare family life, the cleaning up of soil and waste left behind by men and children that we have been charged to do 'for love,' not merely unpaid but unacknowledged by political philosophers. Women are not described as "working" when we create the essential conditions for the work of men: we are supposed to be acting out of love, instinct, or devotion to some higher cause than self.[35]

Rich's vivid outcry and the clinical work of members of the Stone Center both focus on women. I want to place their arguments in historical and cross-cultural context and examine the issue of connectedness for both men and women. *I claim that mutuality and interdependence are basic and necessary forms of human social life. They are not biologically linked to one or another gender.* The practice of connectedness is not a universal female responsibility in all societies. Rather, the primary reliance upon females as caregivers is widespread in those societies where work and home are separated geographically and conceptually.

The relegation of mutuality and interdependence to females, even by some feminist thinkers, narrows our analysis. Throughout history, men and women have engaged in activities requiring interdependence. In the last three centuries, especially in societies with an individualistic, Calvinist work ethic, a different notion of human competence emerged. The emphasis on the autonomy, objectivity, and independence of the mature person was associated with economic, technological, and philosophical developments of the post-Renaissance era, the era of discovery and conquest.

The construction of psychology as a discipline is embedded in these broad historical currents. Research into human nature is recent, but many of its issues are rooted in philosophical concerns of the post-Renaissance age. This was the age of optimism, economic expansion, and personal daring. Emphasis on individual rather than communal achievements, supported by Protestant beliefs, characterized capitalist economies at that time. The psychological theories that emerged from this background embody some assumptions about human nature central in Western technological society. The emphasis on male individuation in psychological theories (for instance, in C. G. Jung) reflected these historical realities.

In contrast, in a world with shrinking resources, mutuality and interdependence are increasingly needed in collaborative endeavors and in the transformation of human possibilities. In the face of such historical challenges, our psychological theories must be broadened to recognize that mutuality of connections are generative for both men and women. After centuries of insisting on solo endeavors, theories that deal with the complexities of working interdependently are called for.

In the earliest periods of homo sapiens, interdependence among members of small bands—in hunting and gathering and in sharing food and tools—allowed them to survive and to migrate with changing climate conditions. Paleontologist Richard Leakey wrote of primates' "social intelligence," their ability, through empathy and reasoning, to monitor social alliances.[36] This theme was echoed by students of the !Kung in the Kalahari desert, where male hunters rely on scouting information supplied by women gatherers. The nomadic !Kung have a high degree of equality, including the sharing of childcare.[37] But with the development of agriculture and the influence of neighboring Westernized societies, class and gender stratification have appeared among the !Kung.

In other "egalitarian" societies, for instance, the Montagnais-Naskapi of Labrador, anthropologist Eleanor Leacock found more examples of gender flexibility in roles and responsibilities. While some division of labor by sex is common in preindustrial society, she argued that such division is more flexible than in advanced, economically stratified societies of the West. She distinguished between flexible task assignments in egalitarian societies and the social division of labor (starting with advanced horticultural societies) in which productive contributions are evaluated hierarchically. Thus, she sees important variations in women's roles in different societies, powerfully affected by social and economic factors.[38] Other cross-cultural studies support her argument. For instance, Whyte concluded:

> We do not find a pattern of universal male dominance, but much variation from culture to culture in virtually all aspects of the position of women relative to men. Our findings do lead us to doubt that there are cultures in which women are totally dominant over men. Rather, there is substantial variation from societies with very general male dominance to other societies in which broad equality and even some specific types of female dominance over men exist.[39]

Writer Riane Eisler developed this argument further in *The Chalice and the Blade*. She made a distinction between dominator societies, such as the modern West, and partnership societies, which were prevalent in the Near East 7,000 to 8,000 years ago. Eisler reported no evidence of inequality between men and women in partnership societies. She quoted archeologist Gimbutas: "The world of myth was not polarized into female and male as it was among the Indo-Europeans and many other nomadic and pastoral peoples of the steppes. Both principles were manifest side by side. . . . Neither is subordinate to the other: by complementing one another, their power is doubled."[40] In Crete, an even more advanced civilization has been unearthed in which both men and women played crucial roles, and where sustained warfare was absent for more than 1,500 years.[41] But with the invasion by northern tribes of the more fertile regions of Europe, beginning around the fourth millennium B.C.E., a dramatic change took place. Instead of the relatively peaceful and egalitarian partnership societies, new social systems arose in which hierarchical power, male dominance, and warfare became common. Historian Gordon Childe described this change: "As competition for land assumes a bellicose character, and weapons such as battle axes became specialized for warfare, not only the social but the ideological organization of European society underwent a fundamental alteration."[42]

These archeological and ethnographic examples show that our contemporary gender arrangements are not universal. Mutuality and interdependence have been major components of social arrangements in many communities. These communities are counterexamples to the ahistorical, universalistic, often sociobiological version of male-female roles and characteristics which makes male competitiveness a primary model of emotional health.

In Western society, women's labor has often been devalued, including the labor of reproduction and caregiving. In addition to limiting the importance of women's authority, leadership, and social contributions, this devaluation affects the human qualities needed for nurturing interpersonal bonds.

I claim that mutuality and interdependence have been and continue to be widely practiced in many communities by both men and women. In Western society, which is the context for mainstream psychological theorizing, these crucial human processes are relegated to the private sphere of women's caregiving activities. In the last two decades, authors within feminist and cultural-historical thought communities have challenged this assumption, raising important questions about interdependence as crucial to personal development, creativity, and the construction of knowledge. These two thought communities conceive of human growth as a dialectical process of cultural transmission both between and within individuals, a process of transformation of self and knowledge within communities of care and practice. They provide a base for discussing women's approaches to collaboration that are different from the dominant theories.

Until now, books on collaboration have ignored gender. The following accounts of collaboration among influential writers on gender illustrate the complexities of mutuality at work in contemporary institutions. These authors confronted received ideas to examine them from different perspectives and construct new approaches. They worked collaboratively, not only relying on each other, but also developing ideas across groups. They co-constructed an emerging paradigm of women's psychology through collaborative work.

Their working methods illustrate some of their theoretical concepts. They described their activities from the early stages of their joining, through productive periods together, until the completion of their major shared work. They further chronicled how they separated and reconnected, which was part of their trajectories.

BEGINNINGS: DISCOVERIES OF MUTUALITY

Anthropologists Elinor Ochs and Bambi Schieffelin first met at a meeting of the American Anthropological Association in Mexico City. After Ochs presented a paper, Schieffelin realized the relevance of Ochs's work to her own research: "It just flipped the whole thing for me." In an interview, Ochs recalled: "We just talked and we sat next to each other at lunch and then we just kept on talking throughout the whole conference. And then on the plane—we were on the same charter plane going back to California. It stopped first in Los Angeles and then in Berkeley. Bambi sat next to my seat on the floor."[43]

The two decided to spend a few weeks together at UCLA and write a joint paper. From the very beginning, they developed a careful discipline by using their time away from family responsibilities in a well-planned manner. Everyday, they went to a small room in the library with no windows. They talked. They took turns taking notes. They analyzed child language transcripts together. They met other people and attended seminars, but their joint work was the focus:

> We would always have the typewriter right there and we would switch off writing and talking. . . . We did not ever allocate parts of the paper to one person or another person but we actually . . . every single sentence we discussed. The typewriter would be between the two of us, and we both had visual access. . . . And then one person would be saying the line over and over again . . . and then we would both kind of think of the next thing to say and then . . . paraphrase one another. . . . It was definitely constructed on the phrasal level together.

The speed with which they established a shared framework and effective working style is exceptional. In most cases, a strong collaboration takes time for adjustment of different work styles. Such an adjustment was necessary for social psychologist Michelle Fine and her co-worker, writer Pat MacPherson. They first met at a feminist conference. They realized that they share common values and have complementary qualities. In linked interviews, they described their interaction as intensely dialogic.[44] They rely on each other to deepen their work before it is published. In the beginning, MacPherson did not know that Fine writes a draft quickly and then rewrites it many times. "I do threads," Fine said, "and spit something out, and then I work it and work it. . . . That is where I really do my work. I really don't know what I am thinking until I have written a draft of it." In contrast, MacPherson makes detailed notes before she writes a first draft. At first she tried to work too closely with Fine's early drafts. She was taking them too seriously, not appreciating the exploratory nature of Fine's "writing aloud" process. As they came to know each other's methods better, MacPherson has learned to lift ideas out of Fine's draft. Now she feels free to reorganize and shape them. Fine is at ease with her partner's rewording. She deeply respects her judgment and her craft. This collaboration combines two patterns identified in recent work that I and my collaborators have done: the complementary pattern, in which participants bring different skills to each other, and the integrative pattern, in which participants develop a shared vision and strive for a common voice.

Another example of an integrative collaboration is the four authors of *Women's Ways of Knowing*: Mary Belenky, Blythe Clinchy, Nancy Goldberger and Jill Tarule. Through several interviews in the last few years, they reconstructed the beginning of their joint endeavor. Goldberger was trained as a clinical psychologist and has done research on cognitive style. Tarule's background is in developmental theory with a focus on stage transitions. She has also done administration and teaching. The two women first met in Indiana as evaluators of projects for the Fund for the Improvement of Post-Secondary Education (FIPSE). They enjoyed their meetings with a group of innovative, collaboration-oriented staff and researchers. During their informal talks after the daily sessions, they discovered common interests in women's development. Both had worked on female students' concerns in higher education.

Goldberger knew Clinchy from a network of researchers at the Harvard Graduate School of Education. They shared an interest in William Perry's 1970 scheme of intellectual and ethical development. Both were involved in longitudinal research tracing students' development — Goldberger at the experimental Simon's Rock College and Clinchy at the more traditional Wellesley. Tarule had known Clinchy for many years. They both lived in the same town in Vermont for more than a decade; they both taught at Goddard College; they both commuted to the Harvard Graduate School of Education; and, while working on their dissertations the same year but on different topics, they spoke to each other every morning. Perry was also influential on Tarule's work, serving as advisor for her dissertation on developmental transitions for adult learners. Belenky's dissertation research on abortion choice was done at Harvard, where she was involved with Gilligan's research group. There were threads of common interests and social connections among these women, but they had different concerns. Goldberger suggested that the four get together. They chose White River Junction in Vermont, a spot central to all their home locations. In the new introduction to the tenth anniversary publication of *Women's Ways of Knowing*, they reconstructed that first meeting, describing how each had qualms approaching their time together in Vermont: How much did they really share?

Belenky had worked with college women at Goddard and in her study of abortion choice, but now she was interested in poor young mothers raising small children. In her interview, as she thought about working in this new group, she remembered worrying: "I had been certain that these three women would have little interest in the questions I wanted to pursue. They were immersed in studies looking at the impact of college experience on women's development; I wanted to study poor mothers raising small children— one of the most marginal and demeaned groups in society. . . . How would these women deal with me and my interests?"[45] She was not the only one concerned about how they would work together. Although Clinchy shared the others' interest in adult development, she felt she hardly knew them: "She was pretty sure she was the last to be chosen, and wasn't sure why she had been chosen. . . . But her qualms receded as soon as she arrived at the motel. . . . Clearly, all three of these women cared deeply and thought hard about research, my kind of research."[46]

In a joint interview, Belenky and Clinchy expressed that "at the beginning, we each talked about what we longed to do in a very open way . . . and very quickly we discovered that we were close enough that we could pull something together." The first resolution of the tension between individual interests and common commitments came as a breakthrough insight: "Women don't just learn in classrooms; they learn in relationships, by juggling life demands, by dealing with crises in families and communities." Goldberger further recalled, "We realized together, at a particular moment, that 'education' need not be narrowly defined. I remember feeling as exhilarated by the collaborative discovery—the group 'aha'—as I was by naming what we wanted to do: Education for Women's Development."

After their first meeting, they decided to apply for a grant from FIPSE. This agency was sympathetic to their objectives and their choice to work collaboratively—to have four equal investigators rather than the standard "principal investigator" and associates. This meshing of the group's perspective with that of a part of the field was important for their eventual success.[47]

Goldberger and Belenky wrote the proposal, which included funds for frequent meetings away from their home institutions. Among the early tasks was designing an interview schedule that was broad yet would take no more than an hour and a half to administer. They paid close attention to choosing interview sites at social agencies as well as educational institutions. They were committed to working with a broad range of women, including welfare mothers, rural women, and women of varied educational attainment. Their research was not driven by specific hypotheses but by broad questions dealing with individuals' assumptions about knowledge. In the beginning, they used Perry's model of adult development as the defining framework for their studies, but they found it constricting. Part of their work was overcoming their deep socialization in the domains in which they had been trained.

A similar process of jointly examining and overcoming their socialization was described by the clinicians associated with the Stone Center of Developmental Services and Studies at Wellesley College. After Miller published *Toward a New Psychology of Women*, she was approached by some Boston-area psychotherapists who wanted to develop alternative treatments for women and, ultimately, an alternative model of human development. These collaborators worked individually, in dyads, and in small groups. Eventually they brought their work together in a book, *Women's Growth in Connection*. In the preface, the editors, Judith V. Jordan, Alexandra G. Kaplan, Jean Baker Miller, Irene P. Stiver, and Janet L. Surrey, wrote:

We initially came together in a group to explore issues in the clinical treatment of women. . . . As we discussed clinical dilemmas together, we were energized and excited. We began to let go of more and more of the strictures of our traditional psychodynamic training . . . [including] theories of "human development" which espoused increasing capacity for separation, autonomy, mastery, independence, and self-sufficiency as indications of health and maturity and [which] consistently portrayed women as too emotional, too dependent, lacking clear boundaries, and so forth.[48]

At their first informal meetings, they started questioning the theories that had been formative in their training. Then came a more organized structure of interactions at the Stone Center and at conventions of mental health professionals, through which they used colloquium presentations to start study groups whose members frequently prepared working papers. These working papers were then criticized and elaborated upon by the larger group. Their book of coordinated articles, in which they develop a relational/cultural approach to human understanding, was published ten years after their first meeting, but their working papers became known even before that and have been widely circulated among psychotherapists and feminist scholars. Members of the Stone Center see their ability to generate new concepts as linked to their own mutuality and to developments in the broader domain of relational/cultural approaches to psychological development. Although, in *Women's Growth in Connection*, the authors wrote individual chapters, their volume presented a shared theory:

These ideas have grown from and feed back into a nourishing process of group exchange. It has not always been clear where the ideas came from and in some way the question of authorship of these papers mirrors the very perspective we are exploring: there are individual ways of organizing the thoughts, and individual effort, time and sometimes "angst" has gone into making each chapter, but the generation of ideas, the expansion of the work has sprung from the group.[49]

Some aspects of how this group worked together show a looser structure of collaboration than that of the authors of *Women's Ways of Knowing*. This looser structure may be a reflection of the distributed collaborative mode: people participate because of shared interests, but have considerable latitude in the extent of their joint activity. As the Stone Center collaborators started to co-articulate a series of shared concepts, they moved into a more integrative pattern.

Gilligan's way of collaborating is different from the complementary, distributed, or integrative modes already described. She and her partners engage in what is called the family model. Roles are flexible, and people of different ages and stages of development are easily integrated into an informal, caring structure. In an interview during the summer of 1996, Gilligan recalled the beginning of this activity, which resulted in two books, *Making Connections*, co-edited with Nora Lyons and Trudy Hammer, and *Meeting at the Crossroads*, written with Lyn Brown.[50] After Gilligan's well-known, solo-authored book *In a Different Voice* was published, she wanted to start something new:

> I was consistently misheard. . . . I wanted to get out of that difference argument because I did not think it was going anywhere. . . .
> I got interested in reconstructing the trajectory from girls to adult women and was astonished to discover that there was so little about girls in the adolescent literature. I decided to do a longitudinal cross-sectional study of girls. That was conceived initially as a collaborative project.[51]

She called for help from students at the Harvard Graduate School of Education. Graduate students joined eagerly. Gilligan was very comfortable with an open structure where participants connected based on values and interest, not power hierarchies. In 1981, she began a study of the "relational worlds" of adolescent girls at the Emma Willard School in Troy, New York. The first participants were two graduate students whom she had been advising. Soon twelve to fourteen graduate students had joined the project and started traveling to Troy together. They were interviewing large numbers of girls. At Harvard, they would say to their fellow graduate students, "You are interested in this? Come join us. Here is training in how to interview." They stayed together in the dorms and even exercised together to Jane Fonda's videotapes.

Collaboration was not new for Gilligan. As a graduate student, she had worked with anthropologists Beatrice and John Whiting and, later, was part of a group around developmental psychologist Lawrence Kohlberg. She was also a member of an improvisational theater group and a long-term political activist. All these experiences prepared her to research collaboratively. The family style of interaction worked well. The participants shared their enthusiasm about the newness and relevance of their topic. Gilligan did not set herself up as an expert: "We were all novices."

JOINT AUTHORSHIP

All the women I interviewed describe the experiences of collaborative work in rich detail. Michelle Fine described collaboration:

I do better work; it allows me to travel intellectually. I think Pat and I import different perspectives to the conversation but from there forward it feels like we are doing experimental cooking. That is, we can crack eggs and we can take them out. We do a lot of playing with each other's language, although at the beginning there was a lot of hesitancy to do that. But I am not so proprietary. I do not feel that ideas and words are private property.

Pat MacPherson agreed with many of Fine's insights, but revealed some tension about writing in the midst of their many stimulating projects. She admires Fine's ability as a dynamic public speaker who can move between different worlds, who can switch from teacher to researcher to collaborator. She likes the experience of being pushed in that direction herself since, like many writers, she is a more solitary person. When asked whether their complementarity can sometimes occasion dissonance, MacPherson replied:

I would say that it is the tension in myself that I feel. The more I don't have time to write by myself at length, the more frustrated I get. I feel like I am kind of getting to be removed from what I most want to do and what I most want to be. . . . The projects that Michelle brings along which are collaborative sound great, and tie into all sorts of useful public networks. And yet there comes a time when there are too many of those. And I don't want to lose the connection, but I feel like the quality of my input is not good enough because I have not had time to think. So I sort of go back and forth in thinking about my own balance about how I want to play it with Michelle.

Listening to MacPherson, I think about my own collaborators. I have often worked with people who are more solitary than I am, who live intensely, passionately with the written word, and who, at times, feel distressed about the multitude of projects in which I am engaged. They bear with me, they rescue me, and they share a part of themselves that I can only admire but never fully appropriate. Fine responded in her usual honest, principled way to her partner: "What do I want to say about this? I want to take it in a slightly different direction. Some of it has to do with the nature of our working together. It is really incredibly wonderful. I realize that intellectually . . . in lovely ways, as a woman who says she is not dependent on anybody, I am incredibly dependent on you." MacPherson responded, "That is quite a compliment, Michelle," to which Fine added, "I never speak of this work without checking with Pat. . . . There are moments when I feel we plagiarize each other because our thinking is so integrated. Yet I know clearly what we bring to each other. . . . And I can't do Pat's part but I also feel I can't do my part."

Their interaction, according to them, is most stimulating in the early stages of a project when ideas fly. Fine asserted, "I think there's no one else I can rely on who's willing to go to all the places I need to go to make sense in a day. So, you know, a kid who is pregnant and just got mugged, to a teacher who you wish was better, to sexual harassment, to feminist theory, to a publication deadline." And as with most intellectual work, at the later stages, details have to be attended to and final drafts decided on: some tensions appear. Fine continued, "And then there is a burden between us about deadline. Who's just gonna do it? . . . But it's like we've got another week. Who's gonna do just the last cut? I'm sick of it, you're sick of it, you do it, you know? And so I think that does kind of sit uneasy, like it doesn't quite speak to our collective voices. It's a single decision." But these collaborators explicitly address their concerns. They can speak about their different strengths, their deep caring for each other, their willingness to push each other into realizing more fully their individual and joint possibilities—a relationship that Fine characterized as an "affair of the mind."

Shifting concerns at different stages of a collaboration is also exemplified by the authors of *Women's Ways of Knowing*. They called their first meeting a wonderful "pajama party" and their mode of interaction as "working in the women's way." In the introduction to their new edition, they described their pattern: "Usually, meeting in each other's homes for three-to-four-day meetings to discuss the design of the project, the piloting of the interviews, and, ultimately, the interview data we collected. We sat around living rooms and kitchen tables as we worked. Dogs barked in the background; children wandered through. We took long walks, talking, always talking. Sometimes our husbands cooked for us."[52] They recalled the vastness of their concerns and the challenge of finding a clear focus: "How do we make sense of all this? Of all the questions in the world you could ask in an interview, how do you choose which questions you are going to ask in an hour and a half?" In addition to collecting interviews, they set up educational programs in their own institutions. That part of the work was easily divided, as each person knew her own environment. Clinchy at Wellesley combined a discussion of interview materials with faculty educational seminars. Belenky in Vermont worked with parent programs reaching out to young rural and African American women. And they all continued to collect, read, and try to understand their interviews.

Once they started to write, they faced the issue of a common written voice—how to construct a sense of "we." Each of the dyads and groups I have interviewed for this chapter has struggled with this concern. The concept of "we" varies among them, manifesting in the way they planned their writing. The most dramatic example of a shared mode of text construction is that of anthropologists Ochs and Schieffelin, whose "enduring collaborative partnership" has spanned more than twenty years.[53] As described above, they never assign part of the paper to one or another; they write every sentence together.

The authors of *Women's Ways of Knowing* were also committed to speaking in a single voice: "An exercise that was difficult but in the end successful, we thought. Throughout the writing, we kept in mind the metaphor of a chorus of voices that was to sing the story we wanted to tell; there were to be no solos."[54] But to achieve the "we"-ness of their prose, the four women did not sit next to each other. Each wrote a first draft and passed it on to another for comment. They had different rhythms. One needed a lot of time to explore the interviews and deepen the writing; another was more concerned with deadlines. Sometimes they experienced these differences as pressure. Other times they welcomed their complementarity because it contributed to their effectiveness. As in the Fine-MacPherson partnership, these women varied in the extent to which they were comfortable in the limelight of the public world. They learned from each other to develop a balance between quiet writing time and planning and fighting for their book. Their "we"-ness was made possible by their playfulness with each other, their careful planning for a lot of protected time together, and their shared values. Clinchy recalled: "We became hard-nosed with each other once the writing started. By that time we had done so much thinking together, we had so much confidence in each other, that we were not too shaken when challenged." Belenky remembered being unsure about one of her drafts. Another member of the collaborative said it was practically perfect. Belenky was so relieved, she has never forgotten that praise. For these women, criticism came from the inside as a really loving thing.

The authors wanted the book to be beautiful. They cared about the language, so they produced many drafts. Goldberger recalled that their computers were not compatible, so they had to recopy each other's drafts many times:

> Of all the many memories of our collaboration, one particular experience always comes to mind when I am asked to describe what it was like. I am sitting before my new computer. I have Blythe's or Jill's or Mary's words before me and the marginal commentary from the other two as well. My task is to rewrite, but first I must type the words from my colleague into my word processor. I decide to edit as I type. What astonishes me is the process that evolves; I take someone else's words (someone I respect and trust and who trusts me), slowly read her text, try to understand her intention behind her choice of words, try to place myself in her place, so that I feel inside her mind and heart, search for her

meaning, before I impose new words from meaning of my own, imagine what might be so important to her to say that I must take care not to lose her meaning. Only then do I allow new words to flow from my fingers—the words are mine, yet hers as well. It was this slowed-down process of reading-attending-typing that led me to an understanding of a friend and colleague in a way that I had not attained in conversation or in the initial reading of the text.[55]

Goldberger's description of understanding and adopting the spirit of her author would be accepted by any committed editor. The word-by-word typing, in her case, facilitated this absorption.

It was not always easy to achieve a shared voice by four authors. Each had a somewhat different relationship to the theory and to the chapter for which she had primary responsibility. Their collaboration was a process—a trajectory that required rewriting and help from outsiders. Interestingly, in the recently completed volume of essays inspired by *Women's Ways of Knowing*, each member of this partnership expanded, in a solo-authored chapter, on some of her particular interests and ideas. In a co-authored chapter together they wonder: "Was a single voice impossible? Maybe we were going to have to choose one of us to write the last draft, smoothing out the bumps and filling in the gaps for the sake of the book. But I hoped not. We have worked too hard to join our voices and pool our thoughts to give that up. And, anyway, if collaborative writing is possible at all, we wanted to prove we could carry it through to the end."[56] And they did; they stayed with the writing and rewriting long enough to achieve a single voice.

Gilligan described a somewhat different mode of writing. Her metaphor was an orchestra in which flutes, violins, and oboes play together: "Each instrument is affected by the resonances of the others, yet there is a distinctive voice. . . . That was the guiding image of our collaborative." Gilligan's group divided the writing assignments according to interest: the writer of a particular part might be someone who was going to write her thesis on the topic, or a postdoc, or the project director. They negotiated the tasks and the order of authorship. Chapters and articles were frequently co-authored. Then they would set the voice of the paper in the first few paragraphs: "It is like saying, 'We are writing in A major, and here is the key, and here is the tempo.'" When they wrote together, they kept in mind the guiding metaphor of the orchestra, which allowed them to shift from individual voices to a duet or trio. "It was a very fluid boundary situation," Gilligan remembered.

In all these groups, in spite of their shared values, they experience times when tension between the relational and the competitive modes lead to difficulty. When they are not under external pressure, the collaborators know how to resolve those tensions. But American universities are not constructed to support groups over long periods of time, nor do they value joint authorship when a young faculty member comes up for tenure.

Schieffelin was criticized when she came up for tenure at the University of Pennsylvania because too many of her publications were authored jointly with Ochs. Up to that time, they did not bother to record which was the first author of their papers and books. From then on, they felt compelled to carefully alternate authorship. As the research of Gilligan's group progressed at the Willard School, the group became stronger at Harvard as well. They had adjacent offices and referred to themselves as the "Feminist Research Collaborative." Their funding increased, and their work extended to different sites. But in the 1990s, outside support for research became harder to get. The graduate students finished their degrees; the postdoctoral students finished their projects. There were no new faculty positions for Gilligan's collaborators. As a consequence, it became difficult to maintain their full-scale collaboration, although they fought hard to preserve it.

These histories seem to follow a pattern. In the beginning, while the collaborators are developing new ideas and learning to work with each other, they are not too seriously affected by the "system," which has little regard for collaboration. But ultimately, however strong their internal bonds, they encounter external pressures that compel concessions in their style of work.

FORGING A THEORY

A crucial advantage of collaboration is the strength it provides to overcome one's socialization into a discipline and a thought community. Ludwik Fleck wrote that knowledge is constructed among a "community of persons mutually exchanging ideas and maintaining intellectual interaction."[57] In joining such a group, the new member must appropriate its governing ideas. These ideas become part of the belief system of the participant. When faced with new facts, it is difficult, sometimes wrenching, to loosen the hold of these concepts and frameworks. The authors of *Women's Ways of Knowing* had such an experience. It was about one's relationship with mentors and "distant teachers." In the beginning, they relied heavily on Perry's developmental scheme, which he based on a longitudinal study of Harvard undergraduates. But their own data was collected from "a very broad net" of women from different walks of life and educational backgrounds. The answers the women gave to the "Perry questions" about how they knew what they knew and what they expected from education did not fit into his developmental schemes. So they needed to change their approach: "When the data the women provided diverged from the theories we had brought to the project, we forced ourselves to believe the women and let go of the theories. It was surprisingly painful to let go of the theories that had served as scaffolding for the project and that we had come to cherish as parts of ourselves."[58]

In a similar vein, Gilligan spoke of the role of her collaborative, the Harvard Project on Women's Psychology and Girls' Development, as crucial in overcoming the legacy of their socializing experiences. While interviewing adolescent girls, members of the group made important discoveries about themselves. They, too, had faced the "relational impasse" described by their young subjects. As mentioned above, a striking finding of the research group was a "going underground" experienced by many adolescent girls of their freer, agentive, younger selves, a "normalized covering over of a conflicted and complicated world."[59] The collaborators discovered together their own experiences of dissociation: "In other words, knowing things that we knew from our own history and then learned not to know. And if we had not been working collaboratively, we could not have done it."[60]

In earlier chapters, I focus on collaboration as a means to overcome existing paradigms of thought in artistic and scientific domains. Picasso and Braque's struggle to see and depict the world differently from their Impressionist predecessors is one example. The paradigm shifts that occurred in physics when classical physics was being subsumed, expanded, and even contradicted by emerging relativity and quantum mechanics is another illustration. Gilligan's account of her collaboration on girls' development broadens this understanding. She said that it is not possible to overcome by oneself the legacy of one's ambivalence in mid-adolescence. It can be done with the support, insight, and multiple perspectives provided by a group. She portrayed a paradigm shift that goes beyond cognitive restructuring and discovery. It takes place at an emotional and intellectual level where one's understanding of the world is linked to a new understanding of oneself: "The collaboration became very deep at the point when we realized that we are all carrying this history. But we were also 'discovering' it, when we were starting to have experiences with the young girls that were resonating with us personally . . . things we knew and then did not know we knew. So the collaboration became an essential part of the research."

The collaborators thought of the members of the research groups as well as the people they worked with as part of the collaborative. And they continued to discover a complex web of connections between their own work and that of other groups committed to the construction of a new women's psychology.

One of the challenges the different groups shared was the issue of the researchers' relationship with the girls and women who participated in their work and the issue of whose voices they were rendering on paper. They kept searching for ways to stay connected to each other and to the young people in their inquiry without "objectifying" their participants. This dilemma became particularly difficult when these feminist writers addressed the challenge of presenting the voices of the girls and women with whom they have worked while constructing theories based on what they have learned. MacPherson described this dilemma: "In a fast moving conversation . . . it is easy to overwhelm them and shut them up. There is a lot of my experience that is not relevant to them now. . . . Trying to select out what would be helpful, I constrain myself a lot because I am very aware of not wanting them to feel like I have some agenda here and that I am trying to fit them into [it]."

The authors of *Women's Ways of Knowing* also confronted this quandary:

> But wasn't it the women's voices that mattered? After all, we had decided to write a book because we found their voices so moving. We came to see, however, that in serving merely as conduits for the women's voices, we were behaving with the double-edged "selflessness" common among women, exhibiting an appropriately humble respect for the wisdom of others, but also a cowardly reluctance to construct and communicate our own knowledge.[61]

Working collaboratively, these authors helped each other overcome some of their conflicts of identity: how to be researchers who do not exploit their "subjects," who respect and are true to what they hear without negating their own strengths. They pushed each other to create "better and better concepts."[62]

Theory construction is still, to a large extent, a male province. Women find it difficult to attain the sense of authority and willingness to argue for one's position since, in our socialization, we have witnessed only the confrontational style of defending a theoretical stance. The narratives above depict a different mode, akin to Evelyn Fox Keller's "dynamic objectivity": "a form of knowledge that grants to the world around us its independent integrity but does so in a way that remains cognizant of, indeed relies on, our [connectedness] with the world."[63]

These collaborators provide several models of their working methods. There are interesting differences among them: for example, in the way some of them strive to construct a single voice, while others orchestrate solo and joint endeavors. Their words evoke a felt knowledge and the courage to practice a human connectedness still rare in today's conflict-ridden world.

At the beginning of this chapter, I ask whether the collaborative experience eloquently described by Kaplan and Rose is particularly congenial to women. To answer that question, I argue that mutuality and interdependence are part of all human life, male and female. But in modern America and other industrialized Western nations, many males experience a powerful push toward independence, competition, and autonomy. Women, on the other hand, have been made responsible for maintaining the social fabric. Today, however, the recognition of shrinking resources is making people think seriously about a turn toward less wasteful, more collaborative modes of work. These modes are varied: some are based solely on division of labor, whereas others require easing traditional hierarchies toward more flexible roles.

Women's primary responsibility for private life, especially childcare, has contributed to their awareness of interdependence. Ways of knowing and ways of structuring working relationships are shaped by recurrent, culturally formed practices. Feminist scholar Sara Ruddick suggested that the "knowing that arises out of practices is also gendered. To the extent that women and men engage more extensively and intensively in certain practices than others, the thinking that arises out of these practices will have a masculine or feminine aspect."[64] To date, because of their socialization, women are more widely engaged than men in practices—both in the public and private spheres—that require relational skills: nurses, teachers, and secretaries; and among physicians, women are disproportionately pediatricians. As a consequence of these recurrent activities, many women become more interested in and more comfortable with collaborative modes of work than do men trained in fields requiring aggressive behavior. In answer to the original question, I argue that women face fewer barriers than men when attempting collaboration. Collaboration is a mode that in modern life has been more adaptive in the private than in the public domain. This gendered division of attitudes and experiences is a result of past practices, but it is subject to further historical and technological changes. These changes make possible the implementation of joint endeavors in more settings and an increase in participation by both men and women, which in turn creates a more gender-equal and collaborative world.

5

FELT KNOWLEDGE:

EMOTIONAL DYNAMICS OF COLLABORATION

The increasing prevalence of joint activities in the arts and sciences presents practical and theoretical challenges to creativity researchers. The importance of mutuality and "a matrix of support" is acknowledged by psychologist Howard Gardner. He considers these connections influential at times of creative breakthroughs:

> My claim, then, is that the time of creative breakthroughs is highly charged, both affectively and cognitively. Support is needed at this time, more so than at any other time in life since early infancy. The kind of communication that takes place is unique and uniquely important, bearing closer resemblance to the introduction of a new language early in life, than to the routine conversations between individuals who already share the same language. The often inarticulate and still struggling conversation also represents a way for the creator to test that he or she is still sane, still understandable by a sympathetic member of the species.[1]

Gardner's depiction of these supportive connections included affective and cognitive dimensions. In addressing the former, he relied on a Freudian framework of early relationships, in which the mother's role in childhood is echoed by the creator's trusted partner. The supportive partner provides legitimization of the new language that is part of the creative breakthrough. There is an interesting analogy between childhood experiences and the experience of the adult in the throes of creation. But the Freudian framework is different from the description in cultural-historical and feminist theories in which human interconnectedness and self-in-relation take a variety of forms. The central role of the biological family in providing experiences of connectedness cannot be minimized, but it is restrictive to make it the prototype for all intense relationships.

In this study of collaboration, I use both feminist and cultural-historical theories to examine the cognitive and motivational aspects of mutuality. Approaches to mutuality need to take account of the person as an agent as well as a recipient. Cultural-historical theorists are rethinking notions of the person as they criticize the traditional, Cartesian emphasis upon the primacy of the individual. In *The Social Self,* edited by David Bakhurst and Christine Sypnowich, the authors wrote about socially constructed, embodied persons who are "the focus of the events which constitute a life."[2] In these non-Cartesian theories of self, thinking and language have been the primary topics of analysis, as in the work of philosopher Ludwig Wittgenstein, literary critic Mikhail M. Bakhtin, psychologists Lev S. Vygotsky and James Wertsch, anthropological linguist George Lakoff and his co-author, Mark Johnson, and neuroscientist Antonio Damasio.

It is clear from this and previous chapters that *collaboration is complex; it is charged both cognitively and emotionally.* A variety of supportive, loving, and conflicted relationships are depicted in this book. There are differences between complementary partnerships, family partnerships, and integrative partnerships in structure, in roles, and in working methods. These patterns also present different emotional dynamics, ranging from caring, respectful companionship, present in most complementary relationships, to the passionate connections in many integrative, transformative partnerships.

Some of the motivational sources of collaboration have been discussed in previous chapters. These include the desire to overcome the limitations of the self and a response to the alienation widespread in modern life. In collaborations resembling extended families, the ties of solidarity and shared vision are accompanied by the participants' longing for the security of a caring community. In many partnerships, participants experience emotional connectedness and a revival of purpose in shared work. They also find reassurance in the spreading of risks when facing challenging, innovative endeavors. I will next identify some additional emotional themes of collaboration in both their supportive and their occasionally destructive aspects.

COMPLEMENTARITY IN TEMPERAMENT

Many scientific husband-wife teams owe part of their success in work and in marriage to their constructive differences. Helena Pycior describes Marie Curie as a thinker-doer who was more concerned than her husband with worldly success. Pierre Curie, on the other hand, was the "thinker-dreamer who reveled in broad reflections on nature."[3] Their daughters were aware of the complementarity of their parents; Irene Joliot-Curie described her father as "an excellent experimenter (and) also a thinker. . . . [The] thought of my mother was more often directed toward immediate action, even in the scientific domain."[4] She further reflected: "Pierre Curie was attracted above all by the fascinating problems posed by the . . . mysterious rays emitted by these materials . . . Marie Curie had the stubborn desire to see salts of pure radium, to measure radium's pure weight."[5] Even their handwriting differed: Marie's was careful and clear; Pierre scrawled. While Marie was energetic and vivacious during their early years, she also tended to be overly serious at times. Her husband's delight in nature enriched their lives during their long bicycle rides exploring quiet rural and coastal areas.

Their ability to help each other was important in their joint work: When Pierre was called upon to teach a new course at the École Municipale, she assisted in preparing lectures; when he retreated to the laboratory for hours on end, she conducted her research at his side.[6] Their complementarity was not one of easy gender divisions: Marie, although practical, was better at abstract mathematics, while her husband enjoyed building and designing instruments.[7] Once they jointly received the Nobel Prize in 1903, the popular press tried to cast them into traditional roles, although a few journalists were able to see them as prototypes for equal roles between men and women.

The Curies' older daughter, Irene, also became a researcher in radiochemistry. She married a colleague, Frederic Joliot, a fellow member of her mother's Radium Institute in Paris. Although there were many parallels across these two generations of scientists, there were also some important differences in their roles. Irene was more like her father than her mother, even though the two were exceptionally close after Pierre's early, tragic death. Joliot watched Irene at work before they married; he later described her as "a living representation of her father. . . . I found in his daughter this same purity, this good sense, this tranquillity."[8] Joliot, in contrast, was very outgoing, lively, talkative, and charming. They worked well together, sharing the same scientific culture, but using somewhat different yet complementary technical, theoretical, and interpersonal skills. They jointly won a Nobel Prize in 1935 for identifying an isotope of phosphorus.

Another collaboration, between German-born, Nobel Prize–winning physicist Maria Goeppert Meyer and her husband, American chemist Joe Meyer, exhibited productive temperamental complementarity. They met in 1927 in Goettingen, Germany, where Maria was a much admired member of the famous scientific community. They married three years later. Meyer was thoroughly committed to his wife's scientific career, although she was at times ambivalent. She wanted to be mother and hostess as well as scientist. During their early difficult years in the United States, after emigrating from fascist Germany, she came to trust and build upon her husband's belief in her abilities. As a female, married physicist, it took many years for Maria to gain recognition and a tenured job. Her husband's unfailing optimism, and her continued professional relationship with the major physicists of her time (many of them also émigrés), helped her to meet these challenges. Maria was self-confident with people she knew but shy in new situations. Her husband's vivacity, confidence, and devotion, together with her "quiet firmness . . . her inability to leave a problem until it was clarified,"[9] contributed to her eventual success.

In addition to the Joliets and the Meyers, many more examples of complementarity in temperament have been mentioned in the previous chapters, including the Riekes, the Dreyfus brothers, Bill Conte and Suki John, the directors of the Group Theater, and Braque and Picasso. These differences contribute to the richness of collaboration. They are also important in the way creative individuals understand themselves through an emotional division of labor. In many family and integrative collaborations, roles are not permanent; partners can take over for each other in reaching out to the world, or in providing hope and support within a collaboration. Bennis and Biederman wrote in *Organizing Genius*: "In a Great Group you are liberated for a time from the prison of the self."[10]

While complementarity is most easily identified in skills and disciplinary training, it is not limited to the cognitive domain. It is part of personal growth that frequently takes place in long-lasting partnerships. Csikszentmihalyi described creative individuals as highly complex: "They contain contradictory extremes—instead of being an 'individual,' each of them is a 'multitude.'"[11] His words bring to mind the famous quotation from Walt Whitman: "Do I contradict myself? Very well then I contradict myself. I am large, I contain multitudes."[12] One of a creative individual's complexities is the combination of discipline and playfulness—the joyous exploration of creative ideas. Effective creative outcomes require the rigorous, sustained labor of nurturing, shaping, and developing imaginative leaps. The motivation for such discipline is strengthened through mutual support. Partners take over for each other at times of personal difficulties, and help each other stretch themselves under the duress of deadlines or external criticism. Their temperamental complementarity can make these demanding tasks more manageable.

THE GIFT OF CONFIDENCE

Belief in a partner's capabilities is crucial in collaborative work, as marginality, estrangement, and self-doubt frequently plague creative people. As he was nearing the end of his life, Jean-Paul Sartre remarked to Simone de Beauvoir: "You did me a great service. You gave me a confidence in myself that I shouldn't have had alone."[13] Henry Miller's confidence in Anaïs Nin's literary talent contributed to her tenacity in fighting for her work over decades of rejection. The Dreyfus brothers, joint authors of *Mind over Machine*, relied on their lifelong belief in each other when opposing the "manic" optimism of their colleagues in artificial intelligence. The authors of *The Mathematical Experience*, Phil Davis and Reuben Hersh, provided mutual support when working on their books.[14] Hersh confirmed that the material Davis was working on was interesting, and reflected their joint philosophy. Howard Gardner suggested, in his case study of Picasso, that the admiration of his friends and collaborators contributed to his sense that "there were no limits on what he could accomplish."[15]

Significant Others, a book about creativity and intimate partnerships, gives many examples of "the gift of confidence." The complex relationship between British painters Duncan Grant and Vanessa Bell was sustained, in part, by their commitment to each other as artists. "We should not underestimate what Grant gave Bell as an artist, which was not least, given her sometimes shaky self-esteem, the daily, and confident assumption that she was one; a worthy collaborator, one with whom day after day on equal terms he would leave the breakfast table for the studio.[16]

Mexican painters Frida Kahlo and Diego Rivera also shared a powerful bond: their limitless belief in each other's talent. Kahlo suffered a very serious accident as a young woman. She found solace in painting on canvases and on small sheets of tin (akin to the Mexican retablos). Her work, which was personal, intense, and dramatic, has been increasingly honored. Painting was hard for a woman who had undergone many operations and had suffered the emotional loss of miscarriages. But her husband encouraged her. He loved her often shocking, self-revealing paintings. He urged her to continue even when she was in pain, and he pushed her to show and sell her work. Kahlo first fell in love with Rivera as a painter, but her belief in him grew until it encompassed the whole man. As in many creative partnerships, her criticism was essential to him. Like Sartre and de Beauvoir, they respected each other's talent, and they listened to each other's comments. They thought of their partners as demanding but fair critics.[17]

The co-construction of ideas is helped by a listening ear. Innovative works of literature, drama, choreography, and art are nourished by emotional support. Building a resilient sense of identity is aided by a self that is stretched and strengthened in partnership. The gifts of confidence and support may outlast a creative partnership: even after Sartre's death, de Beauvoir carried within her Sartre's belief in her.

In order to put this observation in a more theoretical form, I am expanding Vygotsky's notion of the *zone of proximal development* to the emotional sphere. He proposed that, in interaction with more experienced others, individuals can go beyond their existing level of development. His work focused on children and on psychological functions that, in the course of development, are scaffolded by the assistance of those with more knowledge and experience.[18] I am suggesting that the facilitating role of the social, participating other need not be limited to the cognitive sphere. It is also relevant to the process of appropriating emotional experiences. Developing children, as well as developing adults, expand their affective resources by appropriating the consequences of shared experience. Such a process includes identification, scaffolding, expansion by complementarity, and constructive criticism. In this discussion, I am focusing on the implications of the emotional zone of development for adult partnerships.

Emotional scaffolding is multifaceted; it includes the gift of confidence, and the leaning on that gift by creative people during periods of self-doubt and rejection by those in power. It creates a safety zone within which both support and constructive criticism between partners are effectively practiced. Collaborative partners can build on their solidarity as well as their differences; complementarity in knowledge, working habits, and temperament adds to the motivation needed for effective partnerships. It stimulates and challenges the individual whose efforts are expanded by watching a partner, trying to keep up with him or her, and absorbing the other's belief in one's capabilities. Feminist writer Janet Surrey described such a process in her analysis of effective mother-daughter relationships. She referred to these relationships as the "capacity to learn to 'see' the other and to 'make oneself known' [which] highlights one's own self knowledge and fosters growth in the other and in the self. Thus, 'mutual care-taking' is a fundamental aspect of learning."[19]

The lifelong partnership of Sartre and de Beauvoir exemplified the efficacy of intellectual and emotional complementarity. As philosophers and writers, they were sensitive to inconsistencies and errors, and they used these skills for each other. For instance, when Sartre was in a prison camp during World War II, he sent his fiction to her in Paris. In a note to de Beauvoir he wrote that "she had full power to cross out, obliterate, and erase anything you care to but write back about more substantive passages that don't work."[20] He also encouraged her to put herself more fully into her writing.[21]

The fifty-year relationship of these two important French intellectuals continues to fascinate biographers and feminists. Their enduring commitment to each other, while also engaged in other intimate relationships, is part of that fascination. Sartre characterized their connection as follows: "What we have . . . is an essential love; but it is a good idea for us also to experience contingent love affairs. We were two of a kind, and our relationship would endure as long as we did."[22]

Early in their lives together they decided not to marry, as they opposed that traditional form of commitment. They lived close to each other, but had separate quarters. De Beauvoir achieved financial independence as a teacher of philosophy and a writer. Sartre taught, and wrote plays, philosophical treatises, novels, and even screen scripts. Their identity as a couple was of paramount importance to them. Creativity and intimacy rather than traditional family concerns were central.

Their unwavering commonality sustained them in ways that made each a more effective thinker/writer. Emotionally, the partnership took a toll on de Beauvoir. She feared overdependence on a man who wanted multiple sexual relationships. In order to avoid that danger, de Beauvoir preserved her independence within this committed relationship by traveling, taking jobs outside Paris, and developing important relationships with both men and women in addition to her primary commitment to Sartre.

Their placing honesty at the center of their relationship was not always easy, but it remained a crucial feature of their partnerships. During the last decade of his life, when Sartre was close to blindness, he explained in interviews with de Beauvoir the ways in which he saw his existence. He spoke of his involvement with women, of the importance of affect and sensibility that women have, and how that quality added to his life:

> The woman's role was on the emotional plane. It is a very usual state of affairs, but I did not look upon that emotional side as inferior to the practice and exercise of reason. It was a question of different dispositions. That did not mean that women were not capable of exercising reason as men, or that a woman could not be an engineer or a philosopher. It simply meant that most of the time a woman had emotional and sometimes sexual values; and it was that aggregate which I drew toward myself because I felt that having a connection with a woman like that was to some extent taking possession of her affectivity. Trying to make her feel it for me, feel it deeply, meant possessing that affectivity—it was a quality I was giving myself.[23]

Sartre speaks here of an *appropriation at the emotional level* that enriched many relationships. Yet while these relationships added to his life, the basic, lasting connection was with de Beauvoir. As he said: "The real world, that was what I lived in with you."[24] The Sartre–de Beauvoir relationship raises important questions about interdependence, autonomy, will, and commitment. Part of the couple's legacy is that they succeeded in maintaining their intellectual and emotional connection through challenges that many others found overwhelming.

In most psychological analyses, personal and emotional qualities are thought to be established early in life and highly resistant to change. Such a stand is based in part on the greater plasticity of the human nervous system in early life, which does decrease with age. Some argue that temperament—an important source of emotional dispositions such as optimism/pessimism, energy level, and extroversion—is genetically determined. At the same time, students of development have shown that children's behavior is highly context-dependent; for instance, children and adults behave differently with different partners.[25] When we compare individuals in single situations using standardized tools, we focus on stability. When we study persons over time and observe them in multiple settings, we become aware of plasticity.

Social and cultural arrangements can contribute to both stability and plasticity. For instance, in historical periods in which gender stereotypes are strongly enforced, male and female behaviors reveal greater across-situation stability than in our contemporary society, in which there is greater sex-role fluidity. Individuals whose lives are lived within very narrow confines, interacting with few others, may have few opportunities to experience the challenges of lifelong change.

In one example illustrating personality change in midlife, Mihaly Csikszentmihalyi described the experiences of psychologist and foundation president John Gardner. As an academic psychologist, Gardner was somewhat introverted. Once he became chairman of Common Cause, he started to systematically modify his behavior. He realized that it was important in his new post to become a responsive and effective communicator. Gardner was able to cultivate previously neglected aspects of his personality. He shared his belief with his interviewer "that we all have much deeper reserves than we know we have and generally it takes an outside challenge or opportunity to make us aware of what we actually do. A lot of our potential, he believes, is buried, hidden, imprisoned by fears, low self-esteem, and the hold of convention."[26]

In this work, I present personality as a system rather than as a collection of traits. Like all adaptive systems, humans change in altered social and physical environments. Participants engaged in sustained, working partnerships can develop emotional resources different from those needed when working in isolation. In the course of integrative partnerships, for instance that of the Curies, complementarity became the source of enrichment—the experiencing of new possibilities, both intellectually and emotionally. It is interesting that Picasso, who was well known for his substantial ego, was willing to join Braque in an endeavor that the latter described as follows: "We are inclined to efface our personalities in order to find originality."[27]

In the chapter on women and collaboration, I portray the role of complementarity between social psychologist Michelle Fine and writer Pat MacPherson. Fine's dynamic personality contributes to her visibility as a teacher and public speaker, and the arrangement of settings and networks needed for their joint efforts. MacPherson is a more introverted person, whose quiet, patient, editorial efforts shape their joint drafts and add to the impact of their writings. These partners are aware of these differences and can, at times, support each other to expand and appropriate qualities they treasure in the other. What is of particular interest in this partnership is the willingness of Fine to admit her intellectual dependence on her partner, an admission that is unusual for a woman who considers herself very independent. Mutuality and interdependence are carefully negotiated between them. There are times when they are prudent with criticism. At other times, the work becomes independent of their selves and their egos. It needs tending. Their shared responsibilities provide them with greater resources to enact their strengths and to become maximally tuned to the voices and concerns of the young women with whom they explore "difference."[28]

In the chapter on scientific partnerships, I describe disciplinary complementarity and how it expands each person's ability to relate and think with the tools of a discipline not his or her own. I also refer to complementarity in temperament, for instance, between Einstein and Bohr. Such differences can contribute to productive tensions and intense, dialogical exchanges, particularly during periods of rapid, paradigmatic changes in a domain. In some cases, methodological and stylistic differences are so great that a third person is needed to mediate among scientists addressing basic, theoretical issues. This was Freeman Dyson's role in combining Feynman's and Schwinger's theories. They were looking at the same set of ideas, but as Dyson later wrote, from different perspectives. In succeeding to discover and combine these two perspectives, Dyson made a major contribution to physics. In addition, he communicated with Feynman, whose trust he had gained, and consequently was able to "translate" his somewhat personalized thinking and language. In this, his efforts were similar to Howard Gardner's description at the beginning of this chapter, in which he emphasizes the interpretive role of a trusted other person at times of creative breakthroughs. Contemporary physicists have appropriated Feynman's diagrams, they have internalized his mode of thinking. And in this way, they have broadened their modes of generativity in their domain.[29]

In describing collaboration among intimates, examples of emotional complementarity are also available. But these are harder to specify than complementarity and mutual appropriation in the cognitive sphere. The question arises: Is cognitive flexibility greater than emotional flexibility on the part of creative adults? Csikszentmihalyi suggested, based on his study of older creative individuals, that it is difficult but not impossible to change personalities. He portrayed traits as interesting polarities, and recommended that, in enhancing personal creativity, individuals should "keep exploring what it takes to be the opposite of who you are."[30]

In the accounts presented in previous chapters, there are examples of partnerships that depict change in both cognitive and emotional spheres. These case histories support the claim of a profound connection between thought and feeling. In Chapter 2, I discuss the long collaboration between Will and Ariel Durant, and I suggest that their growing interdependence—both intellectual and emotional—was the result of their increasingly equal role in the writing of their multivolumed work, *The Story of Civilization.*

Ariel, as readers may remember, was much younger than Will. During their first years together their lives were quite different, Will traveled and lectured extensively, while his wife was involved in an active, Bohemian social life. Once they settled in California and started to work together more consistently every day, Ariel appropriated some of Will's habits. While maintaining the zest and enthusiasm her husband cherished, she developed a quieter streak. At the same time, Will internalized some of her emotional daring and joie de vivre.

Collaborative mutuality is most likely to have a lasting impact upon partners who share both their personal and working lives. It also tends to flourish among individuals who rely on dialogue for the development of their thinking. I have referred to these individuals as dialogic thinkers: mathematician Phil Davis, psychologists Michelle Fine and Howard Gruber, physicist Niels Bohr, anthropological linguist George Lakoff (see Chapter 7), and philosopher Hubert Dreyfus. Their pattern differs from individuals who prefer to explore their ideas in a written form and only consequently share these with their partners. It is of interest that these dialogic thinkers' needs for affiliative, intellectual relationships are bolstered by their emotional flexibility, that is, a willingness to make compromises, to let go of the ownership of their particular words, or to modify their ideas to mesh with those of their partners.

In integrative collaborations, the partners' objective is frequently the construction of a novel theoretical approach. Participants in such collaboratives, for instance, the authors of *Women's Ways of Knowing,* engage in what these authors referred to as "real talk." The women authors recalled how, in editing each other's words, they identified with the writer of a particular passage. The identification with the words of the other while writing a new draft was possible for these women because of the high level of trust they developed for each other during the decade of their shared endeavor. They forged the metaphor of "we" guided by a chorus of voices with no solos. At the same time, they were able to be critical of each other, relying on their secure confidence in their partnership.

One aspect of emotional growth is the gaining of insights into one's past. Such insights are not limited to individual lives but may be the outcome of shared experiences within a group. Carol Gilligan described in an interview, summarized in the previous chapter, how she and her research partners were able to confront their own histories while jointly engaged in work with young adolescents. They recognized the experience "of knowing things and then learning to know." Theirs was truly felt knowledge; they understood the personal meaning as well as the societal implications of their common history, of growing up within a culture that expects young girls to succumb to the "tyranny of nice and kind."[31] An understanding of the world, and of themselves, was linked to their collaborative research. Their joint discoveries, which included insights usually kept out of consciousness, deepened their mutuality and trust.

In some collaborative accounts, participants described a balance between the closeness within their partnerships and emotional engagements in relationships outside of their collaboration. Mutuality becomes a more complex and challenging endeavor when partners share work and personal lives. It provides for greater possibilities for appropriating qualities valued in one's intimate partner than in partnerships limited to work. But it also puts strains on participants when they may need solitude and privacy. In the first chapter on collaboration among intimates, I report how Nan Lyons enjoyed reparking the family car in the morning, as it gave her time alone.

But not all couples succeed in resolving tensions that arise from lives that are totally intertwined. As in most intense human relationships, the boundaries between connectedness and possessiveness, equality and power differentials are not always easy to recognize.

When conflicts arise in effective partnerships, the participants work on methods to negotiate resolutions. Some intimate partners, such as Georgia O'Keeffe and Alfred Stieglitz, and Sartre and de Beauvoir, used time away from each other to find a relief from the intensity of shared endeavors. They were able to sustain mutual loyalty while in projects, relationships, and even domiciles separate from their partners. Others, to whose lives I now turn, were unable to resolve tensions between interdependence and personal freedom.

Through the previous chapters I have presented the history of many constructive, transformative relationships. I now turn to a more difficult story, the marriage and artistic partnership of poets Sylvia Plath and Ted Hughes. Their life together ended with Plath's suicide in 1963. However, their relationship is still subject to intense debate, most recently after the publication of Hughes' *Birthday Letters*, devoted to his years with Plath.[32]

Plath, whose parents were of German and Austrian descent, was raised around Boston. Her father, Otto Plath, was a determined, hardworking, able immigrant. He had a lifelong interest in biology, was excellent in languages, and pursued his studies in several universities. His biological family rejected him because he turned down their chosen profession for him, the ministry. Otto first met his wife while working on his dissertation for Harvard University and concurrently teaching German at Boston University. While an admirable man, Otto was profoundly driven, a quality he came to share with his daughter. He imposed a Prussian regime on his family. His personality and early death still preoccupy those who try to understand the life and death of Plath. These scholars argue that the powerful, demonic images of her later work are linked to her father's "desertion" of her, which is how his daughter interpreted his terminal illness from severe, neglected diabetes, including the amputation of one of his legs. His actual death was due to an embolism in his lungs. His complex legacy haunted his daughter. In one of Plath's best-known poems she wrote:

Daddy, I have to kill you.
You died before I had time—
Marble-heavy a bag full of God,
Ghastly statue with one gray toe
Big as a Frisco seal.
And a head in the freakish Atlantic
Where it pours bean green over blue
In the waters of the beautiful Nauset.
I used to pray to recover you.
Ach, du.[33]

At the time of her father's death, Plath was eight years old. Like her father, she was an ambitious, brilliant student and professional. She received encouragement from her mother, who was proud of her complex, difficult daughter. But her mother also hovered over her. Aurelia Plath was a teacher who was helped by her parents when she became a young widow: the grandparents were kind to Plath and her brother. Aurelia was close to her daughter. They maintained a large correspondence with each other until the end of Plath's life. But Plath was uneasy about her mother's example, which, with its heavy responsibilities and domesticity, represented a life that Plath feared. Nevertheless, the young poet internalized some of her mother's skills, which contributed to her many-faceted abilities and personality.

The Plath family drama haunted Hughes until his death. After decades of silence, he presented in *Birthday Letters* his own feelings and memories of his much-celebrated, deceased wife. In his poem "The Shot," he wrote:

Till you real target
Hid behind me. Your Daddy,
The god with the smoking gun. For a long time
Vague as mist. I did not even know
I have been hit.
Or that you had gone clean through me—
To bury yourself at last in the heart of the god.
In my position, the right witch doctor
Might have caught you in flight with his bare hands,
Godless, happy, quieted.
I managed
A whisp of your hair, your ring, your watch, your
nightgown.[34]

Plath and Hughes met in Cambridge, England, soon after she arrived there as a Fulbright fellow. At the time of their meeting, Plath was already a successful young poet, whose work was published in the mass media and in college poetry journals. She had also received a number of academic honors. She was, like her father, an exceedingly hard worker; she fought for a place for herself in this world by being an exceptional student. Through language and the transformation of experience into poetry, Plath overcame some of her isolation and managed her rocky emotional path. In college she approached writing, according to one of her biographers, Anne Stevenson, "with the grim determination of a German bricklayer. Later, when speaking to a friend about the many rejection slips she had already collected, she would boast: 'I've got hundreds. They make me proud of myself. They show me I try.'"[35]

Intense drive gave rise to high expectations. Plath, while very successful as a much-honored scholarship student at Smith College, was also a haunted, emotionally damaged human being. Whether she had some hereditary predisposition for suicidal depression, or whether her descent into her private hell was psychogenic, will never be known. Her need to occasionally escape from her high, self-imposed demands was manifested by the way she responded after a ski accident. She enjoyed the slowed pace of physical recovery and the safety of a protected environment. But such periods of rest were rare in her life. While a college junior, Plath continued to receive honors for her poetry, which appeared in poetry magazines and popular journals. She spent a glamorous, publicly celebrated month in New York City as a college intern at *Mademoiselle* magazine. But the demands of such visibility stretched her beyond her psychic resources.

In general, frantic, public activity and competition kept Plath's inner demons at bay. But during a lonely, quiet summer in her home, the defenses she had constructed throughout her life failed her, and she sank into a serious depression. She was treated by the town psychiatrist, who was a man with limited skills. Although the treatment was severe—she received electric shock treatments from him—he offered no psychotherapy, and she did not improve. At the end of the summer, she attempted a carefully planned suicide. She took sleeping pills and concealed herself in a hidden corner of the family basement. She was found forty-eight hours later and was eventually admitted to McLean Hospital. There she reconstructed a self with the help of professionals, family, and friends, even receiving faithful visits from her high school English teacher. In retrospect, questions have been raised about the effectiveness of the therapy at McLean, which may have been limited in assisting Plath to reinstate her public mask. Beneath this mask, the losses, confusions, and her enormous, possibly insatiable hunger for love remained.

This brilliant, energetic, complex, emotionally rent woman was the one Hughes, an English poet, met at the party celebrating the appearance of a new literary magazine, *St. Botolph's Review*. The magazine had included some of Hughes's poems, which were admired by Plath. She memorized some of them. By the time of their first date, Hughes had completed his studies. He had odd jobs, but still spent time with friends and fellow poets at Cambridge. The relationship between them developed very rapidly. Their attraction to each other was fueled by their joint passion for poetry. They also enjoyed nature and talk and treasured the other's erudition. Plath described their times together in one of her many letters to her mother:

> It is this man, this poet, this Ted Hughes. I have never known anything like it. For the first time in my life I can use all my knowing and laughing and force and writing to the hilt all the time. . . .
> Daily I am full of poems; my joy whirls in tongues of words. . . .
> I do not merely idolize, I see right into the core of him. . . . What a huge humour we have, what running strength.[36]

Hughes was attracted to the wonderful vitality she had at this time, and enjoyed the order she brought to his somewhat haphazard existence. As one of their friends observed:

Ted and Sylvia were a united couple, and they complemented each other. Without Sylvia, Ted might have had to work in rose gardens and warehouses for quite a few more years. Competent and organized . . . Sylvia always had Ted's poems, like her own, meticulously typed and out at English and American magazines. A number, both of his and hers, were being published, and those that were not accepted the first time went right out again. It was Sylvia who got Ted's first book, *The Hawk in the Rain*, to the *Harper's* contest, which it won, making his name.[37]

Hughes was primarily a rural poet raised in Yorkshire, whereas Plath was more sophisticated in the literary world of big cities. They seemed to complement each other very effectively. They married on June 16, 1956, and after a honeymoon on the continent, they returned to Cambridge in the fall. Sylvia managed to juggle her academic work, her writing, the continual promotion of their poetry, and domesticity. In a letter to her mother, she described their time together: "We read, we discuss poems we discover, talk, analyze—we continually fascinate each other. It is heaven to have someone like Ted who is so kind and honest and brilliant always stimulating me to study, think, draw and write. He is better than any teacher, he even fills somehow that huge, sad hole I felt in having no father."[38] Intimacy is frequently seen as meeting all the needs of an emotionally hungry person. But it may fail "to fill all the sad holes." Plath idolized her husband and believed, through their early years together, that he could make her feel complete. Hughes's feelings during these times is less well known.

Friends and biographers have focused on their gifts to each other as poets. In *Sylvia Plath: Method and Madness*, Butscher wrote:

> Their marriage vow above all was a mutual protection pact against the world and for poetry. However temperamentally unsuited they might seem in retrospect, they complemented each other perfectly in their belief that poetry was not only important but absolutely central to their existence. Ted would give her the means and encouragement to move more deeply into her unconscious and free her real self from its stifling inhibitions; and Sylvia would help shape his life into a purposeful whole and see that his work (which she would type and submit for him) reached the proper outlets and that he met the right people.[39]

The portrait of Hughes that emerges in these accounts is modest, generous, and caring to friends and relatives. His wife relied so heavily on him that, according to the recollections of Hughes's sister, he could not go on the simplest of errands without her grabbing a coat and running after him.[40]

Plath liked England in many ways, but she suffered physically and emotionally from the cold winters and the poorly heated apartments. She may have had a form of winter depression (due to the reduced light available), which has only been widely recognized within the last decade. But her depressive episodes were not limited to winters. They occurred when she was under self-imposed or external strain.

The couple moved to the United States in 1957, when Plath accepted a job teaching English at her alma mater. When she first started, she was fearful and seriously self-accusatory, as revealed in her journals at that time: "I have this demon who wants me to run away screaming if I am going to be flawed, fallible. It wants me to think I am so good I must be perfect. Or nothing."[41] Hughes remembered this time at Smith College in one of the poems in *Birthday Letters*:

> You waited.
> Knowing yourself helpless in the tweezers
> Of the life that judged you, and I saw
> The flayed nerve, the unhealable face-wound
> Which was all you had for courage.
> I saw that what gripped you, as you sipped,
> Were terrors that had killed you once already.
> Now I see, I saw, sitting, the lonely
> Girl who was going to die.
> That blue suit,
> A mad, execution uniform,
> Survived your sentence. But then I sat, stilled
> Unable to fathom what stilled you
> As I looked at you, as I am stilled
> Permanently now, permanently
> Bending so briefly at your open coffin.[42]

Though self-critical and frightened, Plath was a successful teacher at Smith. Her students loved her. But teaching was very demanding for her, and she gave it up to devote herself to poetry. She and her husband moved to Boston, where they spent time with fellow poets. Butscher described the commonalities and differences between Hughes and Plath as poets:

> They are obviously deeply in debt to each other, although it becomes nearly impossible after a while to isolate exactly who was indebted to whom. Images and motifs often identical or only slightly altered, crop up continuously and are obviously borrowed from or inspired by each other's efforts. Ted was leading the way certainly, drawing Sylvia out from behind the curtain of stiff

method; but his own poetry was also benefiting from her unique imagery, as it is evident in "Pennines in April," which appeared in *Mademoiselle* [and] reflects Sylvia's fierce reaction to seascapes.[43]

As a wife, Plath struggled hard to put her husband in the best light socially. In many public situations, she was quiet while he carried the conversation. During their year in Boston, as Hughes's fame grew, Plath started to confront the shadow of her father in her poetry. Both in "Colossus" and "The Beekeeper's Daughter," she gave voice to her bitterness about him and some of the things that he represented. These included his harsh self-discipline and his male, dominating role in the family. (These poems eventually became part of Plath's first published volume of poems). While laboring for public recognition, Plath was growing as a poet; with Anne Sexton and two other friends, she attended Robert Lowell's poetry class. His influence was important in moving her from a classic to a more confessional mode of writing.

Subsequently, Plath and Hughes lived in the writer's colony at Yaddo for two months before they returned to England. Plath's journals documented some of her stresses during this time: her fears to reveal the magnitude of her raging, hurting self and her passive dependence on her husband. At the same time, she expressed her envy of him "working away unencumbered by any fake image of what the world expects of him—Ted, so rare, so special . . . how could anyone else stand me!"[44]

When the couple returned to England, Plath was expecting their first child. Hughes had already received a number of honors, so their financial situation had improved. And late in her pregnancy, Plath signed the contract for her first book of poems, *The Colossus and Other Poems*. Their daughter, Frieda, was born on April 1, 1960. It was an easy birth and a happy period for Plath. But soon after, her fears returned. Some of their friends started to comment on Plath's antisocial and frequently jealous behaviors. Her husband was quite discreet about the strains this may have imposed upon him and was able to work productively in crammed quarters sharing child care.

Plath and Hughes had collaborated closely in their work and were helpful to each other in many ways. At times, they even wrote on the same themes. They appeared together on radio programs and shared caregiving tasks. But Plath's fears of losing her husband (at that stage quite unfounded) were so unreasonable that they started to undermine a powerful, committed partnership.

During the winter of 1961, when Ted Hughes returned late from a literary appointment with a woman editor, his wife destroyed some of his writings and one of his favorite books: "Ted could neither forget not forgive this desecration; it seems to have marked a turning point in their marriage."[45]

While Hughes stressed Plath's obsession with her father's death in *Birthday Letters*, I believe he underestimated other aspects of his deceased wife's tortured feelings. Some of these may have been the result of her fear of electro-convulsive therapy. Her frantic efforts to lead a normal life, and her success in achieving it when she felt productive and loved, masked some of her terror.

It was in their house in the English countryside in north Devon that the last act of the Plath-Hughes marriage took place. Here Plath completed the final draft of her novel, *The Bell Jar*, which depicted her suicide attempt in 1953. In January 1962, the Hugheses had a second child, a boy they named Nicholas. After his birth, Plath's poems became more powerful but also more distressed. In "The Elm" and "The Moon and the Yew Tree," she wrote of graveyards and a full "mother moon." These themes were based on joint experiences with Hughes, but the feeling tone of her poems frightened him. Stevenson speculated about the impact of these dark works on her husband: "For someone isolated in close proximity with her in a country village, the effect could not be other than profoundly disturbing. Ted Hughes must have begun to feel himself trapped under the same doomed bell jar."[46]

While isolated in Devon, Plath became more insistently jealous of possible rivals than ever before. Her poetry of the period reflected a dramatic change in her attitude toward her husband. She worked hard to achieve a perfect marriage, but once tensions arose, she was unable to compromise. Subsequently, Hughes started an affair. After he left their home and moved to London, Plath created an extraordinary group of poems, collected under the title of *Ariel*. It was autumn. She got up at dawn each day to write. She used all her experiences for her writing, including her beekeeping. She knew her work had reached a new mastery: "I am writing the best poems of my life."[47]

In December, Sylvia Plath moved to London with her children. They all became ill with the flu, but Plath continued to write poetry. In late January, she told her physician that she was becoming increasingly depressed. He tried to get her into a hospital but was unsuccessful because of the short notice. She was frightened about the possibility of more shock treatments if she had to go to an unfamiliar psychiatrist or hospital. After a very disturbed weekend with friends, who tried to help her but failed to keep her with them, Plath committed suicide on February 11, 1963.

The literary partnership did not end with her death. Hughes became the editor of her late poems, her *Letters Home*, and her *Journals*. Her memory, her fame, their children, and the enormous controversy about her death, continued to preoccupy him. The response to his *Birthday Letters* further extended decades-long debates concerning Hughes's role in her death. Some readers and critics loved the poems, while others found them "self-serving."[48]

Their story raises questions about the limits of intimate partnerships. During their early years, they helped each other very effectively. If Hughes was uncomfortable with his wife's adoration or her excessive dependence on him during those years, he gave little evidence of it to friends. Hughes was a caring father and a devoted supporter and critic of Plath's work. He protected her from destructive criticism and adjusted his working life so that she could have time to write. But once the two of them were isolated in Devon, and Plath's "demons" were increasingly revealed in her poetry, Hughes withdrew. One interpretation of their subsequent separation was that Plath drove her husband away with her anger and jealousies. (This was the position taken by one of her biographers, Anne Stevenson.) Others argued that once Plath had helped Hughes to reach fame, he abandoned her. These two positions may oversimplify a complex pattern, including Hughes's view that he became a substitute for Plath's dead father. Plath's illness was definitely part of their troubles, with the fear of having to undergo shock treatment a second time, adding to the terrors that caused her death.

While Plath's illness made this intimate partnership unusual, there were issues concerning mutuality and collaboration that transcended the particulars of their well-documented lives. One of these was the psychic cost of a hermetic relationship. Once Hughes left, Plath was not able to develop effective attachments to others. Their exceptional closeness during their early years probably contributed to their rapid development as poets, but it also made them more vulnerable. (Plath's poetic as well as emotional impact can still be discerned in Hughes's *Birthday Letters*.) Plath became a more feminist poet after the break-up of her marriage. She also developed a more feverish, cadent, but very powerful voice in her last poems. The violence with which Plath broke away from their shared path at the end of her life may have been more than a personal reaction to Hughes leaving her. It raises the question whether, in excessively intense partnerships, one or both persons may fail to explore diverse, or conflicting, aspects of their talent.

Another possibility is that intimacy offers a solid foundation for an individual who is trying to cope with his or her complexity. In effective, long-term relationships, partners learn to adjust to each other's intensity and may be able to give each other "space" when the need for solitude arises. Intense collaborations are frequently transformative and can provide enormous intellectual and emotional benefits to the participants. But when they become emotionally excessive and splinter, the wounds inflicted by a traumatic ending may be long-lasting. (For instance, it took Anaïs Nin and Henry Miller many years after their intimacy ended to be able to talk to each other about the publication of their letters.)

In another case, that of Picasso and Braque, once their collaboration ceased, Picasso's work became less focused, less grounded in an inner or a shared certainty. He did not cease to collaborate with other artists; for instance, he worked with the Ballet Russe de Monte Carlo. He also relied on the audience provided by and the connectedness with the women he loved by evoking a mutual sensuality in his paintings. At the same time, art critic John Berger suggested that his later works, while frequently extraordinary, reflected a lonely search for a subject. He saw Picasso as most successful in his intensely collaborative Cubist period.[49]

Partnerships are not static; most of them include periods of balanced complementarity as well as interludes of strife. Tensions arise when needs for recognition or true equality are unmet, or when there is an asymmetry in responsibilities that can disrupt the working relationship.

ISSUES OF INTELLECTUAL OWNERSHIP AND INEQUALITY

The way in which credit is assigned in collaborative partnerships varies in different fields and at different historical periods. In the book *Creative Couples in the Sciences*, the authors provided many examples of such variations. Most of their case studies were drawn from the physical sciences. Less is known about the joint work of social scientists, although there are some interesting exceptions. One of these exceptions is the partnership of sociologists Helen and Everett Hughes. They were students together at the University of Chicago at a time when the discipline of sociology was still young. As students, they shared a mentor and many common interests. They were active partners in dialogue with each other and were also involved with their fellow students. Once Everett finished his degree, he left the University of Chicago for an appointment at McGill; but his wife continued her dissertation work at Chicago and obtained her degree years after him. Their different responsibilities involved periods of separation. During one of these, Helen wrote of her husband: "[I] was pained to discover how much a scholar's morale can depend on like-minded associates. At home, of course, Everett and I, both steeped in Chicago sociology . . . used each other as sounding boards."[50] Helen's dissertation was one of the earliest studies of journalism from a sociological point of view. While in Canada, the couple engaged in intensive fieldwork together, resulting in the book *French Canada in Transition*, still considered an influential critical study. But Everett's name appeared as the sole author.

The Hugheses returned to Chicago, where Everett received a tenure-track appointment. His wife first spent a few years at home with their two small children and then started to work in part-time jobs. One of these was as managing editor of the *American Journal of Sociology*, which tested her skills but did not lead to a mainstream professional career. She suffered professionally from being a faculty wife. Only in the seventies did she express her dissatisfaction in print, in an article entitled, "Maid of All Work or Departmental Sister-in-Law? The Faculty Wife Employed on Campus."[51] The Hugheses enjoyed a full, compatible life together. Everett greatly admired his wife, but he did not question the injustice of the gender arrangements prevalent in universities during his career. Helen chose to express her disappointment in her secondary role in the workplace through intellectual analysis rather than within her marriage. Until recently, the great majority of working couples in the sciences followed this gender pattern. The work by the women partners was underestimated and given less or no formal recognition. As P. G. Abir-Am wrote in the series introduction to *Creative Couples in the Sciences*:

> Collaborative marriages . . . were historically the single most important avenue for recruiting women to science and retaining them as active participants. Because the institution of marriage had a monopoly on permissible intimacy, it was the inevitable solution for those men and women who wished to collaborate within socially acceptable boundaries. Yet, marriage posed a real but rarely articulated risk that an individual spouse's work would not get independent recognition. In practice, this almost always meant the wife; legally, economically, and socially, marriage made her dependent upon her husband's name, position, and resources. We cannot account for a woman scientist's achievements and honors —or lack of them—unless we understand that inexorably the social condition of being her collaborator's wife spilled over into every assessment of her work as a scientist.[52]

But in the wake of the women's movement of the sixties, and its widespread reverberations in public and private domains, there is no longer a single pattern of collaborations. Contemporary partnerships show innovations in relationships and in modes of work. The editors of *Creative Couples in the Sciences* identified four patterns among their case studies. The first pattern included relationships in which, after a short but intensive premarital collaboration, marriage ends the wife's scientific career. One of the best-known examples of this model was the life of Mileva Maric, Albert Einstein's first wife. Another pattern was that of the husband as creator and the wife as assistant. It was the prototype of scientific spousal collaboration for centuries. A third pattern involved the husband becoming the assistant or primary helper of his highly productive wife. One of the couples illustrating this arrangement was Canadian biologists Edith and Cyril Berkeley.[53] And the final pattern was that of egalitarian partnerships. The most fully documented of these was the marriage of Pierre and Marie Curie.

Psychologists Howard Gruber and Doris Wallace also fit the egalitarian pattern. They have a clear understanding of how to arrange a division of labor, visibility, and credit. They co-edited the book *Creative People at Work* (see Chapter 1). At the time they decided on this project, Wallace had fewer publications than her husband. In recognition for taking on a larger share of the editorial responsibilities, including some of the "scout" work, Wallace became the senior author. At the same time, Gruber's reputation for his approach to creativity assured them of other benefits. It attracted contributors and provided a comprehensive framework for their book. This couple was able to successfully negotiate issues, which, in many collaborative projects, become troublesome and fail to be resolved.

In the course of writing this book over a number of years, I have encountered collaborative dyads who, at the beginning of their work, experienced few tensions. They viewed each other as equals and concentrated on getting the work accomplished. But once the work was finished, concerns about the listing of the names or the distribution of royalties emerged. Some partners realized that the better-known member or members of a project are more frequently invited to make presentations than are the younger partners. Consequently, a joint project may become associated with a single name. In my own experience, I have been in both the junior and senior positions. In some collaborative work, my name was listed second or third, and I felt that I became somewhat marginal to the project. In more recent years, some of my younger collaborators found themselves insufficiently recognized. In both cases, we found ways to expand on the joint work in new ways and consequently receive recognition both as individuals as well as collaborators.

The authors of *Women's Ways of Knowing* faced a similar challenge. They chose to list their names alphabetically. Many readers and conference organizers focused on Belenky as the senior author. In the preface to a book of essays co-edited by the foursome a decade after the original publication of their important book, Goldberger described this situation:

> When it came time to turn our manuscript [*Women's Ways of Knowing*] over to the publisher, we anguished over how we could communicate the truly collaborative nature of our work in a linear culture that insists the order of authorship as indicating the degree of contribution. The only solution (since the publisher did not think a circle of names would work) was to arrange our names alphabetically. Even so, "Belenky" became known to many as the author; the rest of us often disappeared into the "et al."[54]

After the publication of *Women's Ways of Knowing*, the authors engaged in some solo and separate endeavors. They came together again to prepare a tenth anniversary edition of their, by now, classic book. They also decided to put together a book of essays, *Knowledge, Difference and Power*, and in this book's preface Goldberger wrote:

> This time, however, we decided that individuals would speak in their own voices, narrating the story of the relation of the ways of knowing theory to their own work. . . . While working on this book, the four of us marveled at how easily we fell into old routines and collaborative spirit, even though each of us has "separated" from the group and gone on to work on special interests. This new book, then, is offered in the spirit of "we" as well as "I."[55]

These four experienced collaborators moved flexibly between shared and solo work. They also gracefully addressed the challenge of intellectual ownership and visibility by rotating the listing of authorship. They no longer have to fight tenure battles, a fact that undoubtedly has helped them to resolve issues others find more difficult to address. Their experiences have contributed to my thinking about the "emotional zone of proximal development." This is a concept I propose earlier in this chapter. It refers to the effects of mutuality and growth in the emotional and intellectual domains.

In complex, long-term partnerships, participants change and develop unevenly. One person may be making major theoretical advances and is too absorbed in his or her work to pay much attention to "maintenance or expressive roles" in group interactions. These roles include "moving a group forward on the task by mediating or moderating a conflict, yielding, or conceding a point."[56] Others may be uncomfortable dealing with conflict or feelings and may assume instrumental, task related responsibilities. These roles have been identified by social psychologists who study small-group interactions. They can also be seen as useful differentiations in the study of partnerships. I have suggested in this chapter that part of the power of collaboration is that it provides for mutual appropriations, that is, expansion of skills, roles, leadership, and working styles by close partners. The authors of *Women's Ways of Knowing* engaged in multiple roles during their working together. They were listeners, critics, editors, partners in dialogue, theoreticians, and friends. Their personal styles differed from each other, but they succeeded in blending these as well as stretching themselves as a consequence of their joint engagements. Their emotional dynamics included their willingness to face disagreements and to act on them constructively.

Unfortunately, many productive collaborations falter because the participants are focused solely on instrumental roles—on the cognitive and artistic aspects of their partnership. Rather than confronting issues of possible inequality, financial concerns, differences in writing standards, or issues with deadlines, the partnership dissolves. In collaborations, as in all close relationships, making oneself known and heard is central to emotional survival and growth.

New York City Ballet. George Balanchine and Igor Stravinsky work together in AGON, 1957. Photograph by Martha Swope. Copyright © Time Inc.

The Three Directors (from left): Lee Strasberg, Harold Clurman and Cheryl
Crawford. Photograph by Ralph Steiner and courtesy of the estate of Ralph
Steiner.

Anaïs Nin in her garden at Louveciennes, early 1930s. Copyright © 1967 by
Anaïs Nin. Copyright © 1977 by The Anaïs Nin Trust. Used by permission
of the Author's Representative, Gunther Stuhlmann.

Henry Miller at Louveciennes, early 1930s. Copyright © 1967 by Anaïs
Nin. Copyright © 1977 by The Anaïs Nin Trust. Used by permission of the
Author's Representative, Gunther Stuhlmann.

The Guarneri Quartet. Photograph by Gjon Mili, Life Magazine. Copyright © Time Inc.

Mary Catherine Bateson and Gregory Bateson. Photograph by Polyxane Cobb.

6
COLLABORATION ACROSS GENERATIONS

Our most frequent images of collaborators are of painters with their easels close together looking at each other's work, or of scientists engaged in heated talk while sketching models of their ideas on napkins. But these images are limited to men and women of similar experience and age. An additional and critical form of collaboration occurs when participants of different ages are linked by a desire to bridge time and join their talents.

Collaboration across generations is an expression of hope. For the senior participants, who mentor and work with their younger students and colleagues, it provides continuity, a new embodiment of their knowledge. It also stimulates them to reach for transformative ideas with the help of energetic and questioning young colleagues. For younger partners, the advantages of intergenerational collaboration include a guided entry into the complex worlds of human achievement and the opportunity to closely observe an experienced thinker, indeed to witness that person's modes of thought. Young collaborators may learn from multiple mentors and distant teachers, using processes which are usually intricate—a mixture of admiration, of hard and, at times, repetitive work, and of rebellion. As well, they have the opportunity to appropriate what they have witnessed and been taught.

THE FIRST MENTORS

It is with our families that we first learn to collaborate. As children, we share our parents' attention and love; later, as parents, we share responsibilities. Throughout most of human history and until quite recently, families have been the primary site of knowledge, both shared and acquired.[1] Young people traditionally have learned from their elders, family members, clans, tribes, and villages, taking the accumulated knowledge of generations and making it their own. This is a dynamic process since "learning is never simply a matter of the transmission of knowledge or the acquisition of skill. . . . It is a reciprocal relationship between persons and practice."[2] Although there is a large body of anthropological literature on enculturation and apprenticeships, in this chapter I focus on apprenticeships that are preparations for a "life of the mind."[3]

In many homes where the life of the mind is treasured, conversation centers on books, politics, the arts, and the sciences. Children experience the passions that fire their elders: these include a love of sports, the joy of making exquisite objects, the preparation of food, and the creation of community. Family rituals include reading aloud, taking nature walks, playing instruments, gardening, building, taking road trips, and visiting museums. In one account of family apprenticeship that led to a chosen profession, Lisa Redfield Peattie, an anthropologist and community planner, described her childhood years outside of Chicago in an article entitled "Not a Career: a Life": "My mentor was my father. He read me poetry and took me for walks in the woods in which he had roamed as a boy. When we were out of the country he provided books of history to read. I, too, wrote poetry [as did her father, famous anthropologist Robert Redfield] and thought, as he had, that I might become a biologist."[4]

Peattie's childhood years and her career were influenced by her father. The family's trips to Guatemala, where Redfield was doing fieldwork, prepared her in some ways for her own work in Central America. She studied at the University of Chicago, where he was teaching, and like her father she became an anthropologist. There were some continuing similarities between Peattie and her father: to both of them academic life was more a calling than a career. When he started to doubt himself professionally, ready to quit, he was chosen as the dean of social sciences. Peattie recalled: "In these inconsistencies I followed my father. Put up for tenure, I stacked the cards against myself by growing my hair down to my waist and asking nobody for support; yet when I became one of four tenured women at the Massachusetts Institute of Technology [MIT] I felt very pleased."[5]

In *With a Daughter's Eye*, well-known writer and anthropologist Mary Catherine Bateson evoked the legacy of her parents, Margaret Mead and Gregory Bateson. She, too, chose the profession of her parents. As an adult, she worked with her father as a science writer. Her collaboration with her mother was a lifelong process of mutual teaching, conversations, and co-construction of ideas.

Bateson's relationship with her famous parents was very complex, not only because her parents divorced when she was eight years old, but also because they differed in temperament, family tradition, and lifestyle. Her moving, at times ambivalent, account of parental mentoring by two major figures in twentieth-century social science tells of both the trials and benefits of intergenerational collaboration. In the prologue she wrote:

Worlds can be found by a child and an adult bending down and looking together under the grass stems or at the skittering crabs of a tidal pool. They can be spun from the stuff of fantasy and tradition. And they can be handled and changed, created . . . from all sorts of materials.[6] Through my mother's writings echoes the question, "What kind of world can we build for our children?" She thought in terms of building. She set out to create a community for me to grow up in, she threw herself wholeheartedly into the planning and governance of my elementary school, and she built and sustained work of relationships around herself, at once the shelter in which I rested and the matrix of her work and thought.[7] The mornings of fantasy with my mother in a New Hampshire meadow, the hours spent assembling an aquarium with my father, these are moments shared in the microcosm that will not be exactly duplicated in any other memory but my own.[8]

Bateson learned about people, in their extraordinary personal and cultural diversity, from her mother; and she learned about the intricate patterns of nature from her father. Engagement in talk, fantasy, or new insights was crucial in her special times with her world-renowned mother. The two of them lived in large, changing households with people who shared the responsibility for her upbringing. As a child, when she was alone with Mead, they planned their trips and vacations, spoke of daily life and the future, and relived their shared experiences. Once an adult, the conversations continued; Mead always carried a notebook with her, and her daughter joined with others in contributing to the entries:

That notebook was a tremendously powerful tool, for consciously or unconsciously, we used to try to say things that would stimulate her to get it out and write them, and then one would have the feeling of having contributed a piece to the complex jigsaw puzzle she was putting together. Later you might hear it in a technical lecture or read it recast as deceptively homespun advice in *Redbook*, lectures and articles that echoed hours and hours of conversation in a dozen cities.[9] Always she was taking in, recombining, using and reusing every piece, bringing it out again in a new form and in a new place[10] . . . Sometimes Margaret would announce that she wanted to interview me on some issue, and this was a signal that she wanted rich description. As a result, our first professional collaborations were when I was brought into projects to represent childhood or youth.[11]

Bateson planned and participated in meetings with both of her parents. One of these, the conference "Conscious Purpose and Human Adaptation" organized by her father, became a book entitled *Our Own Metaphor*, written by Bateson as an alternative to the usual conference proceedings. In it she recreated some of the ways she learned from her father as a child. She also tried to make her father's thinking about ecosystems and feedback loops, and about how linear thinking violates the way complex, biological systems operate, accessible to a broad readership. In *With a Daughter's Eye*, she recalled:

> Again and again during the conference, he broke up efforts to write prescriptions for action, arguing that the value of the discussion lay precisely in its diversity and complexity, and that the significance of what had been said lay in the fact that each topic had been discussed in the context of the others. He made it clear that preserving that weave was the essential next step, and that was the task he passed to me.[12]

The process of moving from mentoring to a collegial relationship between parents and children is particularly interesting. The first mentors provide the pleasures of childhood's shared activities, such as the trips Mead and her daughter took together, and the assembling of an aquarium that Bateson undertook with her father.

In a similar vein, physicist Richard Feynman remembered how his father had told him "interesting things about the world." One of the family stories was about his father teaching him, while still a toddler, about patterns: "He had brought home a lot of tiles—and we played with them, setting them out like dominoes. . . . And my father said, . . . I want to show him what patterns are like, and how interesting they are. It's a kind of elementary mathematics."[13] Although Feynman's father was very influential in nurturing his son's love of science, as adults they never collaborated.

There are numerous examples in the literature of creativity illustrating the impact of parents as the first mentors. Writer Susan Cheever described in *Home before Dark*, the impact of her father, John Cheever, a major figure in American literature. She wrote of their intense, often uncomfortable, intellectual discussions starting when she was thirteen and continuing until his death:

> We talked about everything I read. We took long walks and talked. . . . After our return from Italy, we talked in the living room of the house in Scarborough night after night, so that I was groggy in the morning and bored with school. How could my teachers compete with my father's stories, his discussions of books and language? . . . and when he got sick we talked in my old bedroom where he slept for the last years of his life.[14]

Many young people put a distance between themselves and their first mentors during adolescence. It is part of their struggle to assume a personal, distinct identity. Bateson left the United States with her mother in 1956. First they traveled together, but then she decided to stay in Israel for a year. Her stay gave her new experiences independent of her parents. When Bateson returned to the United States, she studied Arabic at Radcliffe. She recalled her interdependence tempered by her independence: "Over the years my parents sometimes held me and drew me back to them, and sometimes helped launch forth with the courage or the indifference to let me fly free. Often the decisions that seemed to set a course that would take me far away have brought me back to closeness."[15]

Once an adult, Bateson spent a lot of time away from the United States, but her relationship with her parents remained crucial throughout her life. When she received her Ph.D., her mother addressed her letter of congratulations as "Chère Colleague." Bateson was part of the dialogues through which Mead synthesized her ideas. She also served as example and proof of Mead's wide-ranging theories of child-rearing: "It seems to me however that because so much of her thought was expressed in my upbringing, there is a sense in which my own happiness has had to carry the burden of proof of her many ideas."[16]

Gregory Bateson would have happily involved his daughter in sustained conversations concerning his work at the expense of her own endeavors. Although she was proud of her father's belief in her abilities and of her work on *Our Own Metaphor*, she was committed to her own path. She was careful to establish her own professional identity while remaining connected to each of her parents. Collaborating with them was a process of sustained learning, changing roles, and enduring love.

Another example of intergenerational mentoring that became a partnership was that of the scientists Marie and Irene Curie. Mother and daughter were deeply attached to each other throughout Irene's and her sister Eve's childhood, especially after Pierre Curie's death. The two daughters had different interests; it was Irene who was drawn to science. She identified with her father's legacy, was very attached to her father's brother, Jacques, also a scientist, and was always a good student of mathematics. At age eighteen, after finishing her *lycée* studies at the time of World War I, she joined her mother in establishing a mobile radiological unit for the French army. After demobilization, Irene entered the Radium Institute, headed by Marie, while studying chemistry at the Sorbonne. "Though she started in the modest position as a beginner in the laboratory, Irene soon became Marie's favorite assistant because her early immersion in science at home made her particularly skilled in the lab."[17]

Parental mentoring is both implicit and explicit. Irene benefited from the sustained conversations in her parents' home, from the private education she received from her mother and some of her mother's colleagues, and by her participation in the Radium Institute. Once she started her own career, she was able to build on her tacit knowledge and her self-confidence as a young scientist. She was inspired by the example of her father and nourished by her devoted, extraordinary mother.

Learning through immersion, conversations with parents, and the opportunity to observe them at work endows young people who follow the paths of their parents with an exceptional ease in their subject matter. In a recent article in the *New York Times*, "When Creativity Runs in the Family,"[18] parental influence was described as children seeing "creativity as alternatively joyful, challenging, and painful." Young jazz musician Julian Fleisher observed his musician father's unremitting self-discipline while he was also absorbing the musical richness of his home. The children of playwright Horton Foote followed him into the theater. His daughter, Hallie, an actress and film producer, internalized her father's high standards. She and her sister, Daisy, listened to him try out his lines, and they also learned about female characters from his plays. Now they collaborate with each other.

The benefits of these special, familial experiences are hard to match by those whose childhood lives do not include intimate mentors. Young artists may search for a long time to establish fine-tuned, effective relationships with caring teachers. They frequently have to develop their professional identities in structured rather than intimate settings. At the same time, many children born into families of high achievement express little interest in their parents' work. They construct a professional path independently of their parents. To students of collaboration, parental mentoring is of particular interest as it illustrates patterns of family life where the participants are thoughtful reporters. The relationship between parents and children is akin to that of mentors and apprentices. In both situations, at the start the novices are the primary beneficiaries. But as the relationship develops, it becomes more symmetrical; the older members are renewed and stimulated by their interaction with the former apprentices who have become their colleagues. When the "apprentice" is also one's child, these connections are even more striking.

The dual roles of mentor and parent were powerfully evoked by my friend, anthropologist Constance Sutton. She chronicled some of the changes in her life in "Motherhood Is Powerful: Embodied Knowledge from Evolving Fieldwork."[19] Connie went to the University of Chicago in the late forties and early fifties, a time when the graduate faculty was all male. Since she was married to a laboratory-bound research psychologist, the faculty assumed she would be unable to go away to do fieldwork for her doctoral thesis. This seemed to pose difficult choices between family life and becoming a professional anthropologist. However, Connie resolved the dilemma when her husband, Sam Sutton, took a job in New York. There Connie met Margaret Mead and Eleanor Leacock, who both encouraged her to go into the field on her own, a decision that her husband totally supported. And it was in Barbados while doing fieldwork that she first encountered a cultural ideology and set of practices based on the assumption that having children gave women power in the community and that having children did not preclude pursuing work outside the home.

Her son, David, was born in 1963. He experienced lively discussions and debates of the sixties around his parents' kitchen table. He also joined them during trips to Barbados and other Caribbean islands: "Exposed to these varied cultural settings, David was fascinated to find that the value of currencies differed, food was different, and that language not only differed but would often have no exact translation. David's growing awareness of cultural differences was part of his intellectual and emotional development."

As an adolescent, David visited his mother while she was doing fieldwork in Nigeria. His presence underscored Yoruba cultural patterns with their emphasis upon children and human continuity. During their months of separation, mother and son engaged in weekly correspondence. Connie believes that those letters were the start of their future exchanges about anthropology and kin-based continuity "which began to inform both of our lives." David followed his parents' example and studied at the University of Chicago, where he chose anthropology for his doctoral work. "Soon the balance of knowledge shifted, and I was learning as much as I was imparting. We became colleagues." A few years later, Connie visited her son and his family while he was doing fieldwork in Kalymnos, Greece. His dissertation topic, historical consciousness, developed an important theme in his mother's work on kin-based human continuity. In his book, *Memories Cast in Stone*, David offers her his gratitude:

> . . . To my mother, Connie Sutton, who first afflicted me with the "culture" bug, who took me to many "fields" before Kalymnos, who has guided me through the often murky waters of anthropological theory and practice, and like a good mother has been merciless in her criticism of this manuscript.[20]

These exchanges illustrate the mutuality so crucial to effective mentoring, and the shifting, exciting benefits to both generations involved in the process.

Parents as first mentors frequently experience a joined conscious-ness, or intersubjectivity, when they choose to extend their relation-ship beyond ordinary family ties. My colleagues Ronald Gallimore, Roland Sharp, and I wrote of "intersubjectivity" as a way of experi-encing "the world in similar basic dimensions, processes and content. To the degree that intersubjectivity is present, that values are alike, and that goals are alike, the more cooperation is possible . . . The de-velopment of intersubjectivities is a consequence of profound impor-tance for individual development, for a satisfying community life and for the perpetuation of culture."[21] The twin processes of individua-tion and connection were powerfully captured by Bateson and Cheever. The benefits of parental mentoring for both generations are described by the Suttons. Shared ways of thinking and the lending of emotional support to each other enriched the lives of the Curies. Par-ents and children who make these choices do take some risks. As Bate-son described it, the process is a complex one, which includes periods of distancing as well as closeness. Most sustained collaborations ex-hibit alternating rhythms of intimacy and withdrawal, and shifts be-tween joint and solo work. For parents and children, these rhythms are deeply and emotionally loaded, and also exceptionally fulfilling.

SHARED PASSIONS ACROSS GENERATIONS

Mentoring is a commitment to the future, and for many creative indi-viduals, it is also an opportunity for the revival of purpose. Psycholo-gists Doris Wallace and Howard Gruber, whose partnership I describe in Chapter 1 emphasize the importance of purpose in creative work:

> Think of the kind of high human purpose that begins with a vision
> of things as they are not, that anticipates difficulties—surmounting
> some and avoiding others—that responds to surprises without
> losing sight of its goals. A system exhibiting purposes such as these
> can come into being only in response to the imperfections of
> adaptation, the uncertainties of the world, and the inadequacies
> of our knowledge and skills. When someone is "purposeful," we
> mean that he or she cannot be easily deflected from the pursuit of
> a chosen course.[22]

For experienced thinkers, mentoring can revive their purpose that may have become depleted after years of struggles or habituated be-havior. It can make the challenge of a break with tradition more real as it is confronted jointly with a younger person. This was the expe-rience of Wallace and Gruber, who saw their roles with graduate stu-dent mentees as strengthening their own engagement with their case-study approach to creativity. In transmitting the consequences of their experience to their students, they also informed and encouraged their junior partners. In the book *Creative People at Work*, edited by Wallace and Gruber, some of the chapters were written by their students whose dissertation work was using the case-study approach. Gruber's support of his young colleagues includes pushing them to present their work in public, to have them function as a group at professional meetings, and to construct a "thought community" larger than the usual one-to-one relationship between faculty and a single junior partner.

Whether the mentorship experience includes two individuals or a whole group, it is always a dynamic, changing connection across generations. Gruber wrote of these shifts in mentoring relationships as illustrated in Charles Darwin's life:

> An interesting example is the transformation of the mentor-mentee relationship between Charles Lyell and Charles Darwin into one of friendship and collegiality. During the voyage of the "Beagle," Darwin served, in effect, a five-year apprenticeship under Lyell. They had never met, but Darwin was heavily dependent on Lyell's *Principles of Geology* for his theoretical orientation. Later on, they met and became good friends. Indeed, when Darwin explained his theory of the formation of coral reefs, which surpassed and supplanted Lyell's own theory, the latter "was so overcome with delight that he danced about and threw himself into the wildest contortions," as was his manner when excessively pleased.[23]

The shift from mentorship to collegiality is particularly well documented within the field of music. One of the most legendary mentors of young composers was Nadia Boulanger, who taught in Paris. In the twenties, her students included Virgil Thompson and Aaron Copland, who became two of the most important American composers of the twentieth century. In his autobiography, Copland described his years with Boulanger.[24] He first started to study with her when he was twenty years old, and their relationship lasted for the rest of their lives. "Twentieth century music was nurtured in her old-fashioned salon,"[25] he wrote.

> "The composition of music cannot be taught," she used to say—then went ahead and taught it anyway. She knew everything about music—what came before Bach, Stravinsky's latest works, what came after Stravinsky, and everything in between. Technical skills —counterpoint, orchestration, sight-reading—were second nature to her. She believed in strict discipline, and she worked hard herself.[26]

In addition to sharing her technical skills, Boulanger provided her students with careful criticism and a deep commitment to their work. Copland wrote, "Mademoiselle had the sensitivity of the finest musician and the matchless gift of conveying her understanding with such enthusiasm that it made me try harder, which was all she really wanted."[27]

Boulanger's famous Wednesday afternoon teas provided an inspiring environment for young composers who were moving in new directions. She received in manuscript the scores by some of the most influential masters of the day. The works of Stravinsky, Mahler, Milhaud, and Honegger were available to her students, who discussed and analyzed them. They also met writers, poets, and musical performers in her weekly salon. And most important, she encouraged public performance by her talented pupils. This was a great experience for Copland, who was in his early twenties during his apprenticeship.

In Paris, Copland realized he could follow Stravinsky's example of including folk elements in his music: "It was easy to see a parallel between Stravinsky's powerful Slavic rhythmic drive and our American sense of rhythmic ingenuity. The most important thing for me, though, was that Stravinsky proved it was possible for a twentieth century composer to create his own tradition."[28]

With Boulanger's connections among musical publishers, Copland had opportunities to get his early work published as well as performed. He became part of a community of modern composers who found inspiration from their elders and companionship with each other. Conductor Serge Koussevitzky was a bridge between the avant-garde music of Paris in the twenties and the slowly emerging modernist American scene. The Maestro's appointment as conductor of the Boston Symphony Orchestra in 1924 contributed greatly to new musical developments in the United States and to Copland's career. Koussevitzky facilitated a continuing collaboration between Copland and Boulanger by suggesting that Copland write an organ concerto for her, which she subsequently performed in the United States.

Copland returned to the United States in 1924 and started work on the promised organ concerto. He stayed in touch with Boulanger, who urged him on and whose corrections he requested. Her help, participation, and connections continued to be as significant in Copland's own country as they had been during his apprenticeship with her in Paris. While his relationship with Koussevitzky started through Boulanger, it developed further through their joint efforts. The Maestro was an unwavering supporter of young composers. The foundation that he established in 1942, on which Copland served for many years, gave financial support to gifted students and commissioned new works. These two men were very influential in nurturing the modern

American musical world. Copland introduced promising young composers to conductors and to editors of musical journals. He enjoyed the companionship of his colleagues. In 1928, Copland and his composer-friend Roger Sessions started a series of concerts featuring the work of their American colleagues, including Virgil Thomson, Carlos Chavez, Walter Piston, Ruth Crawford, Marc Blitzstein, and George Antheil. Thus, he practiced what he first learned in Boulanger's home: building a community of artists who share ideas, support each other, and put collegiality ahead of competition. As Virgil Thomson described him, "He always did his best to help his fellow composers."[29]

As Copland's career progressed, he undertook increasingly more complex works, some of which were hard to conduct, even by his steady admirer, Koussevitzky. The Maestro needed to immerse himself in the jazz-derived American idiom, and he did so eagerly with Copland's assistance. At the same time, Boulanger's sustaining support and understanding of Copland's work contributed to his own belief in the new directions his music was taking. The decades of the late twenties through the thirties were crucial for Copland. He developed many new forms of his music and collaborated with writers, choreographers, actors, and composers.

In 1937, he established one of the most important artistic relationships of his life with Leonard Bernstein. The two musicians were nearly a generation apart; when they met, Copland was 37 and Bernstein was still an undergraduate at Harvard University. Writing from his room in Eliot Hall, Bernstein conveyed his admiration after hearing Copland's music: "The concert was gorgeous. . . . I still don't sleep much from the pounding of [some of Copland's notes] in my head. In any event, it's a secure feeling to know we have a master in America."[30] From that early meeting, their relationship spanned many decades. It started with Copland's mentorship and continued later with Bernstein's frequent conducting of Copland's music. Bernstein described Copland's influence on him, which included Copland's mentoring him as a young composer and helping him with his career:

> And thereafter, whenever I came to New York I went to Aaron's, . . . All during those years I would bring him my own music for criticism. I would show Aaron the bits and pieces, and he would say, "All that has to go. . . . This is just Scriabin. You have got to get that out of your head and start fresh. This is good; these two bars are good. Take these two bars and start from there." And in these sessions he taught me a tremendous amount about taste, style, and consistency in music. . . . Through his critical analyses of whatever I happened to be working on at the moment, Aaron became the closest thing to a composition teacher I ever had.[31]

Copland's confidence in Bernstein provided Bernstein with the same solid foundation that years earlier the older composer had received from his mentor Boulanger. In an interview with Bernstein, he described the growing reciprocity of their relationship. He recalled that Copland accepted one of his suggestions about cutting the last movement of *Third Symphony*. At another time, Bernstein wrote a short, jazzy, bar-room piano sequence for Copland's *Rodeo*.

During his younger years, Bernstein particularly benefited from playing Copland's freshly completed scores. Just as his mentor Boulanger had assisted him, Copland assisted Bernstein with contacts, housing, and the loan of a piano. And most important, he gave his unbounded confidence in the younger man's talent. Bernstein's biographer Joan Peyser repeatedly referred to Copland as Bernstein's father figure in "art" music.[32] Once Bernstein became a world-renowned conductor and popular composer, he played Copland's music frequently and with great success. Theirs was an important collaboration across a generation.

Copland also worked with other young composers. He still is remembered as a great teacher and a constructive critic. William Schuman, a distinguished composer who was the president of the Julliard School of Music, recalled, in an interview, some of Copland's qualities:

> Copland would look at your music and try to understand what you were after. He didn't want to turn you into another Aaron Copland. He would sit down at the piano, read through a score, and make comments. When he questioned something, it was in a manner that might make you question it yourself. Everything he said was helpful in making a younger composer realize the potential of a particular work. On the other hand, Aaron could be strongly critical. . . . Because of his agreeable disposition, Aaron is never thought of as being exacting, and this does him an injustice.[33]

Schuman further described how Copland contributed to "the emergence of a truly indigenous American art music. A whole school of composers came into being in this country while Aaron was at the center as teacher, composer, and critic."[34]

Music is a collaborative art form; musicians work with each other, with composers, both living and dead, and with professionals from related disciplines. But musical training frequently focuses on the young performer's or composer's individual talents without helping him or her learn to work with others. In a recent interview, Professor Nancy Uscher of the University of New Mexico spoke of these tensions in her field.[35] She is a violist who combines concert performances in the United States and abroad with her teaching. As a young child, she heard a lot of music at the Berkshire Music Center at Tanglewood, as her family included many avid music lovers. At first, her training was in her public school with teachers who were devoted, but who were not specialists in string technique. Uscher received a lot of encouragement, and at times she played pieces beyond her readiness. More important, she had the opportunity to play with more highly trained musicians. During our talk, she recalled, "It became so natural for me to sit down with people and play, whether [or not] I could do it perfectly. I learned to sight read, just because I was terrified that I would lose my place."

Uscher had many experiences playing in string orchestras for children in school and in summer music camps. As a young violist, she learned to work well with other musicians. She believes that to be a well-rounded musician you need to be able to recognize what is the right instrument for you, to identify really good training, to have a vision for music that goes beyond narrow professionalism, and to enjoy musical collaboration. Her choice of the viola as her instrument was a recognition of a bond with its rich, dark, mellow tones:

> I feel my own personal voice is the viola, I think it is something very deep if you are a musician. . . . If you find the right voice you go on with an incredible drive. . . . The violin was very pleasant, I still play the violin and I teach it, but I never felt the same connection. . . . [The viola evokes] a more mellow, a more obviously emotional mood. It is like a darker red, less yellow. I think about higher notes as lighter colors and darker colors as being very rich, very mild, or muted tones.

Together with a deep personal attachment to her instrument, Uscher has a broad vision of the role of music in society. She and her students have played in elementary schools, and she has taken the university's student chamber ensemble to the Women's Correctional Facility in Grants, New Mexico. She also sees collaboration across disciplines as fresh air, as pushing one's boundaries: "For me, it is almost a desperate need to do that."

KNOWLEDGE TRANSMISSION AND TRANSFORMATION

Through most of this book I have focused on artists and physical scientists engaged in joint work. But my personal experience is primarily with social scientists. In this section, I present some collaborative patterns described by my colleagues. In universities, some of the closest bonds are between professors and doctoral students. In this relationship, we experience the temporary inequality between expert and novice. In time, the relationship changes. The mentor learns new ideas and approaches from his apprentice; he adds to what he learns and transforms it. As their relationship matures, the younger and older participants build a more equal connection. But the journey is not always easy. There is mutual dependence, but there are different needs. The senior members are involved in many projects. They are driven by deadlines and are concerned about the quality of their work. They are struggling with competition for funds and with the difficulty of developing close relationships with colleagues who evaluate them for promotion. The junior members are facing all of the insecurities of careers in the making.

The connection is crucial for both generations, but managing the relationship is complex. In some ways, they are similar to relationships in biological families. Both can involve loyalty, mutual caring, conflict, separations, and the subsequent development of new connections.

Harvard psychologist Howard Gardner described his collaborative practices during our interview in his office. One mode is with his colleagues, who include developmental psychologist David Feldman, creativity scholar Mihaly Csikszentmihalyi, and co-director of Project Zero David Perkins. He has also worked extensively with his wife, Ellen Winner, who has studied gifted adolescents. Gardner differentiates between his sustained, lively intellectual interactions with his colleagues and his solo work. Generative and critical dialogue with his colleagues has been influential in sharpening his ideas and in developing long-term research agendas. But Gardner writes most of his books without collaborators.

He participates in a second form of collaboration: large-scale projects that include both novice and experienced participants:

> That began with the most important experience in my life, which I did not realize until I wrote *To Open Minds*. It was the summer of '65 when I worked under Jerome Bruner's direction on *Man: A Course of Study*. I was not particularly into work groups. . . . But then I went to work with Bruner with about fifty people, about twenty teachers and administrators and thirty researchers. We were designing this new curriculum, and in the mornings we would watch it being taught in the classrooms. In the afternoons we would very intensively criticize what happened, sit in the basement and talk for hours. And at night we would have these big parties at Bruner's house. It was a wonderful mix of social events—meeting interesting personalities—but doing very hard work. Interestingly, I completely forgot the importance of this whole experience because I had some personal problems with Bruner. [Subsequently, the two men became close again, including the dedication of one of Gardner's books to his former mentor.] It was only

after twenty-five years that I realized that my own large scale collaboration, Project Zero, was modeled after the one created by Bruner.[36]

In our talk, Gardner referred to *Schoolhouse Politics* by Peter D. Bow, a book that documented the development and implementation of *Man: A Course of Study*. From the passages referring to Gardner's contributions to this large undertaking, it is clear that he had an important role. He identified teacher training as critical to an innovative educational program, whereas the attention of the other participants was focused on sophisticated curriculum materials. The MACOS project was a "crystallizing" experience for Gardner. It made him recognize his interests and gifts, and it showed him some major challenges in the field. At that time, Gardner's interests and concerns were not fully met by Bruner's program.

When Gardner was growing up, he played music and wrote poetry. As a young scholar, he became interested in creative cognition. His mentor and collaborator in that endeavor was philosopher Nelson Goodman. Project Zero was established with Goodman's leadership; in the seventies, Gardner became a co-director. Psychological approaches to educational issues became of less concern to Gardner during the time when most of his research focused on children's artistic development. When he returned to an educational topic, writing *To Open Minds*, he realized the extent of Bruner's influence. Then he was able to acknowledge his first mentor's support in helping him transcend the traditional confines of psychological and educational thought.

Lengthy collaboration between more and less experienced individuals may result in too great an identification with a particular mentor. In order to avoid such a danger, a mentor may encourage multiple connections, or an apprentice may search for diverse influences. Illustrating this danger is Gruber's account of Mozart's debt to Haydn: "Haydn's influence was strongest during Mozart's adolescence. His work then imitated Haydn. Later he studied Bach intensely, and integrated the influence of this distant teacher into his emerging personal idiom. At that stage he synthesized the impact of both masters, and was able to fully acknowledge Haydn's influence."[37]

Perhaps a similar dynamic is involved in Gardner's delayed recognition of Bruner's impact. In developing his independent theoretical framework, Gardner succeeded in integrating various influences and, subsequently, he developed an influential theory of mind and intelligence.

The literature of social science and education strongly emphasizes the impact of mentoring and role models on professional novices. But there is no single theoretical framework that accounts for this phenomenon. Most studies and theoretical analyses focus on a single mentor, on learning through identification with a more experienced individual. In one study, however, the effect of different aspects of multiple mentors was observed among psychiatric, medical, and biochemistry trainees. The authors reported that the participants constructed a role model that combined features from different individuals who trained them. They fashioned a combined prototype elaborating on their actual experiences.[38] In a similar vein, I have suggested that *one of the ways in which an individual scientist or artist goes beyond the known is by synthesizing diverse influences while finding his or her own voice.* The ability to push beyond the known or a single model or mentor, is nourished by the novice's intensity of engagement. It is this quality, as well as the novice's immersion in the work of a mentor or mentors, which sustains experimentation.[39]

Successful mentoring is a reciprocal process. Experienced thinkers recognize the commitment, talent, and intensity of some of their young co-workers. Their decisions to include students or younger colleagues in their projects are based on some of these characteristics. In an oft-quoted study, sociologist of science Harriet Zuckerman found that Nobel laureates excelled in their ability to choose promising apprentices. When compared with their colleagues, these men and women collaborated more and published more than others in their fields.[40]

In recalling his own socialization into psychology Mihaly Csikszentmihalyi gave a number of examples of how he synthesized the impact of his mentors and distant teachers into his own emergent professional identity.[41] Csikszentmihalyi was born in Hungary and raised in Rome. He was interested in art, did some drawings and paintings as a young man, and wrote a lot. His father, a diplomat, restored old paintings as a hobby, and his mother wrote about historical and philosophical subjects. While in Europe, Csikszentmihalyi accidentally heard a lecture by Jung: "I was in Switzerland skiing and I did not have money to go to a movie, so I went to a free lecture. The lecturer was Carl Jung, whom I did not know at the time. But he seemed to try to understand what happened to Europe during the war. That related to my own experiences."

This was a crystallizing experience for Csikszentmihalyi, whose concerns were varied. They included art, writing, and working as a reporter for major European newspapers. He had not yet focused sharply on a particular profession. Hearing Jung triggered his interest in psychology. He read both Jung and Freud. But the study of psychology in Italy was not an option at that time, as it was only offered as an academic minor for students of philosophy or medicine. He chose to emigrate.

Even after his arrival in the United States, Csikszentmihalyi was not quite sure what psychology consisted of as a field. He encountered behaviorist teachers whose methodology did not match his broader philosophical and artistic interests. But at the University of Chicago, in the interdisciplinary program of the Committee on Human Development, he found an environment in which he could explore deeper questions. One of his mentors was Jack Getzels, who was interested in gifted adolescents. Early in his graduate studies, Csikszentmihalyi convinced Getzels to include young adults among his subjects. They jointly studied a cohort of art students and developed ingenious ways of assessing their creative potentials. This research was published in their book, *Creative Vision*.

The work of these two men of different generations successfully combined their complementary interests and skills. Getzels was a seasoned researcher and Csikszentmihalyi knew a lot about the art world, having studied art and design earlier in his career. Csikszentmihalyi, in an interview, reflected on Getzels as a mentor:

> I came ready to fuse a lot of interests and a lot of concerns. He kind of focused and channeled these. I appreciated that very much and still do. What I mostly owe Getzels is his great professional integrity and his concern for accuracy. He was a great critic and editor, and without him I probably would not have developed a professional identity. He was always very gruff and very private, but at the same time he would praise in no uncertain terms. When he praised, he was generous.

The fact that Csikszentmihalyi entered graduate school with a broad set of personal and professional experiences behind him helped him make thoughtful, independent choices in what he studied. Now, he is concerned that students who pursue graduate studies now tend to remain bound by the conventions of the field: "I never felt that, I never thought I had to accept the viewpoints of any field. . . . I think part of that was based on some of my early disenchantment of what the elders knew." We further talked about some possible differences between the physical and social sciences as to the way in which knowledge is produced, replicated, and taught. The big labs in physical science where work is frequently pursued around the clock tend to promote solidarity among the participants. Senior and junior scientists together address demanding and timely problems. Social scientists are more isolated and are more likely to compete for the limited resources available to them. In these situations, collaboration is frequently vertical. Faculty members rely on their students as dialogue partners.

Csikszentmihalyi worked hard to establish a community of young scholars interested in broad issues of human creativity. After receiving his doctorate, he first taught at Lake Forest College. He liked his students, but his contact with them was short. At this institution, he first thought about "flow." Later he defined flow as optimal experiences, "activities which require the investment of psychic energy, and that could not be done without the appropriate skills."[42] The flow state includes "a deep but effortless involvement that removes from awareness the worries and frustrations of everyday life."[43] He also wrote: "The best moments usually occur when a person's body or mind is stretched to its limits in an effort to accomplish something difficult and worthwhile."[44] In reconstructing the way he came to understand optimal experiences, Csikszentmihalyi talked about some of his endeavors in the seventies: "It started with my work with artists. . . . they were so completely taken by their work, that they were not really interested in the paintings when they were finished. That, then, posed the interesting question, what was their reward? What sustained their activity?" These questions led him to explore play, which resulted in an article he wrote with a student at Lake Forest. But he realized that he needed more sustained interactions with a larger group of graduate students to pursue his first insights. At that point, he received an offer from his alma mater, the University of Chicago. There, with the help of young partners, he started to interview artists, athletes, musicians, and chess masters. Eventually, the work was replicated cross-culturally with the help of many colleagues in Asia, Europe, and the United States. The findings were summarized in a volume co-edited with his wife, Isabella Selega. The two of them share a European background and strong academic training (Isabella studied history at the University of Chicago). She used her considerable intellectual and editorial abilities to work with him. He particularly values her facility in identifying central and necessary ideas in his own and in his co-workers' manuscripts. He acknowledged his wife's support: "her loving, if critical help" throughout his career, and specifically her involvement with his book on creativity.[45]

At the University of Chicago, Csikszentmihalyi had a suite of offices. One of these served as a conference room with a large table in the middle where his students could share their work with him and where they frequently lunched together. Work with graduate students is very important to him. His professional contacts are dispersed over two continents. Half of his many publications are co-authored with students. He referred to this as *vertical collaboration* and commented a little wryly about the process:

> There are many ways of doing this collaborative thing wrong. My way is to give too much recognition to my colleagues too early. At first I thought you can't give too much recognition, but now I know differently. There was this cartoon in the *New Yorker* that epitomizes this situation in my mind. These elderly men are talk-

ing to each other, and one says, "You know what is wrong with the younger generation? It is that you treat them as equals, and then they believe you."

Since he likes to work with people with unusual backgrounds, he frequently chooses students whom his colleagues may avoid. Most of the time his intuition is correct, and he has mentored many exceptional young men and women. Occasionally, he makes a mistake. Csikszentmihalyi is unusually candid about his strengths and weaknesses and acknowledges his infrequent faux-pas.

Students who have worked with Csikszentmihalyi for several years benefit from his generosity, his sustained caring, and the pleasure of participating in his bold explorations. Csikszentmihalyi respects the different skills and domain knowledge that the students bring. Some have backgrounds in history and sociology, others in music or the visual arts. At the beginning of their studies, the younger members of his team take responsibility for the details of the project. As they advance, they shift to more theoretically contributory roles. The students' connection is primarily with their mentor, but during his absences they rely more on each other.

Working with a famous collaborator provides many advantages for those starting in their careers: it gives them access to research settings and experience in analyzing shared data, and they learn how to take general questions and make them more specific and researchable. There are disadvantages as well. When famously mentored young professionals look for their first jobs, they are severely questioned concerning their own, independent ideas. One of Csikszentmihalyi's students described to me such an experience during her job interviews. She had to demonstrate her autonomy as well as her connectedness to her mentor.

In a similar vein, my own students have told me of their need for separation after long periods of interdependence. This is crucial while they are establishing independent professional identities. At times, the process is smooth and comfortable; at other times, it can be a painful rupture. The separation that ensues need not be permanent. In some cases it is followed by interesting new joint endeavors in which collaborators across generations build on their common interests and values, and their well-honed complementarity.

Developmental psychologist Barbara Rogoff works very effectively with graduate students and research associates in her cross-cultural studies. A few years ago, we gathered in the living room of her Spanish colleague, Pilar Lacasa, to talk about collaboration.[46] The group included a student from the former Soviet Union, one from Guatemala, an American student, and our Spanish hostess.

Barbara first discussed some of her own experiences as a young scholar and how they influenced her in the way she works with junior partners. During her training at Harvard University, she was part of several large projects in which the principal investigators had little time for field research. In addition, the work they undertook involved a great number of people at varying sites who had limited contact with each other. Once on her own, Rogoff decided to construct projects that were smaller and more tightly knit, to work closely with her co-participants, and to stay very familiar with her data.

She realized early in her career that psychology's dominant paradigm was closely linked to Western cultural assumptions about individual development. These assumptions contributed to some researchers distinguishing between "regular" (i.e., Western) and "exotic" (non-Western) children. Her fieldwork in Guatemala made her question these distinctions and contributed to her favoring ethnographic methods over standardized tests used in assessing cognitive development. Such work required group effort. Rogoff gave much thought to how to develop collaborative endeavors where the participants are personally committed to a joint project. Her current team includes graduate students from culturally diverse backgrounds, students who help her discover new directions. Rogoff commented: "What I gain from these collaborations is a step back from my own perspective to hear questions that take me to new places."

Her Guatemalan graduate student, Pedro Chavajay, was, two decades before our talk, a child participant in one of Rogoff's first studies. He recalled how that experience, and Barbara's presence in his village, contributed to his decision to study in the United States. His English was limited when he started his studies. He realized that he needed to develop a different relationship to his American professors than the highly deferential one that he was used to and which is prevalent in Latin America and the Far East. In his new environment, Chavajay was ready to ask searching questions about methodology and about the meaning of cross-cultural research to indigenous people who are considered the "subjects" in such studies. He soon realized that in Rogoff's group, the attitude toward research participants is mutual respect and reciprocity.

Each graduate student that joined the group had a somewhat different academic and cultural background. This contributed to some productive tensions in the way the group functions. For instance, one Russian participant, Eugene Matusov, was used to dialogic interaction as critical and intense. When asked whether he saw differences between his discourse experiences in his country of birth and his new home, he replied: "I think the main difference is that U.S. discourse values precision of expression while Russian discourse focuses on movements of thought. These movements may involve argument, even contradiction, but they are deemed useful if they contribute to the development of one's thinking." He appreciated acquiring new forms of discourse in interaction with Rogoff and her colleagues in Salt Lake City and, subsequently, in Santa Cruz, California.

The newcomers to this group faced interesting challenges in dealing with their previous academic socialization. As developmentalists, many of them came from departments steeped in the work of Jean Piaget and in laboratory-based research. Their work in Rogoff's group was primarily in "naturalistic" environments (schools, Girl Scout groups, family, and work settings). This approach required learning new techniques of data gathering.

Lacasa discovered the same thing after she joined Rogoff in Salt Lake City and started a study of Girl Scouts' planning activities. Her previous work was Piagetian and stressed primarily cognitive variables. In accord with her background, she carefully prepared maps of the routes the girls were to use, expecting their planning to be a highly cognitive endeavor. But she found that the children negotiated their activities through social interaction and engaged in shifting cognitive strategies. These results supported a view of learning and cognition which Rogoff and her co-workers refer to as the "transformation of participation model."[47] It is linked to the work of Lave and Wenger;[48] Newman, Griffin, and Cole;[49] and others. Rogoff and her collaborators' cross-cultural framework differs from Piaget and the behaviorists. For instance, observations of Mayan children in Guatemala pointed to the engaged participation of very young learners in their families' cooperative activities. Mayan parents participated in adult group functions while also performing caregiving activities; their children learned "through engagement with others (in a system of ongoing guidance and support) in the everyday mature activities of their community."[50] This participatory model was described by Rogoff in the journal *Mind, Culture and Activity*: "In a community of learners, both mature members of the community and less mature members are conceived as active; no role has all the responsibility for knowing and directing, and no role is by definition passive. . . . A community of learners includes asymmetry of roles. Particular roles vary from one situation or one community of learners to another."[51]

While the article did not refer to her own research group, the description quoted above characterizes it very well. The graduate students and postdoctoral fellows working with Rogoff described their collaboration as consensual; each person listened carefully to the others. They built on these ideas and their complementarity. Some of the postdoctoral fellows, for instance, Gilda Morelli, added to the group's cross-cultural breadth by sharing her data collected in Africa. What Morelli gained from her participation with Rogoff's group was a sense of validation that the kind of research that she was doing had a place in psychology; that she was part of a thought community. For Rogoff, discovering the links between the diverse projects constituted "the creative moment."

As I was listening in Madrid to the accounts of these projects, and was interviewing some of Rogoff's collaborators in other settings over the years, I was repeatedly struck by how well the participation model characterizes their interactions. It also fits our own description of a family approach to collaboration in which roles are flexible, newcomers are carefully socialized, and values are negotiated and shared.[52] In Rogoff's group, the membership changes as graduate students finish and more senior collaborators return to their home institutions. But communication continues through face-to-face dialogue and long-distance communication. In any particular year, onsite members contribute ideas for new research during planning meetings. At the same time, their mentor and co-participant uses her skills to guide her apprentices: Rogoff encourages some ideas while pointing out that others may be risky dissertation projects for young researchers. Vertical collaboration requires careful judgments: How will a dissertation that uses a non-paradigmatic theoretical framework or a non-traditional methodology be evaluated by future employers? Rogoff includes these specific concerns for each of her students within the broader network of her enterprises.

Pamela Trotman Reid, who, at the time I interviewed her, was associate provost at City University of New York's Graduate Center, also takes her job as mentor very seriously. She works with many students of color, and, as an African American, she is aware of the multiple pressures that they face as doctoral students. Some of these students struggle with severe economic pressures. They all confront racist attitudes in a white institution. Those who are graduates of large city colleges may have lacked individual attention and encouragement during their undergraduate years. Thus, they question themselves and wonder whether they are ready for the intense competitive pressures of doctoral work. Reid is aware of these conflicts, which are not limited to women and students of color. She provides her students with supervised research experience. She encourages them and urges them to complete their studies. She is a very energetic, warm, optimistic person, an excellent role model for younger professionals. She is also demanding: in the collaboration Q-sort (which we have used in many interviews), she ranked high the item: "I seem to overwhelm my collaborators with my pace and expectations."[53] She laughed at herself when pointing out how hard it is for those around her to keep up with her fast-paced activities. In the midst of a career that includes teaching, administration, intensive mentoring, and family responsibilities, Reid recognizes the importance of collaboration to her scholarly work. She placed the card, "My collaborator spurs me on to complete the project," high in her distribution. She values her connection with strong African American and Euro-American women. Her article with Vanessa Bing, "Unknown Women and Unknowing Research:

Consequences of Color and Race in Feminist Psychology," reflected the powerful bond between these collaborators engaged in an uphill theoretical and educational battle. They wrote of the limited and biased research about women of color: "The primary consequence of this approach is to pathologize women of color, while leaving their concerns unaddressed. The continued exclusion of culturally and economically diverse women from research on ordinary problems and issues allows an entire discipline to remain ignorant of the experiences of these women."[54]

In her work with her students as well as her collaborators, Reid lives the issues raised in her paper with Bing. Her research is conducted in poor, minority communities, and focuses on education and housing. Frequently, new psychological measures different from the many standardized tests which are inappropriate in these settings need to be developed for her work. While these tasks are demanding, the rewards are great for Reid's students and collaborators. They participate in the development and application of a nonracist, egalitarian research paradigm.

Gardner, Reid, Csikszentmihalyi, and Rogoff differ in some of their approaches to mentoring and collaboration. But they share the ability to provide skilled guidance to their younger partners. Theirs is a fine blend of imagination and caution, assessing the benefits of particular projects to both the group and to each individual.

In my own case, I have experienced a great variety of vertical collaborations. I bring to these some of my own needs and try to respond to those of my students and junior partners. As I teach in the Southwest, I am somewhat isolated from new developments in the human sciences by scholars on the East and West Coasts. My students and young collaborators have helped me to construct a lively intellectual community in which expansion and renewal are my rewards. They have also protected me from becoming overwhelmed by the many projects to which I commit myself. They are skillful in creating much needed order out of the tangled network of my enterprises. As an immigrant, I have gained from my partners' native knowledge of the English language and their willingness to closely scrutinize the texts we have crafted together. Their thoroughness contrasts with my desire for quick closure. Thus, I become very dependent on my young collaborators, which puts pressure on them that I sometimes fail to recognize. They usually tolerate these pressures, because they, too, long for an intellectual community that meets their desire to address difficult issues.

One of my greatest pleasures in collaboration has been the chance to speak at the speed of thinking with those who share my theoretical framework. Professors Carolyn Panofsky and Holbrook Mahn, who were at one time my graduate students, are particularly skillful in accompanying me in these flights of thought. Both of them have a love of the written language, while I am a dialogic thinker. As I listened to Michelle Fine (whose collaborative interactions I described in earlier chapters), I identified with her statement: "Pat deepens my thinking." So do my collaborators. They also challenge me and push me to be explicit. This is a strategy that Dr. Michele Minnis, my partner in examining interdisciplinary, large-scale collaborations, has used with exquisite tact.

Jean Baker Miller wrote of temporary inequalities[55] that change over time, including teacher-student relationships. Institutions reinforce such temporary inequalities by granting varied forms of power to teachers, dissertation supervisors, and project directors. But as vertical collaborations move forward, novices gain from their experience and assume increasingly important roles in joint projects. In this way, a shift toward greater equality between partners is realized. There are some collaborations across generations in which the younger collaborative partners have skills and backgrounds which are complementary to that of their mentors. Because these skills are important to their older partners, the "novices" develop a different kind of relationship with their collaborators. They occupy a dual role, that of learners as well as that of equals within the partnership. It is the simultaneous presence of these two positions that contributes to constructive interdependence across generations together with some role ambiguity.

Novice/expert interactions take place in many contexts. Intergenerational collaboration can result in mutual enrichment in dyadic as well as large-scale collaborative environments. An informative example of the dynamics of collaboration comes from a partnership between researchers and students at a large university and surrounding community institutions.

MENTORING WITHIN A LARGE COLLABORATIVE

Three generations of learners and teachers—university researchers, undergraduates, and schoolchildren—are linked in a program called Fifth Dimension, a large collaborative started in the early 1980s at the Laboratory of Comparative Human Cognition (LCHC), University of California, San Diego (UCSD).

Many children in the United States face two challenges: their parents work long hours, and after school there is hardly anywhere that they are safe and well provided for. There are few places where children can learn while they play. In contrast to countries such as France or Japan, their school year is shorter, and instructional time is less. Thus, there is great need to help pupils learn more without putting them under pressure to perform.

Motivated by research and bolstered by theory, the after-school program developed at UCSD responds to some of these problems. It serves children between six and twelve years old, many from low-income, multilingual communities. The program takes advantage of the great variety of computer games and new forms of communication now available. It aims for computer literacy as well as more general cognitive and social skills. The use of computer games creates a setting for both fantasy and learning. Besides the computer games, the children can play chess or produce materials for the World Wide Web.[56]

Fifth Dimension seeks to bring the university and the community together to create nontraditional after-school programs. Michael Cole described the kind of activities wanted: enjoyable for children, appealing to both girls and boys, promoting reading and writing, at once intrinsically rewarding (fun) and educational.

The principal persona of the Fifth Dimension programs is the Wizard. The Wizard lives in cyberspace and chats with the children by modem. S/he is ageless, can be female or male, and is often multilingual. The Wizard advises children on games and on personal matters as well. The Fifth Dimension uses college students as "Wizard Assistants." They receive college credit and gain valuable experience by working with children. Cole described them: "They occupy a real-life position between the researchers and the children. They are like the researchers in being 'big people' from the university. They are like the children in that they are still in school, still being graded, and still struggling with adult authority."[57] Sometimes the college students become novices and are helped by "Young Wizard Assistants"—children who have mastered much of the program. This fluidity of roles, and the distribution of knowledge between "old timers" and "newcomers" of varying ages, creates an unusual democratic learning community. There are more than a dozen programs using the Fifth Dimension model in the United States, Europe, and Mexico. The programs are adapted to local interest and concerns. In different communities and countries, the Wizard is named El Maga, Golem, or Volshebnik.

The theoretical framework of the Fifth Dimension came from psychologists Lev Vygotsky, Jean Piaget, and L. N. Leontiev, and was further developed by Rogoff, Cole, James Wertsch, Yrjo Engestrom, and Sylvia Scribner (this is a short list of cultural-historical thinkers). Philosophers John Dewey and George Herbert Mead also influenced contemporary scholars committed to authentic experience in learning and to the social embeddedness of thought.

In the same vein, studies of working teams are pursued in many settings. Research at the Finnish Center on Work and Activity Theory centers on teachers, hospital staff, and scientific and legal personnel engaged in joint problem solving.[58] The influence of the center's work stretches from Scandinavia to Japan. Additional strands in cultural-historical research include those focusing on communities of practice and communities of learners.

Finally, the work on apprenticeship by anthropologists Jean Lave and Etienne Wenger has become central to discussions of learning communities. The development and application of these theoretical notions are crucial to the work of the LCHC. They are also a focus of the larger thought community of xmca, an e-mail discussion group named after the publication *Mind, Culture and Activity.*

It is hard to identify common themes in a large, international thought community such as xmca. But to better understand the conceptual foundation of the Fifth Dimension as an "activity system," I will make an attempt. Vygotsky's notions are the starting point: "Human activities take place in cultural contexts, are mediated by language and other symbol systems, and can best be investigated in their historical development."[59] In an introduction to Vygotsky's classic volume, *Thought and Language,* psychologist Jerome Bruner wrote: "The internalization of external dialogue . . . brings the powerful tool of language to bear on the stream of thought."[60]

Vygotsky's concept of play also contributed to Cole and Peg Griffin's thinking, researchers who were among the early planners of the Fifth Dimension:

> Play is enjoyable, it is intrinsically voluntary, and it is at the same time an essentially rule-governed activity: Its two essential components are the presence of an imaginary situation and the rules implicit in this imaginary situation. . . . Furthermore, play is always a *learning* activity because it requires learning and grasping these rules, seeing that they form a system. . . . Even simple pretense play—for example, a little girl pretending to be a "mother"—requires attending to and making explicit the normally implicit rules embedded in the role of the "mother."[61]

Using this notion of play, the designers of Fifth Dimension constructed an environment of learning, fantasy, and active participation. Children and undergraduates play together in shifting combinations. To evaluate these activities, Cole and his collaborators use the undergraduates' narratives to examine how knowledge is transmitted from one group to another. Their accounts report the effects of fine-tuned communications—"scaffolded interactions" —as the child's expertise increases.[62] The undergraduates are particularly helpful to the children in games that support phonetic mastery and the use of coordinate systems. Quantitative assessments have been conducted in a number of Fifth Dimension sites. They show that children who participate in these programs gain academic skills.[63]

In the early 1990s, researchers in San Diego found strong differences across two Fifth Dimension sites—one a library setting, the other a Boys and Girls Club. The library fostered more sustained involvement with game-supported learning than the club. But the program spread most effectively in the Boys and Girls Clubs. This unexpected finding raised important questions concerning the program and its impact.

In analyzing the program's impact, Cole and his colleagues faced questions concerning how to measure success: Long-lasting endeavors across traditional divides of academia and community? Education programs which serve as models far from their original sites? Improvements in the academic skills of individual children? Or better undergraduate education in the human sciences? According to Cole, "there is no single 'cause' for failure or success that seems to distinguish the apparently successful or unsuccessful institutions."[64] He argued that programs that best articulate the shared goals of the universities and the community institutions are most likely to be lasting ones. The achievement of common ground is a challenge for all collaborations, whether they involve a small group or large-scale, complex structures. The interface between the collaborative community and broader social and institutional systems affect the direction and eventual outcome of joint endeavors.

People committed to new collaborative ventures stretch the boundaries of institutions. They, like the designers of Fifth Dimension, tend to construct a safe place for creative exploration. But individuals who engage in joint projects, including vertical collaboration, find that some of them fail. Fifteen years ago, I experienced a very painful break-up of a project conducted with two highly experienced and talented graduate students. It has taken the writing of this book to identify what might have been some of the reasons for this failure. I have learned that collaboration requires trust, the freedom to explore and criticize as equals, and a fluid division of labor. In order to engage in these activities within hierarchical institutions, we try to construct a protective structure. This structure can be a combination of physical or mental space, of independent financing, or of minimizing bureaucratic interference. For months and years the structure may hold. Differences in status and roles among collaborators seem irrelevant when participants are engaged in rewarding work. The mutuality that is experienced in the exchange of ideas and the enjoyment of each other's company bolster the partnership. But this may shatter in the heat of a decision that has to be made quickly and where the responsibility falls to the senior member. Tensions erupt and resentment against the institutional realities become personalized. Subsequently, status differences are harder to ignore, and offenses that were ignored may surface. As described in the previous chapter on the emotional dynamics of collaboration, dyads and groups vary greatly in the ways in which they manage conflict. In some partnerships, the shared goals are sufficiently motivating so that tensions due to temperamental, status, or work-load differences are ignored or minimized. In others, conflict is an occasion to examine differences and to create new modes of interaction. In the collaboration I have mentioned above, we were unable to resolve our conflict. It has taken many years to mend the rupture.

Collaborations across generations are not limited to parental mentoring, after-school programs, or the professor–graduate student relationship. There are other partners in thought who enjoy and choose intergenerational collaboration. Their influence upon each other may start with a stimulating professional encounter or a shared project. When the interaction is sustained over years, the partners are likely to share values, intellectual concerns, and modes of thinking.

An example of such a connection is that between cognitive linguist George Lakoff and cognitive scientist Rafael Nuñez. A world-famous author, Lakoff is known for his contributions to linguistics and cognitive science. Regardless of his fame, Lakoff has the eagerness and enthusiasm of a young person starting on a new project. Nuñez, originally from Chile, is at an earlier stage of his career. At the time of our interview, in the summer of 1997, he was ending a postdoctoral fellowship at University of California at Berkeley. He has taught and done research on three continents, always attracted to a new challenge. Both Lakoff and Nuñez have interdisciplinary interests and a common concern with mathematical reasoning. They discovered that they have a shared scientific worldview which helps them to explore a traditional subject in a novel manner.

They both enjoy collaboration: Lakoff remembered that even in high school he liked to do his homework around a table with his classmates. He believes that he gets his best ideas when talking. Nuñez confirmed this: "When we are producing text, George needs to speak without interruption until he completes his thought. It is important for him, as a verbal thinker, as it is useful for both of us, especially when we differ."

Nuñez, on the other hand, is a visual thinker, who sometimes disappears from the room in which they work to make sketches in his notebook. In doing so, he establishes a conceptual connection among his languages and his thinking. For Lakoff, it is in telling stories that some very important points are conveyed, even in a subject as abstract as mathematics.

Both men are basically interested in how the mind works. This pursuit has been a sustaining one for Lakoff. His books co-authored with

Mark Johnson, including *The Metaphors We Live By* and the recent *Philosophy in the Flesh*, present a novel approach to the embodied mind. Nuñez just published a book co-edited with neuroscientist Walter Freeman entitled *Reclaiming Cognition*. During our talk, Lakoff and Nuñez spoke of the different phases of their collaboration.[65] They started with an article on "the metaphorical structure of mathematics: sketching out cognitive foundations for a mind-based mathematics." While working on their first joint publication, they experienced the wonderful rush of creativity that comes when two individuals discover that they are "friends of the mind."[66] As Nuñez explained, "In our collaboration, we have the chance to deeply explore the conceptual foundations of amazing philosophical and cultural traditions and we can talk, create, and do things together." Both men like to walk or to sit in a cafe and plan their next chapter. They build on their breadth, and their interest in several disciplines contributes to the richness of their thinking. They love the beauty and diversity of Berkeley; they both placed the card, "There must be an aesthetic quality to the project in order for me to work on it," high on their Q-sort distribution.

One way to explore a new topic is to teach it in a seminar. Both Lakoff and Nuñez are very passionate about ideas that engage students. They like to be part of the development of a new domain (that of mathematical cognition), and they like to experience his incredible intellectual energy. In the spring of 1997, they taught a graduate seminar together which led to the development and re-arrangement of some of the topics Lakoff and Nuñez planned to include in their upcoming jointly authored book, *Where Mathematics Comes From: How the Embodied Mind Brings Mathematics into Being*. Exploring topics for the book with students meant that they learned many new things, faced complex issues, and had to slow down their pace of writing together. In the context of their course, these writing partners faced the challenge of collaboration across generations. Lakoff was laboring under many demanding commitments. The pressure of these resulted in his having to make some rapid, on-the-spot decisions in their classroom. He was not always able to discuss these decisions with his collaborator. Nuñez's life was a little freer at that time, and he would have liked to have more joint time to plan the necessary changes in a course neither of them had taught before.

These partners are able to resolve temporary disagreements very well, as they enjoy their work, their lives, and their partnership. Currently, Nuñez is teaching in Europe, and their large book is now completed. Their collaboration has succeeded in bridging differences in their native languages, styles of life, age, and status. They are both enthusiasts who have chosen to mix work and pleasure in an appealing way. Lakoff ended the interview by saying, "Why do something that is not fun?"

Another collaboration across generations is that between professors of education Courtney Cazden of Harvard University and Sarah Michaels of Clark University. As the three of us talked in Cambridge, Mass., they recalled how they used to finish each other's sentences. Michaels was a graduate student at Berkeley when they first met. Her training was in sociolinguistics with a primary interest in children's language interactions. During their second meeting at a small conference at Stanford University, they discovered very quickly their many shared interests and commitments. Cazden was impressed with Michaels's doctoral research and asked her to join her at Harvard. Here, these two women, who differed in age and academic status, started a multiyear collaboration. Their first joint project focused on children's verbal communications during "sharing time" (when young learners exchange accounts of their recent experiences). Subsequently, before these topics became popular, they worked together on the use of computers in upper elementary school and on kids' e-mail communications.

In recalling their shared endeavors, they emphasized the importance of their connection: "We got each other's thought." Michaels recalled that in their collaboration "it was more than just getting a job done. It was building. It was more about a relationship and building an environment that was nurturing, it was bigger than just the paper."

Both of them differentiate between cooperative activities, in which a task is divided and then completed, and more personally meaningful joint activities. The forging of a common vision is part of what made their shared activities important. They also recognize some of the urgent political issues that affected their work. The personal and the professional is closely linked in this friendship across generations. They know and care about each other's families; they celebrate each other's achievements. When I asked them how status and age have affected their relationship, Michaels replied:

> This relationship was different from some of my other collaborations. I very much wanted to please Courtney, I cared and I still care tremendously about how she assesses what I am doing. I really felt somewhat amazed and surprised that she valued what I had to say. It does not strike me as a junior-senior relationship, rather that I hold Courtney in such high regard, . . . We have similar aesthetics and similar, easy sensibilities. . . . But I did not want to encroach on some of her boundaries, so I was careful to respect these.

Cazden added, "You came as an expert in looking at data in a certain way. There was a sharing time over two to three years."

In describing their work together, they recalled that they did not actually write in the same room. One person would assume the primary responsibility for a particular paper, and the other would look over the draft and make corrections. They were not concerned with issues of ownership of either ideas or text. While Michaels is a person who engages in many diverse forms of collaboration, Cazden finds that her best work is done when she can fully concentrate, alone with her text, without diversions. Although their working styles differ, they meshed easily while they were collaborating. Michaels discussed the pleasures and value of being energized by significant exchanges, of exploring and discussing ideas that are then more fully developed in quiet, private spaces. Their description exemplifies many other reports which suggest that effective collaborations are characterized by productive rhythms.

There are alternating shifts between joint and solo work, each contributing to and fueling the other. Michaels remarked how Cazden, who frequently works alone, is very dialogic in her writing; she articulates multiple voices, "she collaborates in her mind." Cazden added, "That is what I like, synthesizing and analyzing, pulling it apart, and then putting it back together."

The significance of similar values and a sense of trust emerged from these conversations of partners whose relationship transcends differences in age and status. My colleague, Holbrook Mahn, commented on the usefulness of complementarity in skills, talents, and experience that enriches vertical collaboration, "the inquisitiveness" that junior members frequently bring to such partnerships. I find this a welcome challenge as it helps to revitalize our understanding. Vertical collaboration also provides hope for the older partners that their work will be used, extended, and transformed by those who participate in its development.

An interest in the dynamic relationship between continuity and change characterizes Chinese American sociolinguist Lily Wong Fillmore. She described to me a generational chain of influences reaching back to her friend and informal mentor, Susan Ervin-Tripp, and forward to some of her own mentees, who in turn are influencing young women in their twenties.[67] Fillmore is a dynamo who successfully combines teaching, research, advocacy, and family responsibilities. As a child, she helped in her parents' Chinese laundry. As a young woman, she volunteered to teach literacy working with Mexican migrants. A mother of two daughters and a son, she returned to graduate school, studying linguistics at Stanford University. Fillmore is widely admired for her courage, her innovative scholarship, and her unflagging commitment to bilingualism.

I interviewed Fillmore and Ervin-Tripp in the latter's beautiful house overlooking the Berkeley hills and the San Francisco Bay Bridge. Ervin-Tripp, a professor of psychology, was surprised that her friend identified her as a mentor. Fillmore commented that it is usually the recipient, "the mentee," who realizes the impact of a mentor's encouragement and example to a greater extent than the one who provides the mentoring.

Ervin-Tripp served as extern examiner at Fillmore's dissertation defense at Stanford University. When Fillmore joined the faculty at Berkeley in the early 1970s, there were still very few tenured women like Ervin-Tripp who were committed to assisting their younger, female colleagues. Ervin-Tripp's struggle to move an entrenched bureaucracy toward a more equitable institution took many forms. She served in numerous organizations dedicated to improving the position of academic women, which included chairing a faculty senate committee on the status of women and minorities. In the late 1980s, she assumed the role of ombudsperson for the University of California campuses. Ervin-Tripp's active support of younger women, minorities, and students is very important for Fillmore:

> There is a sort of community of mind that focuses on justice, that is what I think of in terms of our relationship. . . . When I think of our friendship over the years, there are things that you may not even be aware of that are taking seed in my own mind. You drop a thought here, and you drop a thought there. And I think this is what Sue is talking about. For example, the question of women in the University. I now work with young women who are the beneficiaries of things you started and worked for, like the Women's Studies program.

These two women share a commitment to humanize their institution —Fillmore refers to it as academic ethics. She realizes that students seek her out, in part, because of their need to have a mentor who combines her professional and personal commitments to social justice. Ervin-Tripp inspires her both in her courage to act on such morality as well as in her theoretical orientation to language acquisition. In contrast to many researchers in this field, Ervin-Tripp emphasizes the critical role of the social context. Her friend and colleague is able to implement that perspective in her own work on bilingualism. The two of them collaborated on a project looking at the interaction of social and personal variables in the acquisition of language. Ervin-Tripp thought her contribution to the project was minimal. But Fillmore reminded her of how her thoughts and her framework permeated the project. This awareness of her friend's contribution is further acknowledged in her high placement of the Q-sort card, "My collaborator creates theoretical models to help our thinking processes."

There are some differences in the working methods of these two women. Ervin-Tripp is a dialogic thinker; she enjoys the process of articulating her ideas with others. She placed the Q-sort card, "With my collaborators I can talk at the speed of thinking," high on her distribution. Fillmore likes to plan ahead and bring notes to a project meeting. She is highly organized and is good in assisting her friends in optimally structuring their working environments. As do many women academics, they both tend to take on a great variety of responsibilities: Ervin-Tripp realizes that collaboration can help one to cope with multiple pressures. She selected the Q-sort item, "My collaborator spurs me on to complete a project," as one that is descriptive of her working pattern.

Regarding their interactions with graduate students, Ervin-Tripp distinguishes between those who become colleagues over time and those who remain one's students "forever." Fillmore thinks that the young individuals who become partners have complementary skills and specific expertise to add to their collaborations with mentors. And most important, they have a brightness of spirit—perceptiveness and commitment—with which they enrich their relationship with their elders. She describes the contradictions one faces with graduate students who are colleagues but who still have to be judged and critiqued as they are finishing their work for their degree. She resolves this tension by including them in her family. She gets to know their relatives, she works closely with them, and, eventually, "they start talking back."

The concept of an extended family, of remaining connected to some of her apprentices for many years, is very vivid for Fillmore. She realizes that it is not possible to include all of one's students in these special relationships, as she invests so much of herself in each one of her mentees.

Fillmore's mentoring bridges decades, communities, and individuals. She is currently working with men and women from Southwestern Pueblo communities who are regarded as leaders in their communities. In this work she is assisted by a former student of hers, Rebecca Blum-Martinez, who is an assistant professor at the University of New Mexico. They met while Rebecca was working on an English-as-a-Second-Language project. Fillmore, who is always eager to interest able young people in furthering their knowledge and career, convinced the younger woman to enter a doctoral program at Berkeley. Once at the university, Blum-Martinez became part of the extended family of which Fillmore spoke during our interview.

Many of their conversations took place in the Fillmore kitchen, preparing dinners for Fillmore's own family and those of her students. In talking about her experiences with her mentor, Blum-Martinez emphasized her teacher's passion, her wide-ranging knowledge about language acquisition and bilingualism, and the way in which she approaches these subjects in an integrative manner. Fillmore's ability to present her point of view is an inspiration to those with whom she works. It took Blum-Martinez a number of years after her return to

New Mexico before she stopped seeing herself as Fillmore's student. Her knowledge about Pueblo communities was important to making their joint work a success. The Southwest is a new and exciting place for Fillmore, who continues to fight for all people who are marginalized and oppressed by the mainstream. At the same time, Fillmore keeps inspiring those with whom she works by expressing hope while others express despair.

Fillmore joined scores of others in contributing to a Festschrift volume celebrating the life and work of Ervin-Tripp, *Social Interaction, Social Context, and Language: Essays in Honor of Susan Ervin-Tripp,* edited by Dan Slobin, Julie Gerhardt, Amy Kyratzis, and Jiansheng Guo.[68] These colleagues and former students expressed their appreciation for Ervin-Tripp in many ways. One of the editors, Kyratzis, wrote that her mentor taught her: "You should always care deeply about your students, colleagues, and important social issues and that by doing so, you also become a better scholar. I left Berkeley a year and a half ago, but my collaboration with Sue continues. She has been a profound influence in my life."[69] Throughout the volume, these sentiments were echoed by contributors who acknowledged her influence on their research and their lives. Mary C. O'Connor wrote:

> Susan Ervin-Tripp deserves more tribute than a paper of mine can offer. Her vital, curious and wide-ranging mind and her accepting, gentle nature have been crucial ingredients in the intellectual development of many students. She has created a research environment in which many people have been able to find their own way, due to her benign scholarly mentoring. Finally, she has made more visible to many the complex and beautiful social fabric that we are all weaving and rending with our every use of language.[70]

In this and other tributes to great mentors and to friends of the mind and heart, we hear of the joys of university life that are often obscured by the problems of academia. In the halls and corners of these large institutions, we can experience genuine, loving relationships. These relations keep us going in the midst of frequent professional strife, bureaucratic impositions, and the pressures of the larger society that privileges money over knowledge.

REACHING TOWARD THE FUTURE

Collaboration across generations reveals some of the most important features of human interdependence. It is built on mutual attraction and the establishment of effective emotional bonds, and on the realization that both learners and mentors can meet their goals and hopes together more fully than by solo activities. These thoughts were expressed in a different way in the article on mentoring jointly authored by Gallimore, Tharp and myself:

> The chemistry laboratory or the construction site or the athletic arena becomes the field of initiation, the Magic Wood where culture is taught, and boys and girls become men and women. Such an apotheosis of the ordinary daily routines can occur because in initiation, apprenticeship, and mentoring, more is learned than is taught, and what is learned is the variousness of being a woman or a man of this time and this kind.[71]

The mentored, in turn, become the guides, the teachers of future generations. The power of these connections is remembered and honored through life. My own mentors, particularly those who were facing the destruction of World War II, taught me to hope through sharing. This chapter is dedicated to their memory.

7

THOUGHT COMMUNITIES

During the years that I have worked on this book, the topic of collaboration has become of even greater interest to science writers, creativity researchers, educators, organization theorists, and art critics.[1] It is in the mass media and in academic journals. I have quoted from the *New York Times*, from dozens of biographies and popular books (for instance, Bennis and Biederman's *Organizing Genius*), and from scholarly publications. In some of these works, the authors made practical suggestions for enhancing collaboration, particularly by using computers. But while this literature grows, and the argument for the timeliness and importance of joint activities is powerfully made, no significant change has appeared in mainstream psychological theories.

Most psychological approaches are shaped by the individual-centered work of Freud, Erikson, and Piaget. In cognitive psychology the focus is similar; for instance, information processing is concerned with activity in the brain. The same is true of evolutionary psychology, which has attracted great popular attention. These theories emphasize biologically driven development. In this concluding chapter, I present a different theoretical framework. It is a life-span approach. Social, cultural, historical, and biological conditions together contribute to the realization of human possibility. Central to such an approach is the principle that *humans come into being and mature in relation to others.*

This stance contrasts with the classical view, the development of the autonomous, rational individual. My differing view is supported by cultural-historical and feminist theories. It is also supported by the literature of collaboration. In the course of intense partnerships, new skills are acquired. The partners may develop previously unknown aspects of themselves through motivated joint participation. The collaboration context provides a mutual zone of proximal development where participants can increase their repertory of cognitive and emotional expression.

In mentioning cultural-historical theory, I refer to the works of Russian psychologist Lev Vygotsky and his followers or "collaborators." Vygotsky believed that thought develops first through interdependence with others and later is internalized. His ideas resemble those of American pragmatist George Herbert Mead. These authors published in the first half of the twentieth century. Since then, their relevance has grown. Modern practice in education, work settings, and creative contexts supports their emphasis on the social sources of development.

Although Vygotsky's influence is growing in many fields, most psychologists still focus on the biologically constrained individual. This largely excludes the psychological study of collaboration. But, there are exceptions. Feminist psychologists have developed alternatives to the individual-centered approach to human growth that was part of their own training as young psychologists. Jean Baker Miller and her thought community at Wellesley College (the Stone Center) proposed that human growth occurs through "agency-in-community."[2] Their rethinking of long-held assumptions about independence and autonomy has been influential among clinicians and developmental theorists.[3] Their ideas, and those of Vygotsky and Russian literary critic Mikhail Bakhtin, are valuable when applied to collaboration.

In these concluding pages, I wish to apply and expand some of these central tenets of cultural-historical and feminist approaches. They deepen our understanding of scientific and artistic collaboration. At the same time, this examination of joined lives and shared work has identified additional themes that can contribute to these theories of human possibilities.

SHARED VISIONS, SHARED GROWTH

In depicting the human life span, psychological theories often posit a developmental endpoint, akin to a physical peak capacity, which is then followed by decline. In studying collaboration, I see a different path: *human beings who are engaged in new, partnered activities learn from the consequences of their actions and from their partners.* Creativity researcher Howard Gruber stresses that joint endeavors allow the risks of creativity to be spread out among the partners. Bennis and Biederman wrote of how members of "Great Groups" are liberated, for a time, from the prison of the self.[4] I would add further that taking risks, buoyed by collaborative support, contributes to a developing, changing self. Through collaboration we can transcend the constraints of biology, of time, of habit, and achieve a fuller self, beyond the limitations and the talents of the isolated individual.

In contrast to a maturational theory of the self, this analysis emphasizes the potential of stretching one's identity through partnership, through sustained and varied action, through the interweaving of social and individual processes. This process is well captured by Vygotsky's concept of the zone of proximal development. In the collaborative context, development is realized in a number of ways. A long-term collaboration can be a mirror for each partner: a chance to understand one's habits, styles, working methods, and beliefs through comparison and contrast with one's collaborator. In Vygotskian terms, partners create zones of proximal development for each other. As I stated in Chapter 2, complementarity is a consequence of a basic and often ignored reality. Each individual realizes only a subset of the human potential that can be achieved at a particular historical period. In partnerships, starting from the youngest age, we broaden, refine, change, and rediscover our individual possibilities. There are different ways human possibilities are realized in partnered endeavors. Some of these possibilities are temperamental: a retiring person may become more daring through the example and support of a more outgoing collaborator. Complementarity in knowledge and skill is extensively discussed throughout this book. The appropriation of one's partner's insights and approaches is particularly well documented in the Picasso-Braque collaboration. They learned from each other's styles: Picasso's sharp focus and Braque's sensuousness crossed the boundaries of their individual paintings. The development of innovative techniques (i.e., *papiers coupés*), once initiated by one of the partners, was quickly incorporated in the work of the other. Differences in modes of thought also create opportunities for expansion. Verbal thinkers learn to visualize when working with partners who rely on diagrams, flow charts, and three-dimensional models. The diversity of modes of thought and representational activities is striking among physicists. Niels Bohr was a dialogic thinker who deepened his understanding verbally as well as geometrically. His younger colleagues were trained to rely on mathematical formulations, but in Bohr's company, they shared his use of words to explore new physical concepts.

When Bohr explained and co-constructed his ideas with his younger colleagues, he gained new ways to build on them. In "Inspired by Bach," Yo-Yo Ma relied on a variety of partners to transform his perception of long-familiar, beloved cello suites. These artists and scientists give new meaning to the notion of sustained ways of stretching the self. They exemplify lifelong zones of proximal development through partnered endeavors.

A joint, passionate interest in a new problem, art form, or societal challenge is crucial to collaborative success. In partnerships, participants expand their commitment and endurance. My collaborator, Michele Minnis, suggests a physical fitness metaphor for this aspect of joint endeavors:

> The metaphor is one of athletic fitness (fitness for the challenges of collaboration, for sustaining it to a point of breakthrough or discovery), and the critical importance to that fitness, not only of

cognitive development, but, at least equally important, of emotional development. Becoming emotionally fit for the rigors of collaboration requires increasing one's capacity for and abilities to offer empathy, support, trust, and hard-headed, constructive criticism. It also means strengthening one's endurance when faced with self-doubt, rejection, and feelings of vulnerability.[5]

The collaborative process of which Minnis speaks requires the lowering of the boundaries of the self. As Braque discovered, "We are inclined to efface our personalities in order to find originality."[6] But to achieve such bonding, partners need to learn to listen carefully to each other, to hear their words echoed through those of the collaborator, and to hear the words of the other with a special attentiveness born of joint purpose. The benefits of a shared focus are captured by mathematician Phil Davis, who explained: "In every single case of collaboration, the project required a contribution that each collaborator could only make. [Working with a partner,] it is almost as though I have two brains."[7]

Living in the other's mind requires trust and confidence. The writers of *Women's Ways of Knowing* forged their sense of "we" by carefully building trust during their decade-long collaboration. In *Indivisible by Four*, author Arnold Steinhardt, first violinist of the Guarneri String Quartet, described the way in which four players constructed their distinctive commonality. After decades of playing together, they are still fine-tuning their complementarity. He wrote about the beginning of his personal journey toward the indivisibility of their foursome:

> Playing quartets was not exactly in the spirit of good old-fashioned American individualism. According to that script, I should have mounted my horse, slung my violin over my left shoulder, and ridden out of Severance Hall into the sunset, looking for solo concerts: tough, independent, self-sufficient. Instead I was banding together with three others in a communal endeavor whose low-action plot played itself slowly over the years. Unspectacular as it might at first be imagined, our new work was in fact quite remarkable and dramatic. I was entering a social unit with no boss, no underlings, and certainly no conductor. What was one to call a group of four men who regarded each other equally, or as equal as they wanted to be?[8]

These men engage in careful, at times exhausting, debates about interpretations of the music they play. Steinhardt recalled: "In the early years, I would sometimes return from a rehearsal dazed and exhausted by the continual process of conflict and resolution."[9] But over the years, they have come to appreciate the benefits of their discussions and to respect their differences: "It pushed you to think clearly about the important issues."[10] The result of their debates has been to hone their connection and to strengthen their trust. Steinhardt evoked the necessity of honoring their interdependence: "I was now connected with and dependent on David, John, and Michael for a good performance. How strange! If I played out of tune; they played out of tune; if they stumbled, so did I; and if I managed to play beautifully, we would all share the credit. . . . My future was their future; theirs was mine."[11]

Chamber groups have often been thought of as a particularly good metaphor for collaboration. Individual differences provide depth to a performing group committed to a shared purpose; they are jointly nourished by the great music written for ensembles. Steinhardt called the power of the quartet communicating with each other in a concert hall "the zone of magic."

The interdependence of the players, and their achievement of a "zone of magic," takes place in a broader supportive community. This involves mentors and friends, critics and managers, what psychologist David Feldman referred to as a "cultural organism." He defined such an organism as "a cooperative structure that is formed and reformed in order to enhance the possibilities for discovery, development, and (occasionally) optimal expression of human talents in various domains."[12] He considered the structures that support the participants in a musical endeavor to be examples of humanly crafted environments. Some of these are major edifices, for instance, the Aspen Music Festival, which "requires monumental effort, superb organization, sustained application, substantial resources, and probably luck as well."[13] The relationship between the "cultural organism" and the development of persons is another manifestation of the dynamics of collaboration, of the interdependence of the social and the individual, of their shared growth.

The study of collaboration supports the following claim: productive interdependence is a critical resource for expanding the self throughout the life span. It calls for reconsidering theories that limit development to a progression of stages and to biologically preprogrammed capabilities. The study of partnered endeavors contributes to cultural-historical and feminist theories with their emphases upon the social sources of development, mutuality, and the generative tension between cultural-historical processes and individual functioning.

The examples of partnerships in this book are drawn primarily from the joint endeavors of creative individuals. These are people who have chosen to pursue artistic and scientific discovery and the co-construction of new knowledge. They face many hardships and reap many joyous rewards. Their well-documented lives reveal some interesting dynamics of "agency-in-community." These dynamics are relevant to people in different walks of life. In collaborative endeavors we learn from each other by teaching what we know; we engage in mutual appropriation. Solo practices are insufficient to meet the challenges and new complexities of classrooms, parenting, and the changing workplace. Creative collaborators provide us with important insights for ways to build joint endeavors. And their practices challenge mainstream theories whose focus is limited to the individual.

JOINED LIVES

In trying to describe in this work how people think together, I was faced with a paucity of language. Some terms, like "group mind," carry a negative connotation of stifling conformity. That term doesn't bring to light the role of dialogue and the diversity of perspectives which, when linked to a common purpose, reveal the power of collaboration. New terms, such as "socially shared (or distributed) cognition"[14] come closer to what I am exploring in this work. As socially distributed cognition is an important new development, I will describe its meaning and some of the debates it has generated before turning to "thought communities."

Increasingly, scholars are describing thinking as social practice. Psychologist Lauren Resnick characterized cognition as "people jointly construct[ing] knowledge under particular conditions of social purpose and interaction."[15] Michael Cole wrote that "joint mediated activity is the proper unit of psychological analysis and hence, is inherently socially shared."[16] In his summary article on a book on socially shared cognition, Cole took note of the many critics of a purely "in-the-head"' individualistic notion of thinking. These scholars challenge the dominant psychological paradigm of the twentieth century.

Anthropologists and organization theorists are also contributing to a rethinking of thought. Among the latter, Levine and Moreland emphasize the ways in which members of work groups "struggle together to answer certain key questions about their group, its members, and the work they perform."[17] Barbara Gary, an organization theorist, wrote of collaboration as "action learning. . . . The potential afforded by using a collaborative process is that the parties will search for a common definition of the problem and generate a wide enough set of possible solutions to find one that incorporates at least some of the interests of each of the stakeholders."[18] Interest in workplace collaboration is growing rapidly. Studies in this domain include communicative interactions in work settings. David Middleton found: "The way participants construct and account for what they do is a resource and a topic for both participants and analysts."[19] Studies also focus on technologically mediated work activities and organizational forms—networks, teams, and what Yrgo Engestrom and collaborators have referred to as "knots."[20] Their examples included healthcare crises during which participants from different professions and ways of life act together. "Knotworking" involves solving urgent tasks where the "combinations of people and the contents of tasks change constantly."[21] Decision making in such situations is distributed, as there is no central authority solely in charge. In fact, most work activities involve what Karl Weick referred to as "collective sensemaking."[22] He wrote of the need "to act in order to think"[23] and of organizational life where shared experience leads to engagement with culture, the need to make sense, telling stories about joint experiences.

An interest in joint learning and problem solving in everyday contexts is shared by anthropologists: Shirley Brice Heath wrote of the interactions between members of Little League teams. She suggested that teams share "many other features of communities, including interaction and mutual dependence, expressive ties through numerous symbol systems, mutual and common sentiments, shared beliefs, and an ethic of individual responsibility to the communal life."[24] In Heath's characterization of team life, the dynamic between the group and individual achievement through collaboration is important. This dynamic is explored by others engaged in the construction of theories of socially shared cognition.

Cognition in the Wild, Edwin Hutchins's study of navigational systems (both Western and Micronesian),[25] is one of the most detailed accounts of joint activity. It has raised some interesting issues about personal agency and the sites of cognitive activities. As reviewer Charles Bazerman wrote: "Hutchins' project to see how much cognition can be found outside the self within the culturally ordered system [of navigation], and in the constraints and affordances of tasks and tools helps demystify our cultural beliefs in individuality, individual intelligence, and imagination beliefs that have often found allies in the cognitive tradition."[26] Another reviewer, French sociologist Bruno Latour, was not quite satisfied: he praised Hutchins's great contribution to a cognitive science "that believes in the wind, in the wild, that claims to represent the real cognitive tasks in an organized and collective work site."[27] But, he wanted more. He wanted to go beyond what Hutchins offers of cognition moving subtly across erasable lines of inside/outside dichotomies. Hutchins focused on collective tasks, on artifacts, on the coordination of representational media, but he did not eliminate the person. Latour, on the other hand, wished to have "psychology swept inside out by the fresh air of the upper deck."[28] He claimed that while Hutchins moved far from traditional accounts of individual cognition, of a crammed and heavily burdened head, he may not have moved far enough. As Hutchins said in his rejoinder, he does not want to sweep the mind clean, but to furnish it differently: "One cannot empty the person by delegating cognitive activity to something or someone else. The work must be done somewhere, and some of the work will be done in regions that lie inside the bounds of persons."[29]

These debates concerning the role of the individual in socially shared and distributed cognition are substantive and lively. They are part of the construction of an emerging, alternative view of cognitive science. This view is in opposition to the more traditional reliance on universal cognitive algorithms.

Cultural-historical contributions to this emerging paradigm share an emphasis on joint thinking which is contextualized. It is also mediated through historically shaped tools and artifacts. According to Cole, "the forms and functions of [cognition] are shared among individuals, social institutions, and historically accumulated artifacts (tools and concepts)."[30] For Vygotsky, language is the most significant of all tools. It has conceptual, auditory, and pragmatic aspects. Language is central to shared creation and is not limited to verbal language (recall the visual, painterly dialogues of Picasso and Braque or Renoir and Monet). For scientists, tools range from blackboards and pens to three-dimensional chemical models to accelerators in high-energy physics. For choreographers, tools include music, space, lighting, and the bodies of dancers.

We shape our tools and are shaped by them. The way human practices are interdependent with tools has intrigued many Vygotskian scholars, including James Wertsch: "I believe that much of what we do in the human sciences is too narrowly focused on the agent in isolation and that an important way to go beyond this is to recognize the role played by 'mediational means' or 'cultural tools' in human action."[31]

He discussed a theoretical stance that rejects the unproductive dichotomy between the individual and the social as its methodological unit. Instead, he proposed a dialectical tension between these two, as both are always present. Human activity requires engagement with cultural tools that are generated in specific cultural-historical settings. Interesting examples of this relationship between cultural tools and human practices are provided by authors writing about the new technologies of collaboration.

In *Shared Minds*, Michael Schrage made a powerful case for collaboration's enhanced role in today's society and described the role of tools in facilitating it: "If there is a core theme to this book, it's that people should understand that real value in the sciences, the arts, commerce, and, indeed, one's personal and professional lives, comes largely from the process of collaboration. What's more, the quality and quantity of meaningful collaboration often depends upon the tools used to create it."[32] Schrage's view of collaborative tools is an ambitious one. He sees them as part of the creation of a shared experience. To him, collaboration goes beyond communication, it requires that "people spend as much time understanding what they are doing as actually doing it. Vocabulary is defined precisely; imagery to illustrate ideas is agreed upon; individuals generate shared understandings that they couldn't possibly have achieved on their own."[33]

Shared Minds was written for a popular audience. Schrage presented a persuasive case for the growing importance of collaborative endeavors. While his primary interest was in the new technologies of shared work, he repeatedly referred to collaborative communities. His use of this term identifies a void in much of the literature on socially shared cognition.

Little is written about communities by cognitive scientists. The word "community" is more widely used among anthropologists, feminists, educators, and social reformers than among cognitive scientists. Heath includes mutual dependence, verbal interaction, and common sentiments in her characterization of communities engaged in learning and problem solving (see quote above). Anthropologist Jean Lave describes learning (and cognition) as participation in communities of practice. In contrast to these authors, the writings of cognitive scientists separate thought from its situatedness within a community, however large or small. They maintain a view of cognition that lacks the complex lived-in qualities of intimacy, engagement, conflict, and negotiation. Their view resembles other analytical dichotomies separating interrelated human experiences, such as the separation of thinking from feeling, or the individual from the social.

When I first used the term *thought communities*, I was not fully aware of its complexities. I adopted it from biologist and sociologist of science Ludwik Fleck, whose work was originally published in 1935. He wrote of cognition as the result of social activity: "When we look at the formal aspect of scientific activities, we cannot fail to recognize its social structure. We see the organized effort of the collective involving division of labor, cooperation, preparatory work, technical assistance, mutual exchange of ideas, and controversy. . . . A well-organized collective harbors a quantity of knowledge far exceeding the capacity of any one individual."[34] He developed these ideas further when he described thoughts as passing from one individual to another "each time a little transformed, for each individual can attach to them somewhat different associations. . . . Whose thought is it that continues to circulate? It is one that obviously belongs not to any single individual but to the collective."[35] He viewed cognition as nourished by a collective fund of knowledge within domains and in specific collectives. The simplest thought collective, he wrote, "exists whenever two or more people are actually exchanging thoughts."[36]

Fleck made a distinction between "thought collectives" and "thought communities." The former are well-established groups with their own thought styles and institutional structures. The latter are less fully described by Fleck. They are not as highly structured as thought collectives. They are formed by individuals with common concerns during focused collaboration. In this analysis of the psychological dynamics of collaboration I have used the term "thought communities" to refer to experienced thinkers who collaborate with an intensity that can lead to a change in their domain's dominant paradigm.

Throughout this book, many different communities of thought are described. Some are highly focused on a particular task, such as the joint work of Albert Einstein and Marcel Grossmann. Their disciplinary complementarity helped them create Einstein's general relativity. Their concerns were clearly defined, and their collaboration was embedded in a lifelong friendship. Other thought communities start with broad shared interests which are jointly shaped into more specific projects. The authors of *Women's Ways of Knowing* illustrate this second pattern.

Thought communities enable participants to engage in the co-construction of knowledge as interdependent intellectual and emotional processes. But most of the literature on shared cognition focuses on cognition at the expense of the relational dynamics of collaboration. Issues of trust, uncertainty, competition, intellectual ownership, financial dependence, equity, emotional fusion, and separation need to be negotiated among partners in long-term collaboration. In order to establish such a group, partners take each other's questions, skills, and personal styles very seriously. They hear their partners' concerns even before they are fully articulated.

PATTERNS OF COLLABORATION

Thought communities are different from cooperating teams as their members take emotional and intellectual risks to construct mutuality and productive interdependence. Their objectives are to develop a shared vision as well as achieve jointly negotiated outcomes. These collaborating groups vary in intensity, duration, interactional processes, and objectives. Through analysis of focused interviews, study of biographical data, administration of a collaborative Q-sort, and reconstruction of partnerships through joint narrative accounts, my collaborators and I identified four patterns of partnerships.[37]

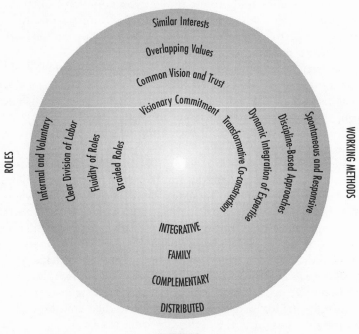

VALUES

Similar Interests

Overlapping Values

Common Vision and Trust

Visionary Commitment

ROLES

Informal and Voluntary

Clear Division of Labor

Fluidity of Roles

Braided Roles

Transformative Co-construction

Dynamic Integration of Expertise

Discipline-Based Approaches

Spontaneous and Responsive

WORKING METHODS

INTEGRATIVE

FAMILY

COMPLEMENTARY

DISTRIBUTED

PATTERNS

Collaborative patterns: Roles, values and working methods

We see collaborative endeavors as dynamic, changing processes. In the diagram we use a circle with gradations to show possible movement among patterns. This classification is not a hierarchy. Collaboration often starts as one pattern and over time changes into another pattern.

The first of these patterns we refer to as *distributed collaboration*. Psychologist Herbert A. Simon described this mode of working in his autobiography:

> To make interesting scientific discoveries, you should acquire as many good friends as possible, who are as energetic, intelligent, and knowledgeable as they can be. Form partnerships with them whenever you can. Then sit back and relax. You will find that all the programs you need are stored in your friends, and will execute productively and creatively as long as you don't interfere too much. The work I have done with more than eighty collaborators will testify to the power of that heuristic.[38]

Distributed collaboration is widespread. It takes place in casual settings and also in more organized contexts. These include conversations at conferences, in electronic discourse communities, and among artists who share a studio space. In these groups, participants exchange information and explore thoughts and opinions. Their roles are informal and voluntary. In electronic discussion groups, for example, one person may assume a more active organizing role, while others may remain "lurkers."

The participants in distributed collaborative groups are linked by similar interests. At times, their conversations may lead to new personal insights. When exchanges become heated or controversial, new groups may form to address issues in greater depth. Other groups splinter or dissolve. But out of such informal connections some lasting partnerships may be built.

The second pattern on the diagram is *complementarity collaboration*, the most widely practiced form. It is characterized by a division of labor based on complementary expertise, disciplinary knowledge, roles, and temperament. Participants negotiate their goals and strive for a common vision. One of the most effective metaphors that captures disciplinary complementarity and mutual understanding is Stravinsky's " visual hearing" of his music. Another is offered by linguist George Lakoff describing his work with philosopher Mark Johnson: "We lived in each other's minds." The insights that collaborators provide for each other may pertain to their craft, to their respective domains, or to their self-knowledge as creators. This is particularly true when the collaboration involves complementarity in scientific fields or in art forms. Differences in modalities—the translation of one's thoughts into a new language of expression or into the developed mode of expression of one's partner—are part of this rewarding process.

I have frequently referred in this book to the personal and professional partnership of Pierre and Marie Curie. Besides their disciplinary complementarity (Marie's background was in chemistry, Pierre's in physics), they also played complementary roles. Marie was a "thinker-doer." She took on a large part of the organizing work in their laboratory. Her husband provided some of the conceptual scaffolding of their research. They were complementary in temperament. He was retiring and cautious, reluctant to publish until completely satisfied with the accuracy of his findings. She was quick, determined, and willing to work with institutions, which required negotiation and compromise. This division of labor remained a flexible aspect of their collaboration.

Their partnership was fueled by their love for each other and their shared passion for their scientific work. Their values were remarkably similar, considering their different early upbringing. After Pierre's untimely death, Marie continued their research. She had closely observed how Pierre worked and made some of his methods and modes of thought her own. This illustrates one of the most important psychological dynamics of collaboration, mutual appropriation, or the stretching of human possibilities through the collaborative partners' shared experiences that sustains their endeavors. This stretching provides personal benefits in addition to the accomplishment of jointly negotiated tasks. In applying the term "appropriation" to creative endeavors, we are stretching a concept first developed by Bakhtin, which Vygotskian scholar James Wertsch described as follows: "the process is one of taking something that belongs to others and making it one's own."[39] He used words as the example of appropriation when he quoted Bakhtin: "The word in language is half someone else's. It becomes 'one's own' only when the speaker populates it with his own intention, his own accent, when he appropriates the word, adapting it to his own semantic and expressive intention."[40]

In collaborative endeavors, mutual appropriation is a result of sustained engagement during which partners hear, struggle with, and reach for each other's thoughts and ideas. This is not only a cognitive process. It is a good example of both intellectual and emotional appropriation. In the preface to the second edition of *Women's Ways of Knowing*, Nancy Goldberger recollected the rewriting of a draft chapter of their book: "My task is to rewrite, but first I must type the words from my colleague into my word processor. I decide to edit as I type. . . . [I] try to understand her intention behind her choice of words, try to place myself in her place so that I feel inside her mind and heart, search for her meaning before I impose new words."[41] This account tells of a cognitive task placed within the relational dynamics of this group. While the language of connectedness is more often employed by feminist writers, it is not limited to women. Cellist Yo-Yo Ma's collaboration with choreographers and others evoked the same unification of heart and mind about which Goldberger wrote.

Mutual appropriation, then, implies a very particular form of human interdependence that takes years to be fully realized. Motivational dynamics are linked with cognitive ones. Some may ask, is it sensible to separately identify these processes? Our answer is yes. Motivation and cognition constitute a complex system, and if some aspects of the system are not identified, the interrelationships among them are ignored.

In planning this book, motivational concerns emerged slowly for me. It was only while working on Chapter 4, the chapter which addresses gender and collaboration, that I realized I had not dealt with them explicitly. I attribute this delayed awareness to my socialization in Central European culture, which values knowledge and language very highly. Cultural-historical theory fits my interests, as it is most explicit about cognitive and linguistic issues. But once I started to interview some of the feminist psychologists, I was struck by the productive way in which they integrated epistemological and relational concerns. Their example was critical to my identifying motivational themes in the interviews and biographic materials I have collected.

Human interdependence is central to Vygotskian thought. There is agreement that survival of human infants requires mutuality and interpersonal synchrony. Born helpless, our young call forth caregiving behavior by adults and older siblings. As they mature, they start to participate in the vast pool of transmitted experiences of their caregivers. Vygotskian scholars have written about cultural variations in caregiving behavior (see Cole, 1996)[42] and have stressed the social sources of cognitive development. Jill Tarule, one of the authors of *Women's Ways of Knowing*, identified commonalities in feminist and cultural-historical theories. She noted their shared emphasis on the role of language in maintaining and developing meaningful connections throughout the life span: "Vygotsky's emphasis, as in connected knowing, is on how thinking and knowledge are mediated through interaction with others. [Vygotsky's approach] values a dialogue that relies on relationships as one enters meaningful conversations that connect one's ideas with others."[43] An additional psychological dynamic of collaboration is empowerment, or what I refer to in Chapter 5 as "the gift of confidence." I quote Jean-Paul Sartre saying to Simone de Beauvoir, "You did me a great service. You gave me a confidence in myself that I shouldn't have had alone." This is echoed by most collaborators whose words are included in this book. They write and speak of leaning on their partners' confidence during periods of self-doubt and rejection. Mutual caretaking is one way this dynamic is described by Janet Surrey. It is crucial when partners present a new, possibly controversial idea. Blythe Clinchy recalled when writing the last sentence of *Women's Ways of Knowing*, how when she first typed it, she wrote: "These are the lessons we think we have learned listening to women's voices." After staring at the sentence, she deleted, "we think." She was able to make an unqualified assertion speaking in the voice of the foursome, rather than speaking for herself alone.

Another aspect of empowerment is revealed in some partners' willingness to face the pain of their own past. Carol Gilligan illustrates this idea in her description of a study of relational impasse among adolescent girls. With a group of Harvard women, she interviewed young girls in private and public schools. They identified ways in which young women feel under pressure "to hide what they most want and value."[44] The researchers realized that they, too, had experienced these feelings; through their collaboration they were able to confront their history. These joint discoveries made them stronger individually and deepened their connections.

A third pattern identified in our work is the *family collaboration*. We characterize it as a mode of interaction in which roles are flexible or may change over time. Such a shift is well documented by Will and Ariel Durant, co-authors of the multivolume *A Story of Civilization.*

Their joint autobiography is based on their letters to each other. It reconstructs the changes in their working and personal relationship. When they married, young Ariel worked on classifying her husband's notes for his books. He was more experienced and more highly educated than she. But with each new volume in the series, Ariel's contributions became more important. She started to do independent research and challenged some of her husband's interpretations of history. Their debates and dialogues were stimulating to both, and her role became significant in their work. Her change from helpmate to fully engaged partner was recognized by her husband in 1957, decades after they first married. He placed both of their names on the title page of *The Age of Reason.*

The Durant partnership during the second half of their marriage is an example of a dynamic integration of expertise. Participants help each other to shift roles, including the move from novice to a more expert level. As in a family, members can take over for each other while still using their complementarity. These groups or pairs tend to be committed to each other for a long time. Roles and responsibilities may shift during their partnerships.

Psychologist Harold Stevenson's metaphor for collaboration came from a Chinese family: "You give up some of your freedom, in a sense. On the other hand, you expand your reach by such a great amount." The Group Theater described in Chapter 3 is an example of the extended family mode of collaboration. The members of this innovative group shared important dramatic and political objectives. One of the theater's founders, Lee Strasberg, was the American adapter of the famous Stanislavsky method. At the beginning, the directors were the primary decision makers for the theater. But as the group developed, the actors participated in the decisions and helped to fashion a more egalitarian structure.

The participants in the Group Theater periodically needed to integrate new members. This required readjustments and the socialization of newcomers into an existing structure. The process was akin to a family adapting to new relatives. While dealing with these challenges, the actors and directors became more aware of what connected them. They shared companionship and a sense of belonging: they aspired to some minimum job and financial security. And sometimes they had the unrealistic belief that their community was an oasis in a difficult world.

In *Organizing Genius*, Bennis and Biederman described a somewhat similar dynamic: "Great Groups become their own worlds. . . . [They] create a culture of their own—with distinctive customs, dress, jokes, even a private language. People who have been in Great Groups never forget them, although most groups do not last very long. Our suspicion is that such collaborations have a certain half-life, that, if only because of their intensity, they cannot be sustained indefinitely."[45]

Harold Clurman documented the decade-long history of the Group Theater in his book *The Fervent Years*. In the late thirties the group faced new financial crises and needed to reorganize once more. The actors took on even more decision-making responsibilities. For a few years their vision was supported by the broader society, and they had some successful seasons. But they had no enduring financial base. Eventually, the Group Theater disbanded.

Two interesting theoretical issues emerge from the history of the Group Theater. One of these is the role of conflict in collaboration. Finnish researcher Yrjo Engestrom puts a great emphasis on "knots" in cooperative interactions, which allow for hidden contradictions to emerge and be confronted by participants.[46] The actors and directors of the Group Theater found themselves in conflict a number of times. But they were willing to confront their differences and, through negotiations, to modify the structure of their organization.

Conflicts between collaborators are not always resolved. In some intense personal partnerships, for instance, in Martha Graham's brief marriage to Erick Hawkins, they failed to resolve the tension between their cooperative and competitive drives. When Hawkins first joined Graham's young company, he added a strong male idiom to a predominantly female group. He had a great impact on Graham's choreography: her themes became more charged and emotional. But Graham's extraordinary abilities overshadowed her husband's. Her biographer, Agnes de Mille, wrote that Hawkins was unable to tolerate the disparity between them. He walked out of the company and the marriage.

The sustainability of a collaboration depends on the supporting structures in which it is embedded. While dyads can draw on their existing resources, larger ensembles such as the Group Theater depend on support from the field. This concept is advanced by Csikszentmihalyi in his analysis of creativity.[47] The field consists of the institutions and individuals that select and support innovations within a domain. In the case of theater, this includes drama critics, foundations, and individual contributors. These, in turn, are affected by the larger socio-political atmosphere, or Zeitgeist, in which an art form is practiced. All these factors contribute to the development and the eventual decline of innovative institutions such as the Group Theater.

Csikszentmihalyi also described domains: "knowledge conveyed by symbols . . . bundled up in discrete domains—geometry, music, religion, legal systems, and so on. Each domain is made up of its own symbolic elements, its own rules, and generally has its own system of notation. In many ways, each domain describes an isolated little world in which a person can think and act with clarity and concentration."[48] Disciplinary and artistic socialization into domains require the appropriation of a dominant mode of thought and the acquisition of certain symbols. But these are not permanent. As Ludwik Fleck argued, great changes of thought styles require changes within communities of experienced thinkers. These transformative changes may be stimulated by periods of social unrest or by creative individuals standing at the intersection of different communities of thought.

I argue, in a similar vein, that *transformative changes require joint efforts*. The weight of disciplinary and artistic socialization is hard to overcome without assistance. One of the central claims in this work is that the construction of a new mode of thought or art form thrives best in *integrative collaboration*, the fourth pattern presented in the diagram above. These partnerships require a prolonged period of committed activity. They thrive on dialogue, risk taking, and a shared vision. In some cases, the participants construct a common set of beliefs, or ideology, which sustains them in periods of opposition or insecurity. Integrative partnerships are motivated by the desire to transform existing knowledge, thought styles, or artistic approaches into new visions.

The partnership of Picasso and Braque is an example of an integrated, transformative collaboration. Together they constructed Cubism, a new, twentieth-century approach to painting that focused on the interrelation of objects. Art historian John Berger argued that the "Moment of Cubism" is one that coincided with profound changes in science, mass communication, and our view of reality. It also coincided with social unrest and far-reaching political changes.

Berger and Fleck sought to place the social processes of knowledge transformation into the broad contexts of history. Vygotsky had a similar commitment. His theory construction was integrative; he worked closely with a number of collaborators. The authors of *Understanding Vygotsky*, van der Veer and Valsiner, wrote of his intellectual interdependency and the "web of other ideas" available to him.[49] Vygotsky relied heavily on the ideas of French, German, English, and American psychology, using and transforming them. He constructed his research approaches and his theoretical ideas jointly with his Russian collaborators, including Luria, Leontiev, Levina, and Shif, among many others. Members of this group traveled together, establishing new psychological laboratories in different parts of the young Soviet Union. They talked and argued, they planned experiments, and they polished their ideas through sustained, intense interactions.

In this collaborative context, cultural-historical theory was born. And the scholars who rediscovered the Vygotskian school, and are expanding it today, also work collaboratively. Some of their interactions follow the distributed pattern, described above, as members of the computer network "xmca." Others write, publish, or teach together. Theoretical issues are of particular interest to them, as are ideas, interpretations, and the co-construction of new knowledge. As a thought community, these scholars have a complex thinking style. They are highly interactive, at times argumentative, and are sustained by a shared vision of historically and culturally constructed human possibilities.

DYNAMICS OF COLLABORATION

This book is devoted to constructing "we-ness" in a world where the separateness of individuals is still highly prized. At the same time, under the pressure of mounting challenges to existing knowledge, collaborative thought communities are growing in numbers and effectiveness. Participants in these thought communities experience a stretching of themselves, as they share the sustained labor of changing their domains. This insight, as well as others gained through this study of creative collaboration, is not limited to the arts and sciences. Collaborative dynamics are relevant to people in diverse walks of life.

The demanding task of building sustained collaborations is particularly worthwhile when we address large questions that cannot be resolved by solo efforts. But in engaging in collaboration in Western societies, partners need to shed some of their cultural heritage, such as the powerful belief in a separate, independent self and in the glory of individual achievement. These are deeply ingrained in us. When partners commit themselves to collaboration, they challenge these beliefs. The very effort to work together, to risk an undertaking that is so different from the norm, is a creative act.

There is a deep and interesting paradox in productive collaboration. Each participant's individual capacities are deepened at the same time that participants discover the benefits of reciprocity. But the achievement of productive collaborations requires sustained time and effort. It requires the shaping of a shared language, the pleasures and risks of honest dialogue, and the search for a common ground.

In collaborative endeavors we learn from each other. By teaching what we know, we engage in mutual appropriation. In partnerships we see ourselves through the eyes of others, and through their support we dare to explore new parts of ourselves. We can live better with temporary failures as we rely on our partners' strengths. By joining with others we accept their gift of confidence, and through interdependence, we achieve competence and connection. *Together we create our futures.*

APPENDIX

The "Collaboration Q-sort" was designed with the assistance of my former graduate student, Kathryn Miller, to elicit information concerning various aspects of collaborators' joint activities. The format of the instrument follows one originally designed by British psychologist William Stephenson, and has been used widely in personality research since its inception.[1]

The Q-sort items were based on early interviews with collaborative partners who were asked about their motivation, collaborative roles, and working methods. Once the items were finalized, they were printed separately on cards. The stack of cards is arranged into a bell-shaped distribution by the individuals, a process that frequently requires a multiple ordering. The participants place items most characteristic of their collaboration at the high end of the distribution and items least characteristic at the low end. This mode of placing the cards allows for easy comparisons across participants and for statistical analyses of placement values both within pairs and among larger populations.

For this study, the comments elicited from collaborative partners reflecting similarities and differences in their sorts provided additional valuable data.

COLLABORATION Q-SORT ITEMS

Note: The items use the singular or the plural of the word "collaborator" based on the specific circumstances of the participant.

1. I rely upon my collaborator to connect observation and data with my theoretical constructs.
2. I don't think a project is as valuable when someone else helps.
3. I meet new potential collaborators at conferences and professional meetings.
4. Clarity and sequential logic are essential to my collaborative work.

5. I like to write down my ideas before I share them with others.
6. My collaborator is more involved in the details than I am.
7. I do my best work alone.
8. My collaborator and I have matched our work rhythms in order to do our work.
9. I don't have the patience to define a problem by thinking with another person.
10. My collaborator needs my total attention when we are discussing an issue, while I can attend to several things at once.
11. When I'm working with my collaborator on a project, my personal life becomes far less important.
12. The female collaborators with whom I work are more nurturing and relationship oriented than male collaborators.
13. My collaborator and I need to schedule ample time for integrating our diverse approaches.
14. Collaboration helps me to overcome the loneliness of individual work.
15. Sometimes it is important to get away from our normal environment to discuss our project and ideas.
16. I try to construct a working climate where our time and privacy are protected.
17. I sometimes need time away from my collaborator and a chance to focus on my individual work.
18. My collaborator is brilliant and also domineering.
19. I prefer to have written specifications of what is to be accomplished.
20. I seem to overwhelm my collaborator with my pace and expectations.
21. Because of our collaboration I frequently fail to receive credit for my accomplishments.
22. There must be an aesthetic quality to the project in order for me to work on it.
23. I wish my collaborator would ask me before discussing our work with other colleagues.
24. My preferred working style does not blend easily with my collaborator(s).
25. My collaborator and I are both capable of working long hours.
26. I don't have to explain myself to my collaborator, I can just use key words.
27. The process of thinking together with my collaborator was informal in the beginning.

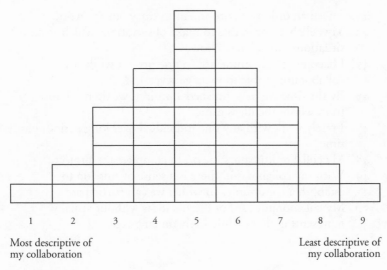

1	2	3	4	5	6	7	8	9

Most descriptive of
my collaboration

Least descriptive of
my collaboration

Q-sort distribution

28. Sometimes my collaborator's visibility affects our relationship negatively.
29. Excessive criticism causes a collaboration to fail.
30. Sometimes my collaborator and I exchange ideas while we walk.
31. In a good collaborative environment, one's ideas can be made explicit through questioning and dialogue.
32. With my collaborator, I am more careful about the way I challenge his/her ideas.
33. Sometimes my collaborator and I do different parts of the same project.
34. My collaborator is able to function amongst clutter, while I need to have everything neat and orderly.
35. I expect my collaborator to be a critic of my work.
36. Sometimes I draw pictures when I start working on a new collaborative project.
37. My collaborator and I rarely argue over methods.
38. I find male collaborators more efficient and product oriented than female collaborators.
39. My collaborator creates theoretical models to help our thinking processes.
40. My collaborator and I write together at the typewriter or word processor.
41. My collaborator and I are committed to state-of-the-art technology.
42. With my collaborator, I can talk at the speed of thinking.

43. I need an orderly environment to carry out my work.
44. My collaborator is able to make observations which make a situation immediately clear.
45. I become totally immersed in one project while my collaborator is able to manage several.
46. By the time we have finished a project, we do not know from whom the ideas came.
47. I rarely work with any one individual over long periods of time.
48. My collaborator spurs me on to complete the project.
49. With my collaborator, there is a sense of mission to establish a community in which we can participate.
50. My collaborator cannot discuss ideas without visually representing them while I rely on language.

NOTES

Introduction

1. As opposed to the word's use during World War II, when "collaboration" referred to the collusion of politicians with German officials in countries occupied by the Nazi regime.

2. Bruffee, K. A. (1993). *Collaborative learning: Higher education, interdependence, and the authority of knowledge.* Baltimore: Johns Hopkins University Press, p. 172.

3. Engestrom, Y., & Middleton, D. (Eds.). (1998). *Cognition and communication at work.* Cambridge: Cambridge University Press. Gray, B. (1989). *Collaborating: Finding common ground for multiparty problems.* San Francisco: Jossey-Bass Publishers. Schrage, M. (1990). *Shared minds: The new technologies of collaboration.* New York: Random House. Weick, K., & Roberts, K. H. (1993). Collective mind in organizations: Heedful interrelating on flight decks. *Administrative Science Quarterly, 38,* 357–381. Weick, K. E. (1995). *Sensemaking in organizations.* Thousand Oaks, CA: Sage Publications.

4. Becker, H. S. (1982). *Art worlds.* Berkeley: University of California Press, p. 25.

5. Kushner, T. (1996). *Angels in America, Part II: Perestroika.* New York: Theatre Communications Group, p. 149.

6. Chadwick, W., & de Courtivron, I. (Eds.). (1996). *Significant others: Creativity and intimate partnership.* London: Thames & Hudson.

7. Ibid., p. 9.

8. Pycior, H. M., Slack, N. G., & Abir-Am, P. G. (Eds.). (1996). *Creative couples in the sciences.* New Brunswick: Rutgers University Press, p. 4.

9. Vygotsky, L. S. (1978). *Mind in society: The development of higher psychological processes.* Cambridge, MA: Harvard University Press. See particularly chapter 6.

10. Wertsch, J. V. (1998). *Mind as action.* New York: Oxford University Press, p. 116.

11. Gilligan, C. (1982). *In a different voice: Psychological theory and women's development.* Cambridge, MA: Harvard University Press.

12. Bakhurst, D., & Sypnowich, C. (Eds.). (1995). *The social self.* London: Sage Publications.

13. John-Steiner, V. (1999). Sociocultural and feminist theory: Mutuality and relevance. In S. Chaiklin, M. Hedegaard, & U. J. Jensen (Eds.), *Activity theory and social practice* (pp. 201–224). Aarhus, Denmark: Aarhus University Press, p. 210.

14. Belenky, M. F., Clinchy, B. M., Goldberger, N. R., & Tarule, J. M. (1997). *Women's ways of knowing: The development of self, voice, and mind* (10th anniversary ed.). New York: Basic Books.

Chapter 1. Joined Lives and Shared Work

1. Beauvoir, S. D. (1968). *Hard times: Force of circumstances, 1952–1962 (Autobiography of Simone de Beauvoir)*. Harmondsworth: Penguin Books, p. 659.
2. Durant, W., & Durant, A. (1977). *Dual autobiography*. New York: Simon and Schuster.
3. Ibid., pp. 178–179.
4. Ibid., p. 179.
5. Damon, W., & Phelps, E. (1989). Critical distinctions among three approaches to peer education. *International Journal of Educational Review, 58*(2), 9–19.
6. Durant & Durant, *Dual autobiography*, p. 261.
7. Ibid., p. 288.
8. Ibid., p. 305.
9. Ibid., p. 318.
10. Ibid., p. 323.
11. Ibid., p. 332.
12. Chadwick, W., & de Courtivron, I. (Eds.). (1996). *Significant others: Creativity and intimate partnership*. London: Thames & Hudson, p. 72.
13. Madsen, A. (1977). *Hearts and minds: The common journey of Simone de Beauvoir and John Paul Sartre*. New York: William Morrow.
14. Beauvoir, S. D. (1984). *Adieux: A farewell to Sartre*. New York: Pantheon Books.
15. Vygotsky, L. (1986). Thought and language (A. Kozulin, Trans.). Cambridge, MA: MIT Press.
16. Tickner, L. (1996). The left-handed marriage: Vanessa Bell and Duncan Grant. In W. Chadwick & I. D. Courtivron (Eds.), *Significant others*, p. 81.
17. Wallace, D. B., & Gruber, H. E. (Eds.). (1989). *Creative people at work: Twelve cognitive case studies*. New York: Oxford University Press.
18. Block, G., & Drucker, M. (1992). *Rescuers: Portraits of moral courage in the Holocaust*. New York: Holmes & Meyer.
19. Ibid., p. 254.
20. Einstein, A., & Maric, M. (1992). *The love letters* (S. Smith, Trans.). Princeton, NJ: Princeton University Press.
21. Pais, A. (1982). *Subtle is the Lord: The science and the life of Albert Einstein*. New York: Oxford University Press.
22. Troemel-Ploetz, S. (1990). Mileva Einstein-Maric: The woman who did Einstein's mathematics. *Women's Studies International Forum, 11*(5), 41–432.
23. McCarthey, S. J., & McMahon, S. (1992). From convention to invention: Peer interaction during writing. In R. Hertz-Lazarowitz & N. Miller (Eds.), *Interaction in cooperative groups: The theoretical anatomy of group learning*. New York: Cambridge University Press.

24. John-Steiner, V. (1997). *Notebooks of the mind: Explorations of thinking* (2nd ed.). New York: Oxford University Press.

25. Ibid.

26. Ibid.

27. Aaron, J. (1991). *A double singleness: Gender and the writings of Charles and Mary Lamb.* Oxford: Claridon Press.

28. Ibid., pp. 207–208.

29. Bank, S., & Kahn, M. D. (1982). Intense sibling loyalties. In E. M. Lamb & B. Sutton-Smith (Eds.), *Sibling relationships: Their nature and significance across the lifespan* (pp. 251–266). Hillsdale, NJ: Lawrence Erlbaum Associates.

30. Weisner, T. S. (1982). Sibling interdependence and child caretaking: A cross-cultural view. In Lamb & Sutton-Smith, *Sibling relationships.*

31. Zukow-Goldring, P. (1995). Sibling caregiving: Being and becoming and giving and getting. In M. H. Bornstein (Ed.), *Handbook of parenting* (Vol. 3). Mahwah, NJ: Lawrence Erlbaum Associates.

32. Stillinger, J. (1991). *Multiple authorship and the myth of solitary genius.* New York: Oxford University Press, p. 72.

33. Wallace, D. (1990). Sibling relationships in creative lives. In M. J. A. Howe (Ed.), *Encouraging the development of exceptional skills and talents.* Leicester: British Psychological Society Books, p. 82.

34. Ibid., p. 85.

35. Ibid., p. 86.

36. Dreyfus, H. L., & Dreyfus, S. E. (1988). *Mind over machine: The power of human intuition and expertise in the era of the computer.* New York: Free Press.

37. Ibid., p. 7.

38. Ibid., p. 11.

39. Hamilton, N. (1978). *The brothers Mann: The lives of Heinrich and Thomas Mann, 1871–1950 and 1875–1955.* New Haven, CT: Yale University Press.

40. Ibid., p. 37.

41. Ibid., p. 168.

42. Ibid., p. 42.

43. Gruber, H. E. (1989). The evolving systems approach to creative work. In Wallace & Gruber, *Creative people at work,* pp. 3–24.

44. Zukow-Goldring, Sibling caregiving, p. 28.

45. Curie, M. (1923). *Pierre Curie.* New York: Macmillan, p. 91.

46. Ibid., p. 104.

47. Pycior, H. M. (1987). Marie Curie's anti-natural path. In P. G. Abir-Am & D. Outram (Eds.), *Uneasy careers and intimate lives: Women in science, 1789–1979.* New Brunswick, NJ: Rutgers University Press, p. 200.

48. Chavkin, A., & Chavkin, N. F. (Eds.). (1994). *Conversations with Louise Erdrich and Michael Dorris.* Jackson: University Press of Mississippi, p. 11.

49. After this chapter was written, Michael Dorris committed suicide. He had a lifelong depressive disorder. In a book written after his death, Louise Erdrich honors his memory and their long partnership in her dedication.

50. Ibid., p. 26.

51. Ibid., p. 26.

52. Ibid., p. 35.

53. Ibid., p. 177.

54. Ibid., p. 179.

55. Ibid.

56. Art Bridgman and Myrna Packer's presentation at Dance with Dance Collaborations, Movement Research Center, New York, March 1993.

Chapter 2. Partnerships in Science

1. Pycior, H. M. (1996). Pierre Curie and his eminent partner Mme. Curie. In H. M. Pycior, N. S. Slack, & P. G. Abir-Am (Eds.), *Creative couples in the sciences.* New Brunswick, NJ: Rutgers University Press, p. 46.

2. Ibid., p. 46.

3. Curie, M. (1923). *Pierre Curie.* New York: Macmillan, p. 48.

4. Pycior, Pierre Curie and Mme. Curie, p. 46.

5. Hadamard, J. (1945). *The psychology of invention in the mathematical field.* Princeton, NJ: Princeton University Press, pp. 142–143.

6. Hoffmann, B. (1972). *Albert Einstein: Creator and rebel.* New York: Viking Press.

7. Holton, G. J. (1973). *Thematic origins of scientific thought: Kepler to Einstein.* Cambridge, MA: Harvard University Press, p. 367.

8. Ibid., p. 368.

9. Einstein, A. (1972, March 27). Unpublished papers of Albert Einstein. *New York Times,* p. 26.

10. Hoffmann, *Albert Einstein,* p. 57.

11. Holton, G. J. (1973). *Thematic origins of scientific thought: Kepler to Einstein.* Cambridge, MA: Harvard University Press, p. 354.

12. Ibid.

13. Pais, A. (1982). *Subtle is the Lord: The science and the life of Albert Einstein.* New York: Oxford University Press, p. 178.

14. Ibid., p. 201.

15. Holton, *Thematic origins of scientific thought,* p. 380.

16. Pais, *Subtle is the Lord,* p. 213.

17. Einstein, A. (1973). *Ideas and opinions.* New York: Dell, p. 235.

18. Miller, A. I. (1984). *Imagery in scientific thought.* Boston: Birkhauser, p. 138.

19. Ibid., p. 142.

20. Weisskopf, V. F. (1991). *The joy of insight.* New York: Basic Books, pp. 48–49.

21. Heisenberg, W. (1971). *Physics and beyond: Encounters and conversations.* New York: Harper & Row, pp. 59–60.

22. Holton, *Thematic origins of scientific thought,* p. 118.

23. Weisskopf, *The joy of insight,* p. 66.

24. Holton, *Thematic origins of scientific thought,* p. 139.

25. Ibid., p. 148.

26. Ibid., p. 118.

27. Weisskopf, *The joy of insight,* p. 65.

28. Ibid., p. 71.

29. Blaedel, N. (1988). *Harmony and unity: The life of Niels Bohr.* Madison, WI: Springer-Verlag, p. 19.

30. Hersh, R. (1997). *What is mathematics, really?* New York: Oxford University Press, pp. 35–37.

31. Sykes, C. (1994). *No ordinary genius: The illustrated Richard Feynman.* New York: W.W. Norton, p. 18.

32. Gleick, J. (1993). *Genius: The life and science of Richard Feynman.* New York: Vintage, p. 131.

33. Sykes, *No ordinary genius*, p. 18.

34. Ibid., p. 78.

35. Ibid., p. 73.

36. Dyson, F. (1979). *Disturbing the universe.* New York: Harper & Row, pp. 63–68.

37. Sykes, *No ordinary genius*, p. 76.

38. McGrayne, S. B. (1993). *Nobel prize women in science: Their lives, struggles, and momentous discoveries.* Secaucus, NJ: Carol Publishing Group.

39. Pycior, Slack, & Abir-Am, *Creative couples in the sciences.*

40. McGrayne, *Nobel prize women in science*, p. 101.

41. Ibid., p. 104.

42. Pais, *Subtle is the Lord*, p. 404.

43. Davis, P. J., & Hersh, R. (1980). *The mathematical experience.* Boston: Birkhauser.

44. Stevenson, H. W., & Stigler, J. W. (1992). *The learning gap: Why our schools are failing and what we can learn from Japanese and Chinese education.* New York: Summit Books.

45. Courant, R., & Friedrichs, K. O. (1948). *Supersonic flow and shock waves.* New York: Interscience Publishers.

46. Pais, *Subtle is the Lord*, p. 412.

47. Ibid., pp. 423–449.

48. Pais, A. (1991). *Niels Bohr's times.* Oxford: Claridon Press, p. 314.

49. Chomsky, N. (1965). *Aspects of the theory of syntax.* Cambridge, MA: MIT Press.

50. Chomsky, N. (1988). *Language and problems of knowledge: The Managua lectures.* Cambridge, MA: MIT Press.

51. Pinker, S. (1994). *The language instinct: How the mind creates language.* New York: William Morrow.

52. Bates, E., Dale, P., & Thel, D. (1997). Individual differences and their implications. In P. Fletcher & B. MacWhinney (Eds.), *The handbook of child language* (pp. 96–151). Oxford: Blackwell Publishers. Berko-Gleason, J., & Weintraub, S. (1978). Input language and the acquisition of communicative competence. In K. E. Nelson (Ed.), *Children's language* (Vol. 1). New York: Gardner Press. Halliday, M. A. K. (1985). *An introduction to functional grammar.* London: Edward Arnold. Slobin, D. I. (1985). *The cross-linguistic study of language acquisition* (Vols. 1–5). Hillsdale, NJ: Lawrence Erlbaum Associates.

53. Langacker, R. (1987). *Foundations of cognitive grammar* (Vols. 1–2). Stanford, CA: Stanford University Press.

54. Deacon, T. W. (1997). *The symbolic species: The co-evolution of language and the brain.* New York: W. W. Norton.

55. Damasio, A. R. (1994). *Descartes' error: Emotion, reason, and the human brain.* New York: G. P. Putnam's Sons.

56. Ibid., p. 183.

57. Ibid.

58. Ibid., p. 200.

59. Holton, *Thematic origins of scientific thought*, p. 118.

60. Vygotsky, L. S. (1978). *Mind in society: The development of higher psychological processes.* Cambridge, MA: Harvard University Press. (See his introduction for a description of the zone of proximal development.)

61. Wertsch, J. V. (1998). *Mind as action.* New York: Oxford University Press.

Chapter 3. Patterns of Collaboration among Artists

1. Louis, M. (1993, July 18). Collaborating with a perfectionist and visionary. *New York Times*, p. 24.

2. Ibid.

3. Kushner, T. (1996). *Angels in America, Part II: Perestroika.* New York: Theatre Communications Group, p. 145. (Emphasis mine.)

4. Ibid., p. 155.

5. Berger, J. (1965). *The success and failure of Picasso.* Harmondsworth, England: Penguin Books, p. 59.

6. Richardson, J. (1991). *The life of Picasso* (Vol. 1). New York: Random House, p. 29.

7. Gardner, H. (1993). *Creating minds: An anatomy of creativity seen through the lives of Freud, Einstein, Picasso, Stravinsky, Eliot, Graham, and Gandhi.* New York: Basic Books, p. 141.

8. Richardson, *The life of Picasso*, p. 55.

9. See John-Steiner, V. (1997). *Notebooks of the mind: Explorations of thinking* (rev. ed.). New York: Oxford University Press, chap. 2.

10. Gardner, *Creating minds*, p. 147.

11. Gruber, H. E. (1989). The evolving systems approach to creative work. In D. B. Wallace & H. E. Gruber (Eds.), *Creative people at work: Twelve cognitive case studies* (pp. 3–24). New York: Oxford University Press, p. 11.

12. Ibid., p. 12.

13. Richardson, *The life of Picasso*, p. 334.

14. Ibid.

15. Ibid., p. 475.

16. Picasso, P. (1986). *Je suis le cahier: The sketchbooks of Pablo Picasso* (A. Glimcher & M. Glimcher, Trans.). Boston: Atlantic Monthly Press.

17. Berger, J. (1965). *The success and failure of Picasso.* Harmondsworth, England: Penguin Books, p. 73.

18. Richardson, *The life of Picasso*, p. 68.

19. Ibid., p. 105.

20. Berger, *The success and failure of Picasso*, p. 59.

21. Picasso as quoted in Richardson, *The life of Picasso*, p. 124.

22. Gilot, F., & Lake, C. (1964). *Life with Picasso.* New York: McGraw-Hill, p. 76.

23. Richardson, *The life of Picasso*, pp. 194–195.

24. Ibid., p. 195.

25. Ibid., p. 236.

26. Ibid., p. 238.

27. Ibid., pp. 245–246.

28. Ibid., p. 249.

29. Ibid., p. 256.

30. Berger, *The success and failure of Picasso*, pp. 69–70.

31. Bennis, W. & Biederman, P. W. (1997). *Organizing genius: The secrets of creative collaboration.* Reading, MA: Addison-Wesley.

32. Becker, H. S. (1982). *Art worlds.* Berkeley: University of California Press, p. 13.

33. Csikszentmihalyi, M. (1996). *Creativity: Flow and the psychology of discovery and invention.* New York: HarperCollins, p. 34.

34. Fischer, E. (1963). *The necessity of art: A Marxist approach* (A. Bostock, Trans.). Baltimore: Penguin Books, p. 13.

35. Ibid., p. 8.

36. Stuckey, C. F. (Ed.). (1985). *Monet: A retrospective.* New York: Hugh Lauter Levine Associates, Inc., p. 27.

37. Ibid., p. 218.

38. Bennis, & Biederman, *Organizing genius.*

39. Hulsker, J. (1990). *Vincent and Theo Van Gogh: A dual biography.* (ed. by J. M. Miller). Ann Arbor: Fuller Publications, p. 162.

40. Bair, D. (1995). *Anais Nin: A biography.* New York: Putnam & Company, p. 235.

41. Nin, A. (1932). *D. H. Lawrence: An unprofessional study.* Paris: E. W. Titus.

42. Bair, *Anais Nin*, p. 97.

43. Martin, J. (1978). *Always merry and bright: The life of Henry Miller.* Santa Barbara, CA: Capra Press, p. 278.

44. Nin, A., & Miller, H. (1987). *A literate passion: The letters of Anais Nin and Henry Miller, 1932–1953.* San Diego: Harcourt Brace Jovanovich, p. 202.

45. Bair, D. (1995). *Anais Nin: A biography.* New York: Putnam & Company, p. 116.

46. Ibid., p. 138.

47. Ibid., p. 153.

48. Jordan, J. V., Kaplan, A. G., Miller, J. B., Stiver, I. P., & Surrey, J. L. (Eds.). (1991). *Women's growth in connection: Writings from the Stone Center.* New York: Guilford Press.

49. Vygotsky as cited in John-Steiner, V., & Mahn, H. (1996). Sociocultural approaches to learning and development: A Vygotskian framework. *Educational Psychologist, 31*, 191–206 (p. 192).

50. John-Steiner, V. (1989). Beyond the transmission of knowledge: A Vygotskian perspective on creativity. In R. Bjorson & M. R. Waldman (Eds.), *The university of the future* (pp. 51–68). Columbus: Center for Comparative Studies in the Humanities, Ohio State University. John-Steiner, V. (1997). *Notebooks of the mind: Explorations of thinking* (rev. ed.). New York: Oxford University Press, p. 234.

51. Gruber, The evolving systems approach to creative work, p. 13.

52. Interview with Bill Conte and Suki John in New York City, November 1992, telephone follow-up interviews, January 1998.

53. Mille, A. D. (1991). *Martha: The life and work of Martha Graham.* New York: Random House, pp. 231–232.

54. Hawkins, E. (1992). *The body is a clear place and other statements on dance.* Pennington, NJ: Princeton Book Company, p. ix.

55. Bennis & Biederman, *Organizing genius*, p. 216.

56. Robinson, R. (1989). *Georgia O'Keeffe: A life.* New York: Harper-Collins, p. 56.

57. Ibid.

58. Interview with Zachariah and Gail Rieke in Santa Fe, NM, February 1997.

59. Zorpette, G. (Summer, 1994). Dynamic duos. *ARTnews,* p. 167.

60. Collaborative research project funded by NSF Grant #SBR-9423277. Participants include Vera John-Steiner, Michele Minnis, Robert Weber, Holbrook Mahn, and Teresa Meehan.

61. Sagan, F. (1985). *With fondest regards* (C. Donougher, Trans.). New York: E. P. Dutton, pp. 99–101.

62. Clurman, H. (1975). *The fervent years: The Group Theatre and the thirties.* New York: Harcourt Brace Jovanovich, p. 72.

63. Ibid., p. 41.

64. Feldman, D. H. (1994). *Beyond universals in cognitive development* (2nd ed.). Norwood: Ablex, pp. 168–169.

65. Ibid., p. 182.

66. Clurman, *The fervent years*, p. 95.

67. Ibid., p. 43.

68. Ibid., p. 44.

69. Ibid., p. 103.

70. Middleton, D. (1998). Talking work: Argument, common knowledge, and improvisation in teamwork. In Y. Engestrom & D. Middleton (Eds.), *Cognition and communication at work* (pp. 233–256). Cambridge: Cambridge University Press.

71. Ibid., pp. 193–194.

72. Ibid., p. 211.

73. Clurman, *The fervent years*, p. 247.

74. Csikszentmihalyi, *Creativity*, pp. 36–50.

75. Clurman, H. (1974). *All people are famous (instead of an autobiography).* New York: Harcourt Brace Jovanovich, p. 103.

76. Lave, J., & Wenger, E. (1991). *Situated learning: Legitimate peripheral participation.* Cambridge: Cambridge University Press.

77. Ibid., p. 98.

78. Engestrom, & Middleton, *Cognition and communication at work.*

79. Goffman, E. (1959). *The presentation of self in everyday life.* Garden City, NY: Doubleday.

80. Chadwick, W., & Courtivron, I. D. (Eds.). (1996*). Significant others: Creativity and intimate partnership.* London: Thames & Hudson, p. 13.

81. Taper, B. (1974). *Balanchine: A biography.* New York: Macmillan, p. 184.

82. Ibid., pp. 104–195.

83. Ibid., p. 267.

84. Ibid., p. 268.

85. Stravinsky, I., & Craft, R. (1966). *Themes and episodes.* New York: Knopf, p. 25.

86. Taper, *Balanchine*, p. 361.

87. John-Steiner, V. (1985). *Notebooks of the mind: Explorations of thinking.* New York: Harper & Row, pp. 52–53.

88. John-Steiner, V. (1997). *Notebooks of the mind: Explorations of thinking* (rev. ed.). New York: Oxford University Press.

89. Taper, *Balanchine.*

Chapter 4. A Chorus of Voices: Women in Collaboration

1. Kaplan, C., & Rose, E. C. (1993). Strange bedfellows: Feminist collaboration. *Signs: Journal of Women in Culture and Society, 18*(3), 565.

2. Ibid., p. 549.

3. Ibid., p. 555.

4. Ibid., p. 556.

5. Ibid., p. 557.

6. Miller, J. B. (1976). *Toward a new psychology of women.* Boston: Beacon Press.

7. Gilligan, C. (1982). *In a different voice: Psychological theory and women's development.* Cambridge, MA: Harvard University Press.

8. Interview with DeWitt-Morette in Austin, Texas, January 1993.

9. Chouguet-Bruhat, Y., DeWitt-Morette, C., & Dillard-Bleick, M. (1977). *Analysis, manifolds, and physics.* Amsterdam: North Holland Publishing Company. Chouguet-Bruhat, Y., DeWitt-Morette, C., & Dillard-Bleick, M. (1982). *Analysis, manifolds, and physics* (2nd rev. ed.). Amsterdam: North Holland Publishing Company.

10. Elbow, P. (1973). *Writing without teachers.* London: Oxford University Press.

11. Ibid., p. 150.

12. Ibid.

13. Clinchy, B. M. (1996). Connected and separate knowing: Toward a marriage of two minds. In N. R. Goldberger, J. M. Tarule, B. M. Clinchy, & M. F. Belenky (Eds.), *Knowledge, difference and power: Essays inspired by "Women's ways of knowing"* (pp. 205–247). New York: Basic Books, p. 207.

14. Traweek, S. (1988). *Beamtimes and lifetimes: The world of high energy physicists.* Cambridge, MA: Harvard University Press, p. 162.

15. Weisskopf, V. F. (1991). *The joy of insight.* New York: Basic Books, p. 324.

16. Midgley, M. (1992). *Science as salvation: A modern myth and its meaning.* New York: Routledge, p. 41.

17. Belenky, M. F., Clinchy, B. M., Goldberger, N. R., & Tarule, J. M. (1986). *Women's ways of knowing: The development of self, voice and mind.* New York: Basic Books, p. 134.

18. Midgley, *Science as salvation*, p. 61.

19. Miller, J. B. (1976). *Toward a new psychology of women*. Boston: Beacon Press.

20. Gilligan, *In a different voice*.

21. Belenky, Clinchy, Goldberger, & Tarule, *Women's ways of knowing*. See also the 10th anniversary edition (1997).

22. Harding, S. (1996). Gendered ways of knowing and the "Epistemological Crisis" of the West. In Goldberger, Tarule, Clinchy, & Belenky, *Knowledge, difference and power*, pp. 431–454.

23. Schor, N. (1994). The essentialism which is not one. In N. Schor & E. Weed (Eds.), *The essential difference*. Bloomington and Indianapolis: Indiana University Press, p. 42.

24. Hutchins, E. (1996). Review symposium: Response to reviewers of "Cognition in the Wild." *Mind, Culture, and Activity, 3* (1), 64–68.

25. Ruddick, S. (1996). Reason's "Femininity": A case for connected knowledge. In Goldberger, Tarule, Clinchy, & Belenky (Eds.), *Knowledge, difference, and power*, pp. 248–273.

26. Ibid., p. 263.

27. Whiting, B., & Whiting, J. W. M. (1975). *Children of six cultures*. Cambridge, MA: Harvard University Press.

28. Cole, M., & Cole, S. (1989). *The development of children*. New York: Scientific American Books.

29. Rubin, J. Z., Provenzano, F. J., & Luria, Z. (1974). The eye of the beholder: Parents' view on sex of newborns. *American Journal of Orthpsychiatry, 44*, 512–519.

30. Miller, J. B. (1991). The development of women's sense of self. In J. V. Jordan, A. G. Kaplan, J. B. Miller, I. P. Stiver, & J. L. Surrey (Eds.), *Women's growth in connection: Writings from the Stone Center* (pp. 11–26). New York: Guilford Press, p. 14.

31. Dyson, A. H. (1995). Writing children: Reinventing the development of childhood literacy. *Written Communication, 12*, 4–46.

32. Brown, L., & Gilligan, C. (1992). *Meeting at the crossroads: Women's psychology and girls' development*. Cambridge, MA: Harvard University Press. Gilligan, C., Lyons, N., & Hamner, T. (Eds.). (1990). *Making connections*. Cambridge: Harvard University Press.

33. Broverman, I. K., Broverman, D. M., Clarkson, F. E., Rosenkrantz, P. S., & Vogel, S. R. (1970). Sex-role stereotypes and clinical judgements of mental health. *Journal of Consulting and Clinical Psychology, 34*, 1–7.

34. Surrey, J. L. (1991). The "Self-in-Relation": A theory of women's development. In Jordan, Kaplan, Miller, Stiver, & Surrey, *Women's growth in connection*, pp. 51–66.

35. Ruddick, S., & Daniels, P. (1977). *Working it out: 23 women writers, artists, scientists, and scholars talk about their lives and work*. New York: Pantheon Books, p. xvi.

36. Leakey, R. E. (1994). *The origin of humankind*. New York: Basic Books.

37. Draper, P. (1975). !Kung women: Contrasts in sexual egalitarianism in the foraging and sedentary contexts. In R. Reiter (Ed.), *Toward an anthropology of women* (pp. 77–109). New York: Monthly Review Press.

38. Leacock, E. (1977). Women's status in egalitarian society: Implications for social evolution. *Current Anthropology, 19*, 247–275.

39. Whyte, M. K. (1978). The status of women in preindustrial societies. Princeton, NJ: Princeton University Press, p. 167.

40. Eisler, R. (1987). *The chalice and the blade: Our history, our future.* New York: Harper & Row, p. 27.

41. Ibid., p. 37.

42. Childe as quoted in Eisler, Ibid., p. 52.

43. Transcript from interview with Ochs and Schieffelin in Palo Alto, CA, April 1990.

44. Transcript from interview with Fine and MacPherson, May 1993.

45. Belenky, Clinchy, Goldberger, & Tarule (1997), *Women's ways of knowing,* p. 3.

46. Ibid.

47. The term "field" was introduced by the creativity researcher Mihaly Csikszentmihalyi. He argues that creativity cannot be understood solely at the individual level. Characteristics of the domain—for instance, geometry, music, or gender studies—have to be analyzed, and the relation of the domain to the culture understood. The "field" means the governing institutions which support or inhibit developments in the domain, such as granting agencies, experts who have decision-making power, patrons, and journal editors. See Csikszentmihalyi, M. (1996). *Creativity: Flow and the psychology of discovery and invention.* New York: HarperCollins.

48. Jordan, Kaplan, Miller, Stiver, & Surrey, *Women's growth in connection,* p. v.

49. Ibid.

50. Gilligan, *In a different voice.* Gilligan, Lyons, & Hamner, *Making connections.*

51. Interview with Carol Gilligan, July 1996.

52. Belenky, Clinchy, Goldberger, & Tarule (1997), *Women's ways of knowing,* p. 5.

53. Schieffelin, B. B., & Ochs, E. (1996). The microgenesis of competence: Methodology in language socialization. In D. I. Slobin, J. Gerhardt, A. Kyratzis, & J. Guo (Eds.), *Social interaction, social context, and language: Essays in honor of Susan Ervin-Tripp* (pp. 251–263). Hillsdale, NJ: Lawrence Erlbaum Associates, p. 251.

54. Goldberger, Tarule, Clinchy, & Belenky, *Knowledge, difference and power,* p. 1.

55. Preface to Belenky, Clinchy, Goldberger, & Tarule (1997), *Women's ways of knowing,* p. 9.

56. Ibid., p. 14.

57. Fleck, L. (1979). *Genesis and development of a scientific fact.* Chicago: University of Chicago Press, p. 158.

58. Belenky, Clinchy, Goldberger, & Tarule (1997), *Women's ways of knowing,* p. 7.

59. Bookman, M. (1996). *Phantoms slain: A Vygotskian reading of Carol Gilligan.* Unpublished manuscript, p. 23.

60. Gilligan interview.

61. Belenky, Clinchy, Goldberger, & Tarule (1997), *Women's ways of knowing*, p. 11.

62. Ibid.

63. Keller, E. F. (1987). *Reflections on gender and science.* New Haven, CT: Yale University Press, p. 117.

64. Ruddick, Reason's "Femininity," p. 265.

Chapter 5. Felt Knowledge: Emotional Dynamics of Collaboration

1. Gardner, H. (1993). *Creating minds: An anatomy of creativity seen through the lives of Freud, Einstein, Picasso, Stravinsky, Eliot, Graham, and Gandhi.* New York: Basic Books, p. 74.

2. Bakhurst, D., & Sypnowich, C. (Eds.). (1995). *The social self.* London: Sage Publications, p. 6.

3. Pycior, H. M. (1996). Pierre Curie and his eminent partner Mme. Curie. In H. M. Pycior, N. S. Slack, & P. G. Abir-Am (Eds.), *Creative couples in the sciences* (pp. 39–56). New Brunswick, NJ: Rutgers University Press, p. 46.

4. Ibid.

5. Quinn, S. (1995). *Marie Curie: A life.* New York: Simon & Schuster, p. 154.

6. Pycior, Pierre Curie and Mme. Curie, p. 48.

7. Quinn, *Marie Curie*, p. 154.

8. Ibid., p. 425.

9. McGrayne, S. B. (1993). *Nobel prize women in science: Their lives, struggles, and momentous discoveries.* Secaucus, NJ: Carol Publishing Group, p. 187.

10. Bennis, W. & Biederman, P. W. (1997). *Organizing genius: The secrets of creative collaboration.* Reading, MA: Addison-Wesley, p. 30.

11. Csikszentmihalyi, M. (1996). *Creativity: Flow and the psychology of discovery and invention.* New York: HarperCollins, p. 57.

12. Whitman, W. (1950). *Leaves of grass.* New York: Modern Library, p. 74.

13. Beauvoir, S. D. (1984). *Adieux: A farewell to Sartre.* New York: Pantheon Books, p. 168.

14. Davis, P. J., & Hersh, R. (1980). *The mathematical experience.* Boston: Birkhauser.

15. Gardner, *Creating minds*, p. 147.

16. Tickner, L. (1996). The left-handed marriage: Vanessa Bell and Duncan Grant. In W. Chadwick & I. de Courtivron (Eds.), *Significant others: Creativity and intimate partnerships* (pp. 65–81). London: Thames & Hudson, p. 80.

17. Ibid., p. 122.

18. See chapter 6 in Vygotsky, L. S. (1978). *Mind in society: The development of higher psychological processes.* Cambridge, MA: Harvard University Press.

19. Surrey, J. L. (1991). The "Self-in-Relation": A theory of women's development. In J. V. Jordan, A. G. Kaplan, J. B. Miller, I. P. Stiver, & J. L. Surrey (Eds.), *Women's growth in connection: Writings from the Stone Center* (pp. 51–66). New York: Guilford Press, p. 58.

20. Madsen, A. (1977). *Hearts and minds: The common journey of Simone de Beauvior and John-Paul Sartre.* New York: William Morrow, p. 91.

21. Ibid., p. 78.

22. Evans, M. (1985). *Simone de Beauvoir: A feminist mandarin.* London: Tavistock, p. 16.

23. Beauvoir, *Adieux*, p. 298.

24. Ibid., p. 304.

25. Maccoby, E. E. (1990). Gender and relationships: A developmental account. *The American Psychologist, 45*, 513–520.

26. Csikszentmihalyi, *Creativity*, p. 313.

27. Richardson, J. (1996). *The life of Picasso* (Vol. 2). New York: Random House, p. 238.

28. MacPherson, P., & Fine, M. (1995). Hungry for an us: Adolescent girls and adult women negotiating territories of race, gender, class, difference. *Feminism and Psychology, 5*, 181–200.

29. Feynman, R. P. (1994). *No ordinary genius: The illustrated Richard Feynman.* New York: W. W. Norton, p. 76.

30. Csikszentmihalyi, *Creativity*, p. 360.

31. Plath, S. (1965). *Ariel.* New York: HarperPerennial.

32. Hughes, T. (1998). *Birthday letters.* New York: Farrar, Straus, Giroux.

33. Plath, *Ariel.*

34. Hughes, *Birthday letters*, pp. 16–17.

35. Butscher, E. (1976). *Sylvia Plath: Method and madness.* New York: Seabury Press, p. 71.

36. Stevenson, A. (1989). *Bitter fame: A life of Sylvia Plath.* London: Viking, pp. 86–87.

37. Ibid., p. 89.

38. Ibid., p. 103.

39. Butscher, *Sylvia Plath*, p. 189.

40. Stevenson, *Bitter fame*, p. 110.

41. Ibid., p. 115.

42. Hughes, *Birthday letters*, p. 68.

43. Butscher, *Sylvia Plath*, p. 233.

44. Stevenson, *Bitter fame*, p. 167.

45. Ibid., p. 206.

46. Ibid., p. 239.

47. Ibid., p. 267.

48. See amazon.com reviews of *Birthday letters*, 1998.

49. Berger, J. (1965). *The success and failure of Picasso.* Harmondsworth, England: Penguin Books.

50. Hoecker-Drysdale, S. (1996). Sociologists in the vineyard: The careers of Helen MacGill Hughes and Everett Cherrington Hughes. In Pycior, Slack, & Abir-Am (Eds.), *Creative couples in the sciences*, p. 223.

51. Ibid., p. 225.

52. Ibid., p. x.

53. Ibid., chapter 8.

54. Goldberger, N., Tarule, J., Clinchy, B., & Belenky, M. (Eds.). (1996). *Knowledge, difference and power: Essays inspired by "Women's ways of knowing."* New York: Basic Books, p. xi.

55. Ibid., p. xii.

56. Aries, E. (1996). *Men and women in interaction: Reconsidering the differences.* New York: Oxford University Press, p. 43.

Chapter 6. Collaboration across Generations

1. Csikszentmihalyi, M., personal communication, 1999.

2. Lave, J., & Wenger, E. (1991). *Situated learning: Legitimate peripheral participation.* Cambridge: Cambridge University Press, p. 116.

3. Arendt, H. (1977). *The life of the mind* (Vol. 1: Thinking). New York: Harcourt Brace Jovanovich.

4. Peattie, L. R. (1991). Not a career: A life. In F. M. Carp (Ed.), *Lives of career women: Approaches to work, marriage, children.* (pp. 173–190) New York: Plenum Press, p. 177.

5. Ibid., p. 178.

6. Bateson, M. C. (1984). *With a daughter's eye: A memoir of Margaret Mead and Gregory Bateson.* New York: Washington Square Press, p. 4.

7. Ibid., p. 5.

8. Ibid., p. 6.

9. Ibid., p. 240.

10. Ibid., p. 241.

11. Ibid., p. 246.

12. Ibid., p. 237.

13. Sykes, C. (1994). *No ordinary genius: The illustrated Richard Feynman.* New York: W. W. Norton, pp. 20–21.

14. Cheever, S. (1991). *Home before dark.* New York: Bantam Books, p. 128.

15. Bateson, *With a daughter's eye,* p. 115.

16. Ibid., p. 288.

17. Bensaude-Vincent, B. (1996). Star scientists in a nobelist family: Irene and Frederic Joliot-Curie. In H. M. Pycior, N. G. Slack, & P. G. Abir-Am (Eds.), *Creative couples in the sciences* (pp. 57–71). New Brunswick, NJ: Rutgers University Press, p. 61.

18. Adamson, L. (1997, August 17). When creativity runs in the family. *New York Times,* pp. 1, 31.

19. Sutton, C. (1998). Motherhood is powerful: Embodied knowledge from evolving field-based experience. *Anthropology and Humanism, 23* (2), 139–145.

20. Sutton, D. E. (1998). *Memories cast in stone: The relevance of the past in everyday life.* Oxford: Berg. David Sutton also acknowledges the mentoring of his father, Sam Sutton (who died in 1986), and emphasizes the issue of continuity by naming his first son after his father and dedicating his book "to the two Sams: past present and present future."

21. Gallimore, R., Tharp, R. G., & John-Steiner, V. (1992). *The development and socio-historical foundations of mentoring* (ERIC Document), pp. 21–22.

22. Wallace, D. B., & Gruber, H. E. (Eds.). (1989). *Creative people at work: Twelve cognitive case studies.* New York: Oxford University Press, p. 10.

23. Gruber, H. (1990). Commentary. *Human Development, 33,* 304–306 (p. 305).

24. Copland, A., & Perlis, V. (1984). *Copland: 1900 to 1942*. (Vol. 1). New York: St. Martin's Press.

25. Ibid., p. 62.

26. Ibid.

27. Ibid., p. 64.

28. Ibid., p. 73.

29. Ibid., p. 201.

30. Ibid., p. 249.

31. Bernstein, L. (1982). *Findings*. New York: Simon & Schuster, p. 332.

32. Peyser, J. (1998). *Bernstein: A biography*. New York: Billboard Books.

33. Copland & Perlis, *Copland*, p. 355.

34. Ibid.

35. Interview with Professor Nancy Uscher, Albuquerque, NM, June 26, 1997.

36. Interview with Howard Gardner, Spring 1993, Harvard University.

37. Gruber, H. E. (1986). The self-construction of the extraordinary. In R. J. Sternberg & J. E. Davidson (Eds.), *Conceptions of giftedness* (pp. 247–263). New York: Cambridge University Press.

38. Bucher, R., & Stelling, J. G. (1977). *Becoming professionals* (Vol. 46). Berkeley, CA: Sage Library of Social Research.

39. John-Steiner, V. (1989). Beyond the transmission of knowledge: A Vygotskian perspective on creativity. In R. Bjorson & M. R. Waldman (Eds.), *The university of the future* (pp. 51–68). Columbus: Center for Comparative Studies in the Humanities, Ohio State University, pp. 62–63.

40. Zuckerman, H. (1977). *Scientific elite: Nobel laureates in the United States*. New York: Free Press.

41. Interview with Mihaly Csikszentmihalyi, University of Chicago, April 1991.

42. Csikszentmihalyi, M. (1990). *Flow: The psychology of optimal experience*. New York: Harper & Row, p. 49.

43. Ibid.

44. Ibid., p. 3.

45. Csikszentmihalyi, M. (1996). *Creativity: Flow and the psychology of discovery and invention*. New York: HarperCollins, p. viii.

46. Interview with Barbara Rogoff and her research group, Madrid, Spain, September 15, 1992.

47. Rogoff, B. (1994). Developing understanding of the idea of communities of learners. *Mind, Culture, and Activity, 1*, 209–229 (p. 212).

48. Lave & Wenger, *Situated learning*.

49. Newman, D., Griffin, P., & Cole, M. (1989). *The construction zone: Working for cognitive change in school*. Cambridge: Cambridge University Press.

50. Rogoff, Communities of learners, p. 216.

51. Ibid., p. 213.

52. John-Steiner, V., & Mahn, H. (1996). Sociocultural approaches to learning and development: A Vygotskian framework. *Educational Psychologist, 31*, 191–206.

53. Interview with Pamela T. Reid, New York City, December 1996.

54. Bing, V., & Reid, P. R. (1996). Unknown women and unknowing research: Consequences of color and class in feminist psychology. In N. Gold-

berger, J. Tarule, B. Clinchy, & M. Belenky (Eds.), *Knowledge, difference and power: Essays inspired by "Women's ways of knowing."* New York: Basic Books, p. 186.

55. Miller, J. B. (1976). *Toward a new psychology of women.* Boston: Beacon Press.

56. Cole, M. (1996). *Cultural psychology: A once and future discipline.* Cambridge, MA: Belknap Press of Harvard University Press.

57. Ibid., p. 297.

58. Engestrom, Y. (1993). Developmental studies on work as a testbench of activity theory. In S. Chaiklin & J. Lave (Eds.), *Understanding practice: Perspectives on activity and context* (pp. 64–103). Cambridge: Cambridge University Press.

59. John-Steiner, & Mahn, Sociocultural approaches, *Educational Psychologist*, p. 191.

60. Vygotsky, L. (1962). *Thought and language.* (E. Hanfmann & G. Vakar, Trans.). Cambridge, MA: MIT Press, p. vii.

61. Nicolopoulou, A., & Cole, M. (1993). Generation and transmission of shared knowledge in the culture of collaborative learning: The Fifth Dimension, its play-world, and its institutional contexts. In E. A. Forman, N. Minick, & C. A. Stone (Eds.), *Context for learning: Sociocultural dynamics in children's development* (pp. 283–312). New York: Oxford University Press, pp. 293–294.

62. Cole, *Cultural psychology*, pp. 309–318.

63. Banton, W., Moorman, G., Hayes, B., & Warner, M. (1997). Effects of Fifth Dimension participation on far transfer. *Journal of Education Computing Research, 16,* 371–379.

64. Cole, M. (1997). From the creation of settings to the sustaining of institutions. *Mind, Culture, and Activity, 4,* 183–190 (p. 188).

65. Interview with George Lakoff and Rafael Nuñez in Berkeley, California, June 1997.

66. The expression "friend of my mind" is borrowed from my mentee, Tasia Young, who in turn borrowed it from the author Toni Morrison.

67. Interview with Sue Ervin-Tripp and Lily Wong Fillmore, June 1997.

68. Slobin, D. I., Gerhardt, J., Kyratzis, A., & Guo, J. (Eds.). (1996). *Social interaction, social context, and language: Essays in honor of Susan Ervin-Tripp.* Hillsdale, NJ: Lawrence Erlbaum Associates.

69. Ibid., p. 10.

70. O'Connor, M. C. (1996). Managing the intermental: Classroom group discussion and the social context of learning. In ibid., p. 495.

71. Gallimore, Tharp, & John-Steiner, ERIC Document, p. 26.

Chapter 7: Thought Communities

1. Becker, H. S. (1982). *Art worlds.* Berkeley: University of California Press.

2. Surrey, J. (1991). Relationship and empowerment. In J. V. Jordan, A. G. Kaplan, J. B. Miller, I. P. Stiver, & J. L. Surrey (Eds.), *Women's growth in connection: Writings from the Stone Center* (pp. 162–180). New York: Guilford Press.

3. Surrey, J. L. (1991). The "Self-in-Relation": A theory of women's development. In Jordan, Kaplan, Miller, Stiver, & Surrey, *Women's growth in connection*.

4. Bennis, W. & Biederman, P. W. (1997). *Organizing genius: The secrets of creative collaboration*. Reading, MA: Addison-Wesley.

5. Personal communication from Michele Minnis, February 26, 1999.

6. Richardson, J. (1996). *The life of Picasso* (Vol. 2). New York: Random House.

7. Interview with Phil Davis and Reuben Hersh, in Albuquerque, New Mexico 1999.

8. Steinhardt, A. (1998). *Indivisible by four: A string quartet pursuit of harmony*. New York: Farrar, Straus, Giroux.

9. Ibid., quotation on the jacket.

10. Ibid.

11. Ibid., p. 115.

12. Feldman, D. H. (1994). *Beyond universals in cognitive development*. (2nd ed.). Norwood: Ablex.

13. Ibid., p. 184.

14. Resnick, L. B., Levine, J. M., & Teasely, S. D. (Eds.). (1991). *Perspectives on socially shared cognition*. Washington, DC: American Psychological Association.

15. Ibid., p. 2.

16. Cole, M. (1991). Conclusion. In ibid.

17. Levine, J. M., & Moreland, R. L. (1991). Culture and socialisation in work groups. In ibid.

18. Gray, B. (1989). *Collaborating: Finding common ground for multiparty problems*. San Francisco: Jossey-Bass Publishers.

19. Middleton, D. (1998). Talking work: Argument, common knowledge, and improvisation in teamwork. In Y. Engestrom & D. Middleton (Eds.), *Cognition and communication at work* (pp. 233–256). Cambridge: Cambridge University Press.

20. Engestrom, Y., Engestrom, R., & Vahaaho, T. (1999). When the center does not hold: The importance of knotworking. In S. Chaiklin, M. Hedegaard, & U. J. Jensen (Eds.), *Activity theory and social practice* (pp. 345–374). Aarhus, Denmark: Aarhus University Press.

21. Ibid., p. 353.

22. Weick, K. E. (1995). *Sensemaking in organizations*. Thousand Oaks, CA: Sage Publications.

23. Ibid., p. 183.

24. Heath, S. B. (1991). "It's about winning!" The language of knowledge in baseball. In Resnick, Levine, & Teasley, *Perspectives on socially shared cognition*.

25. Hutchins, E. (1995). *Cognition in the wild*. Cambridge, MA: MIT Press.

26. Bazerman, C. (1996). Review symposium: "Cognition in the wild." *Mind, Culture, and Activity, 3*(1), 51–54.

27. Latour, B. (1996). Review symposium: "Cognition in the wild." *Mind, Culture, and Activity, 3*(1), 54–63.

28. Ibid.

29. Hutchins, E. (1996). Review symposium: Response to reviewers of "Cognition in the wild." *Mind, Culture, and Activity, 3*(1), 64–68.

30. Cole, Conclusion.

31. Wertsch, J. V. (1998). *Mind as action.* New York: Oxford University Press.

32. Schrage, M. (1990). *Shared minds: The new technologies of collaboration.* New York: Random House.

33. Ibid., pp. 32–33.

34. Fleck, L. (1979). *Genesis and development of a scientific fact.* Chicago: University of Chicago Press.

35. Ibid.

36. Ibid., p. 44.

37. This diagram was co-constructed by Vera John-Steiner, Michele Minnis, Teresa Meehan, Holbrook Mahn, and Robert Weber. Work on this model was supported by a National Science Foundation Grant #SBR-9423277.

38. Simon, H. A. (1996). *Models of my life.* Cambridge, MA: MIT Press.

39. Wertsch, J. V. (1998). *Mind as action.* New York: Oxford University Press.

40. Ibid., p. 54.

41. Belenky, M. F., Clinchy, B. M., Goldberger, N. R., & Tarule, J. M. (1997). *Women's ways of knowing: The development of self, voice, and mind* (10th anniversary ed.). New York: Basic Books.

42. Cole, M. (1996). *Cultural psychology: A once and future discipline.* Cambridge, MA: Belknap Press of Harvard University Press.

43. Tarule, J. M. (1996). Voices in dialogue: Collaborative ways of knowing. In N. R. Goldberger, J. M. Tarule, B. M. Clinchy, & B. F. Belenky (Eds.), *Knowledge, difference and power: Essays inspired by "Women's ways of knowing"* (pp. 274–304). New York: Basic Books.

44. Interview with Carol Gilligan, July 1996.

45. Bennis, W. & Biederman, P. W. (1997). *Organizing genius: The secrets of creative collaboration.* Reading, MA: Addison-Wesley.

46. Engestrom, Y. (1994). Teachers as collaborative thinkers: Activity-theoretical study of an innovative teacher team. In I. Carlgren, G. Handal, & S. Vaage (Eds.), *Teachers' minds and actions: Research on teachers' thinking and practice* (pp. 43–61). Briston, PA: The Falmer Press.

47. Csikszentmihalyi, M. (1996). *Creativity: Flow and the psychology of discovery and invention.* New York: HarperCollins.

48. Ibid., p. 37.

49. Van der Veer, R., & Valsiner, J. (1991). *Understanding Vygotsky: A quest for synthesis.* Oxford: Blackwell Publishers.

Appendix

1. Block, J. (1978). *The Q-sort method in personality assessment and psychiatric research.* Palo Alto, CA: Consulting Psychologists Press.

BIBLIOGRAPHY

Aaron, J. (1991). *A double singleness: Gender and the writings of Charles and Mary Lamb.* Oxford: Clarendon Press.

Adamson, L. (1997, August 17). When creativity runs in the family. *New York Times,* pp. 1, 31.

Arendt, H. (1977). *The life of the mind* (Vol. 1: Thinking). New York: Harcourt Brace Jovonovich.

Aries, E. (1996). *Men and women in interaction: Reconsidering the differences.* New York: Oxford University Press.

Bair, D. (1995). *Anaïs Nin: A biography.* New York: Putnam and Company.

Bakhurst, D., & Sypnowich, C. (Eds.). (1995). *The social self.* London: Sage Publications.

Bank, S., & Kahn, M. D. (1982). Intense sibling loyalties. In E. M. Lamb & B. Sutton-Smith (Eds.), *Sibling relationships: Their nature and significance across the lifespan* (pp. 251–266). Hillsdale, NJ: Lawrence Erlbaum Associates.

Banton, W., Moorman, G., Hayes, B., & Warner, M. (1997). Effects of Fifth Dimension participation on far transfer. *Journal of Education Computing Research, 16,* 371–379.

Bates, E., Dale, P., & Thel, D. (1997). Individual differences and their implications. In P. Fletcher & B. MacWhinney (Eds.), *The handbook of child language* (pp. 96–151). Oxford: Blackwell Publishers.

Bateson, M. C. (1984). *With a daughter's eye: A memoir of Margaret Mead and Gregory Bateson.* New York: Washington Square Press.

Bazerman, C. (1996). Review Symposium: Cognition in the wild. *Mind, Culture, and Activity, 3* (1), 51–54.

Beauvoir, S. D. (1968). *Hard times: Force of circumstances, 1952–1962 (Autobiography of Simone de Beauvoir).* Harmondsworth, England: Penguin Books.

Beauvoir, S. D. (1984). *Adieux: A farewell to Sartre.* New York: Pantheon Books.

Becker, H. S. (1982). *Art worlds.* Berkeley: University of California Press.

Belenky, M. F., Clinchy, B. M., Goldberger, N. R. & Tarule, J. M. (1986). *Women's ways of knowing: The development of self, voice, and mind.* New York: Basic Books.

Belenky, M. F., Clinchy, B. M., Goldberger, N. R., & Tarule, J. M. (1997). *Women's ways of knowing: The development of self, voice, and mind* (10th anniversary ed.). New York: Basic Books.

Bennis, W., & Biederman, P. W. (1997). *Organizing genius: The secrets of creative collaboration.* Reading, MA: Addison-Wesley.

Bensaude-Vincent, B. (1996). Star scientists in a nobelist family: Irene and Frederic Joliot-Curie. In H. M. Pycior, N. G. Slack, & P. G. Abir-AM (Eds.), *Creative couples in the sciences* (pp. 57–71). New Brunswick, NJ: Rutgers University Press.

Berger, J. (1965). *The success and failure of Picasso.* Harmondsworth, England: Penguin Books.

Berko-Gleason, J., & Weintraub, S. (1978). Input language and the acquisition of communicative competence. In K. E. Nelson (Ed.), *Children's language* (Vol. 1) (pp. 171–222). New York: Gardner Press.

Bernstein L. (1982). *Findings.* New York: Simon and Schuster.

Bing, V., & Reid, P. R. (1996). Unknown women and unknowing research: Consequences of color and class in feminist pychology. In N. Goldberger, J. Tarule, B. Clinchy, & M. Belenky (Eds.), *Knowledge, difference and power: Essays inspired by "Women's ways of knowing"* (pp. 175–202). New York: Basic Books.

Blaedel, N. (1988). *Harmony and unity: The life of Niels Bohr.* Madison, WI: Springer-Verlag.

Block, G., & Drucker, M. (1992). *Rescuers: Portraits of moral courage in the Holocaust.* New York: Holmes & Meyer.

Block, J. (1978). *The Q-sort method in personality assessment and psychiatric research.* Palo Alto, CA: Consulting Psychologists Press.

Bookman, M. (1996). Phantoms slain: A Vygotskian reading of Carol Gilligan. Unpublished manuscript.

Broverman, I. K., Broverman, D. M., Clarkson, F. E., Rosenkrantz, P. S., & Vogel, S. R. (1970). Sex-role stereotypes and clinical judgments of mental health. *Journal of Consulting and Clinical Psychology, 34,* 1–7.

Brown, L., & Gilligan, C. (1992). *Meeting at the crossroads: Women's psychology and girls' development.* Cambridge, MA: Harvard University Press.

Bruffee, K. A. (1993). *Collaborative learning: Higher education, interdependence, and the authority of knowledge.* Baltimore: Johns Hopkins University Press.

Bucher, R., & Stelling, J. G. (1977). *Becoming professionals* (Vol. 46). Berkeley: Sage Library of Social Research.

Butscher, E. (1976). *Sylvia Plath: Method and madness.* New York: Seabury Press.

Chadwick, W., & Courtivron, I. D. (Eds.). (1996). *Significant others: Creativity and intimate partnership.* London: Thames & Hudson.

Chaiklin, S., Hedegaard, M., & Jensen, U. J. (Eds.). (1999). *Activity theory and social practice.* Aarhus, Denmark: Aarhus University Press.

Chang-Wells, G. L. M., & Wells, G. (1993). Dynamics of discourse: Literacy and the construction of knowledge. In E. A. Forman, N. Minick, & C. A. Stone (Eds.), *Contexts for learning: Sociocultural dynamics in children's development* (pp. 58–90). New York: Oxford University Press.

Chavkin, A., & Chavkin, N. F. (Eds.). (1994). *Conversations with Louise Erdrich and Michael Dorris.* Jackson: University Press of Mississippi.

Cheever, S. (1991). *Home before dark.* New York: Bantam Books.

Chomsky, N. (1965). *Aspects of the theory of syntax*. Cambridge, MA: MIT Press.

Chomsky, N. (1988). *Language and problems of knowledge: The Managua lectures*. Cambridge, MA: MIT Press.

Chouguet-Bruhat, Y., DeWitt-Morette, C., & Dillard-Bleick, M. (1977). *Analysis, manifolds, and physics*. Amsterdam: North Holland Publishing Company.

Chouguet-Bruhat, Y., DeWitt-Morette, C., & Dillard-Bleick, M. (1982). *Analysis, manifolds, and physics* (2nd rev. ed.). Amsterdam: North Holland Publishing Company.

Clinchy, B. M. (1996). Connected and separate knowing: Toward a marriage of two minds. In N. R. Goldberger, J. M. Tarule, B. M. Clinchy, & M. F. Belenky (Eds.), *Knowledge, difference and power: Essays inspired by "Women's ways of knowing"* (pp. 205–247). New York: Basic Books.

Clurman, H. (1974). *All people are famous (instead of an autobiography)*. New York: Harcourt Brace Jovanovich.

Clurman, H. (1975). *The fervent years: The Group Theatre and the thirties*. New York: Harcourt Brace Jovanovich.

Cole, M. (1991). Conclusion. In L. B. Resnick, J. M. Levine, & S. D. Teaslet (Eds.), *Perspectives on socially shared cognition* (pp. 398–417). Washington, DC: American Psychological Association.

Cole, M. (1996). *Cultural psychology: A once and future discipline*. Cambridge, MA: Belknap Press of Harvard University Press.

Cole, M. (1997). From the creation of settings to the sustaining of institutions. *Mind, Culture, and Activity, 4,* 183–190.

Cole, M., & Cole, S. (1989). *The development of children*. New York: Scientific American Books.

Copland, A., & Perlis, V. (1984). *Copland: 1900 to 1942* (Vol. 1). New York: St. Martin's Press.

Courant, R., & Friedrichs, K. O. (1948). *Supersonic flow and shock waves*. New York: Interscience Publishers.

Csikszentmihalyi, M. (1990). *Flow: The psychology of optimal experience*. New York: Harper & Row.

Csikszentmihalyi, M. (1996). *Creativity: Flow and the psychology of discovery and invention*. New York: HarperCollins.

Curie, M. (1923). *Pierre Curie*. New York: Macmillan.

Damasio, A. R. (1994). *Descartes' error: Emotion, reason, and the human brain*. New York: G. P. Putnam's Sons.

Damon, W., & Phelps, E. (1989). Critical distinctions among three approaches to peer education. *International Journal of Educational Review, 58*(2), 9–19.

Davis, P. J., & Hersh, R. (1980). *The mathematical experience*. Boston: Birkhauser.

Deacon, T. W. (1997). *The symbolic species: The co-evolution of language and the brain*. New York: W. W. Norton.

Draper, P. (1975). !Kung women: Contrasts in sexual egalitarianism in the foraging and sedentary contexts. In R. Reiter (Ed.), *Toward an anthropology of women* (pp. 77–109). New York: Monthly Review Press.

Dreyfus, H. L., & Dreyfus, S. E. (1988). *Mind over machine: The power of human intuition and expertise in the era of the computer.* New York: Free Press.

Durant, W., & Durant, A. (1977). *Dual autobiography.* New York: Simon and Schuster.

Dyson, A. H. (1995). Writing children: Reinventing the development of childhood literacy. *Written Communication, 12,* 4–46.

Dyson, F. (1979). *Disturbing the universe.* New York: Harper & Row.

Einstein, A. (1972, March 27). Unpublished papers of Albert Einstein. *New York Times,* p. 26.

Einstein, A. (1973). *Ideas and opinions.* New York: Dell.

Einstein, A., & Maric, M. (1992). *The love letters* (S. Smith, Trans.). Princeton, NJ: Princeton University Press.

Eisler, R. (1987). *The chalice and the blade: Our history, our future.* New York: Harper & Row.

Elbow, P. (1973). *Writing without teachers.* London: Oxford University Press.

Engestrom, Y. (1993). Developmental studies on work as a testbench of activity theory. In S. Chaiklin & J. Lave (Eds.), *Understanding practice: Perspectives on activity and context* (pp. 64–103). Cambridge: Cambridge University Press.

Engestrom, Y. (1994). Teachers as collaborative thinkers: Activity-theoretical study of an innovative teacher team. In I. Carlgren, G. Handal, & S. Vaage (Eds.), *Teachers' minds and actions: Research on teachers' thinking and practice* (pp. 43–61). Bristol, PA: Falmer Press.

Engestrom, Y., Engestrom, R., & Vahaaho, T. (1999). When the center does not hold: The importance of knotworking. In S. Chaiklin, M. Hedegaard, & U. J. Jensen (Eds.), *Activity theory and social practice* (pp. 345–374). Aarhus, Denmark: Aarhus University Press.

Engestrom, Y., & Middleton, D. (Eds.). (1998). *Cognition and communication at work.* Cambridge: Cambridge University Press.

Evans, M. (1985). *Simone de Beauvoir: A feminist mandarin.* London: Tavistock.

Feldman, D. H. (1994). *Beyond universals in cognitive development* (2nd ed.). Norwood, NJ: Ablex.

Feynman, R. P. (1994). *No ordinary genius: The illustrated Richard Feynman.* New York: W. W. Norton & Co.

Fischer, E. (1963). *The necessity of art: A Marxist approach* (A. Bostock, Trans.). Baltimore: Penguin Books.

Fleck, L. (1979). *Genesis and development of a scientific fact.* Chicago: University of Chicago Press.

Gallimore, R., Tharp, R. G., & John-Steiner, V. (1992). *The development and socio-historical foundations of mentoring* (ERIC Document).

Gardner, H. (1993). *Creating minds: An anatomy of creativity seen through the lives of Freud, Einstein, Picasso, Stravinsky, Eliot, Graham, and Gandhi.* New York: Basic Books.

Gilligan, C. (1982). *In a different voice: Psychological theory and women's development.* Cambridge, MA: Harvard University Press.

Gilligan, C., Lyons, N., & Hamner, T. (Eds.). (1990). *Making connections.* Cambridge, MA: Harvard University Press.

Gilot, F., & Lake, C. (1964). *Life with Picasso*. New York: McGraw-Hill.

Gleick, J. (1993). *Genius: The life and science of Richard Feynman*. New York: Vintage Books.

Goffman, E. (1959). *The presentation of self in everyday life*. Garden City, NY: Doubleday.

Goldberger, N., Tarule, J., Clinchy, B., & Belenky, M. (Eds.). (1996). *Knowledge, difference and power: Essays inspired by "Women's ways of knowing."* New York: Basic Books.

Gray, B. (1989). *Collaborating: Finding common ground for multiparty problems*. San Francisco: Jossey-Bass Publishers.

Gruber, H. E. (1986). The self-construction of the extraordinary. In R. J. Sternberg & J. E. Davidson (Eds.), *Conceptions of giftedness* (pp. 247–263). New York: Cambridge University Press.

Gruber, H. E. (1989). The evolving systems approach to creative work. In D. B. Wallace & H. E. Gruber (Eds.), *Creative people at work: Twelve cognitive case studies* (pp. 3–24). New York: Oxford University Press.

Gruber, H. (1990). Commentary. *Human Development, 33*, 304–306.

Hadamard, J. (1945). *The psychology of invention in the mathematical field*. Princeton, NJ: Princeton University Press.

Halliday, M. A. K. (1985). *An introduction to functional grammar*. London: Edward Arnold.

Hamilton, N. (1978). *The brothers Mann: The lives of Heinrich and Thomas Mann, 1871–1950 and 1875–1955*. New Haven: Yale University Press.

Harding, S. (1996). Gendered ways of knowing and the "Epistemological Crisis" of the West. In N. R. Goldberger, J. M. Tarule, B. M. Clinchy, & M. F. Belenky (Eds.), *Knowledge, difference and power: Essays inspired by "Women's ways of knowing"* (pp. 431–454). New York: Basic Books.

Hawkins, E. (1992). *The body is a clear place and other statements on dance*. Pennington, NJ: Princeton Book Company.

Heath, S. B. (1991). "It's about winning!" The language of knowledge in baseball. In L. B. Resnick, J. M. Levine, & S. D. Teasley (Eds.), *Perspectives on socially shared cognition* (pp. 101–126). Washington, DC: American Psychological Association.

Heisenberg, W. (1971). *Physics and beyond: Encounters and conversations*. New York: Harper & Row.

Hersh, R. (1997). *What is mathematics, really?* New York: Oxford University Press.

Hoecker-Drysdale, S. (1996). Sociologists in the vineyard: The careers of Helen MacGill Hughes and Everett Cherrington Hughes. In H. M. Pycior, N. S. Slack, & P. G. Abir-Am (Eds.), *Creative couples in the sciences* (pp. 220–231). New Brunswick, NJ: Rutgers University Press.

Hoffmann, B. (1972). *Albert Einstein: Creator and rebel*. New York: Viking Press.

Holton, G. J. (1973). *Thematic origins of scientific thought: Kepler to Einstein*. Cambridge, MA: Harvard University Press.

Hughes, T. (1998). *Birthday letters*. New York: Farrar, Straus, Giroux.

Hulsker, J. (1990). *Vincent and Theo Van Gogh: A dual biography*. (ed. by J. M. Miller). Ann Arbor: Fuller Publications.

Hutchins, E. (1995). *Cognition in the wild*. Cambridge, MA: MIT Press.

Hutchins, E. (1996). Review symposium: Response to reviewers of "Cognition in the wild." *Mind, Culture, and Activity, 3*(1), 64–68.

John-Steiner, V. (1985). *Notebooks of the mind: Explorations of thinking.* New York: Harper & Row.

John-Steiner, V. (1989). Beyond the transmission of knowledge: A Vygotskian perspective on creativity. In R. Bjorson & M. R. Waldman (Eds.), *The university of the future* (pp. 51–68). Columbus: Center for Comparative Studies in the Humanities, Ohio State University.

John-Steiner, V. (1997). *Notebooks of the mind: Explorations of thinking* (2nd ed.). New York: Oxford University Press.

John-Steiner, V. (1999). Sociocultural and feminist theory: Mutuality and relevance. In S. Chaiklin, M. Hedegaard, & U. J. Jensen (Eds.), *Activity theory and social practice* (pp. 201–224). Aarhus, Denmark: Aarhus University Press.

John-Steiner, V., & Mahn, H. (1996). Sociocultural approaches to learning and development: A Vygotskian framework. *Educational Psychologist, 31*, 191–206.

Jordan, J. V., Kaplan, A. G., Miller, J. B., Stiver, I. P., & Surrey, J. L. (Eds.). (1991). *Women's growth in connection: Writings from the Stone Center.* New York: Guilford Press.

Kaplan, C., & Rose, E. C. (1993). Strange bedfellows: Feminist collaboration. *Signs: Journal of Women in Culture and Society, 18*(3).

Keller, E. F. (1987). *Reflections on gender and science.* New Haven, CT: Yale University Press.

Kushner, T. (1996). *Angels in America, Part II: Perestroika.* New York: Theatre Communications Group.

Langacker, R. (1987). *Foundations of cognitive grammar* (Vols. 1–2). Stanford, CA: Stanford University Press.

Latour, B. (1996). Review symposium: "Cognition in the wild." *Mind, Culture, and Activity, 3*(1), 54–63.

Lave, J., & Wenger, E. (1991). *Situated learning: Legitimate peripheral participation.* Cambridge: Cambridge University Press.

Leacock, E. (1977). Women's status in egalitarian society: Implications for social evolution. *Current Anthropology, 19*, 247–275.

Leakey, R. E. (1994). *The origin of humankind.* New York: Basic Books.

Levine, J. M., & Moreland, R. L. (1991). Culture and socialisation in work groups. In L. B. Resnick, J. M. Levine, & S. D. Teasley (Eds.), *Perspectives on socially shared cognition* (pp. 257–279). Washington, DC: American Psychological Association.

Louis, M. (1993, July 18). Collaborating with a perfectionist and visionary. *New York Times*, p. 24.

McCarthey, S. J., & McMahon, S. (1992). From convention to invention: Peer interaction during writing. In R. Hertz-Lazarowitz & N. Miller (Eds.), *Interaction in cooperative groups: The theoretical anatomy of group learning* (pp. 17–35). New York: Cambridge University Press.

Maccoby, E. E. (1990). Gender and relationships: A developmental account. *American Psychologist, 45*, 513–520.

McGrayne, S. B. (1993). *Nobel prize women in science: Their lives, struggles, and momentous discoveries.* Secaucus, NJ: Carol Publishing Group.

MacPherson, P., & Fine, M. (1995). Hungry for an Us: Adolescent girls and adult women negotiating territories of race, gender, class, difference. *Feminism and Psychology, 5*, 181–200.

Madsen, A. (1977). *Hearts and minds: The common journey of Simone de Beauvoir and John Paul Sartre*. New York: Morrow.

Martin, J. (1978). *Always merry and bright: The life of Henry Miller*. Santa Barbara, CA: Capra Press.

Middleton, D. (1998). Talking work: Argument, common knowledge, and improvisation in teamwork. In Y. Engestrom & D. Middleton (Eds.), *Cognition and communication at work* (pp. 233–256). Cambridge: Cambridge University Press.

Midgley, M. (1992). *Science as salvation: A modern myth and its meaning*. New York: Routledge.

Mille, A. D. (1991). *Martha: The life and work of Martha Graham*. New York: Random House.

Miller, A. I. (1984). *Imagery in scientific thought*. Boston: Birkhauser.

Miller, J. B. (1976). *Toward a new psychology of women*. Boston: Beacon Press.

Miller, J. B. (1991). The development of women's sense of self. In J. V. Jordan, A. G. Kaplan, J. B. Miller, I. P. Stiver, & J. L. Surrey (Eds.), *Women's growth in connection: Writings from the Stone Center* (pp. 11–26). New York: Guilford Press.

Newman, D., Griffin, P., & Cole, M. (1989). *The construction zone: Working for cognitive change in school*. Cambridge: Cambridge University Press.

Nicolopoulou, A., & Cole, M. (1993). Generation and transmission of shared knowledge in the culture of collaborative learning: The Fifth Dimension, its play-world, and its institutional contexts. In E. A. Forman, N. Minick, & C. A. Stone (Eds.), *Context for learning: Sociocultural dynamics in children's development* (pp. 283–312). New York: Oxford University Press.

Nin, A. (1932). *D. H. Lawrence: An unprofessional study*. Paris: E. W. Titus.

Nin, A., & Miller, H. (1987). *A literate passion: The letters of Anaïs Nin and Henry Miller, 1932–1953*. San Diego: Harcourt Brace Jovanovich.

O'Connor, M. C. (1996). Managing the intermental: Classroom group discussion and the social context of learning. In D. I. Slobin, J. Gerhardt, A. Kyratzis, & J. Guo (Eds.), *Social interaction, social context, and language: Essays in honor of Susan Ervin-Tripp* (pp. 495–509). Hillsdale, NJ: Lawrence Erlbaum Associates.

Pais, A. (1982). *Subtle is the Lord: The science and the life of Albert Einstein*. New York: Oxford University Press.

Pais, A. (1991). *Niels Bohr's times*. Oxford: Claridon Press.

Peattie, L. R. (1991). Not a career: A life. In F. M. Carp (Ed.), *Lives of career women: Approaches to work, marriage, children* (pp. 173–190). New York: Plenum Press.

Peyser, J. (1998). *Bernstein: A biography*. New York: Billboard Books.

Picasso, P. (1986). *Je suis le cahier: The sketchbooks of Pablo Picasso* (A. Glimcher & M. Glimcher, Trans.). Boston: Atlantic Monthly Press.

Pinker, S. (1994). *The language instinct: How the mind creates language*. New York: William Morrow.

Plath, S. (1965). *Ariel*. New York: HarperPerennial.

Pycior, H. M. (1987). Marie Curie's anti-natural path. In P. G. Abir-Am & D. Outram (Eds.), *Uneasy careers and intimate lives: Women in science, 1789–1979*. New Brunswick, NJ: Rutgers University Press.

Pycior, H. M. (1996). Pierre Curie and his eminent partner Mme. Curie. In H. M. Pycior, N. S. Slack, & P. G. Abir-Am (Eds.), *Creative couples in the sciences* (pp. 39–56). New Brunswick, NJ: Rutgers University Press.

Pycior, H. M., Slack, N. G., & Abir-Am, P. G. (Eds.). (1996). *Creative couples in the sciences*. New Brunswick, NJ: Rutgers University Press.

Quinn, S. (1995). *Marie Curie: A life*. New York: Simon and Schuster.

Resnick, L. B., Levine, J. M., & Teasely, S. D. (Eds.). (1991). *Perspectives on socially shared cognition*. Washington, DC: American Psychological Association.

Richardson, J. (1991, 1996). *The life of Picasso*. (Vols. 1–2). New York: Random House.

Robinson, R. (1989). *Georgia O'Keeffe: A life*. New York: HarperCollins.

Rogoff, B. (1994). Developing understanding of the idea of communities of learners. *Mind, Culture, and Activity, 1,* 209–229.

Rubin, J. Z., Provenzano, F. J., & Luria, Z. (1974). The eye of the beholder: Parents' view on sex of newborns. *American Journal of Orthopsychiatry, 44,* 512–519.

Ruddick, S. (1996). Reason's "Femininity": A case for connected knowledge. In N. R. Goldberger, J. M. Tarule, B. M. Clinchy, & M. F. Belenky (Eds.), *Knowledge, difference, and power: Essays inspired by "Women's ways of knowing"* (pp. 248–273). New York: Basic Books.

Ruddick, S., & Daniels, P. (1977). *Working it out: 23 women writers, artists, scientists, and scholars talk about their lives and work*. New York: Pantheon Books.

Sagan, F. (1985). *With fondest regards* (C. Donougher, Trans.). New York: E. P. Dutton.

Schieffelin, B. B., & Ochs, E. (1996). The microgenesis of competence: Methodology in language socialization. In D. I. Slobin, J. Gerhardt, A. Kyratzis, & J. Guo (Eds.), *Social interaction, social context, and language: Essays in honor of Susan Ervin-Tripp* (pp. 251–263). Hillsdale, NJ: Lawrence Erlbaum Associates.

Schor, N. (1994). The essentialism which is not one. In N. Schor & E. Weed (Eds.), *The essential difference*. Bloomington and Indianapolis: Indiana University Press.

Schrage, M. (1990). *Shared minds: The new technologies of collaboration*. New York: Random House.

Scribner, S. (1984). Cognitive studies of work. *The Quarterly Newsletter of the Laboratory of Comparative Human Cognition, 6*(1 & 2), 1–41.

Scribner, S., & Cole, M. (1984). *The psychology of literacy*. Cambridge, MA: Harvard University Press.

Simon, H. A. (1996). *Models of my life*. Cambridge, MA: MIT Press.

Slobin, D. I. (1985). *The cross-linguistic study of language acquisition* (Vols. 1–5). Hillsdale, NJ: Lawrence Erlbaum Associates.

Slobin, D. I., Gerhardt, J., Kyratzis, A., & Guo, J. (Eds.). (1996). *Social interaction, social context, and language: Essays in honor of Susan Ervin-Tripp*. Hillsdale, NJ: Lawrence Erlbaum Associates.

Steinhardt, A. (1998). *Indivisible by four: A string quartet pursuit of harmony.* New York: Farrar, Straus, Giroux.

Stevenson, A. (1989). *Bitter fame: A life of Sylvia Plath.* London: Viking.

Stevenson, H. W., & Stigler, J. W. (1992). *The learning gap: Why our schools are failing and what we can learn from Japanese and Chinese education.* New York: Summit Books.

Stillinger, J. (1991). *Multiple authorship and the myth of solitary genius.* New York: Oxford University Press.

Stravinsky, I., & Craft, R. (1966). *Themes and episodes.* New York: Knopf.

Stuckey, C. F. (Ed.). (1985). *Monet: A retrospective.* New York: Hugh Lauter Levine Associates, Inc.

Surrey, J. L. (1991). Relationship and empowerment. In J. V. Jordan, A. G. Kaplan, J. B. Miller, I. P. Stiver, & J. L. Surrey (Eds.), *Women's growth in connection: Writings from the Stone Center* (pp. 162–180). New York: Guilford Press.

Surrey, J. L. (1991). The "Self-in-Relation": A theory of women's development. In J. V. Jordan, A. G. Kaplan, J. B. Miller, I. P. Stiver, & J. L. Surrey (Eds.), *Women's growth in connection: Writings from the Stone Center* (pp. 51–66). New York: Guilford Press.

Sutton, C. (1998). Motherhood is powerful: Embodied knowledge from evolving field-based experience. *Anthropology and Humanism, 23*(2), 139–145.

Sutton, D. E. (1998). *Memories cast in stone: The relevance of the past in everyday life.* Oxford: Berg.

Sykes, C. (1994). *No ordinary genius: The illustrated Richard Feynman.* New York: W. W. Norton.

Taper, B. (1974). *Balanchine: A biography.* New York: Macmillan.

Tarule, J. M. (1996). Voices in dialogue: Collaborative ways of knowing. In N. R. Goldberger, J. M. Tarule, B. M. Clinchy, & B. F. Belenky (Eds.), *Knowledge, difference, and power: Essays inspired by "Women's ways of knowing"* (pp. 274–304). New York: Basic Books.

Tickner, L. (1996). The left-handed marriage: Vanessa Bell and Duncan Grant. In W. Chadwick & I. D. Courtivron (Eds.), *Significant others: Creativity and intimate partnerships* (pp. 65–81). London: Thames & Hudson.

Traweek, S. (1988). *Beamtimes and lifetimes: The world of high energy physicists.* Cambridge, MA: Harvard University Press.

Troemel-Ploetz, S. (1990). Mileva Einstein-Maric: The woman who did Einstein's mathematics. *Women's Studies International Forum, 11*(5), 41–432.

Van der Veer, R., & Valsiner, J. (1991). *Understanding Vygotsky: A quest for synthesis.* Oxford: Blackwell.

Vygotsky, L. (1962). *Thought and language* (E. Hanfmann & G. Vakar, Trans.). Cambridge, MA: MIT Press.

Vygotsky, L. S. (1978). *Mind in society: The development of higher psychological processes.* Cambridge, MA: Harvard University Press.

Vygotsky, L. (1986). *Thought and language* (A. Kozulin, Trans.). Cambridge, MA: MIT Press.

Wallace, D. (1990). Sibling relationships in creative lives. In M. J. A. Howe (Ed.), *Encouraging the development of exceptional skills and talents.* Leicester: British Psychological Society Books.

Wallace, D. B., & Gruber, H. E. (Eds.). (1989). *Creative people at work: Twelve cognitive case studies.* New York: Oxford University Press.

Weick, K. E., & Roberts, K. H. (1993). Collective mind in organizations: Heedful interrelating on flight decks. *Administrative Science Quarterly, 38,* 357–381.

Weick, K. E. (1995). *Sensemaking in organizations.* Thousand Oaks, CA: Sage Publications.

Weisner, T. S. (1982). Sibling interdependence and child caretaking: A cross-cultural view. In E. M. Lamb & B. Sutton-Smith (Eds.), *Sibling relationships: Their nature and significance across the lifespan.* Hillsdale, NJ: Lawrence Erlbaum Associates.

Weisskopf, V. F. (1991). *The joy of insight.* New York: Basic Books.

Wertsch, J. V. (1998). *Mind as action.* New York: Oxford University Press.

Whiting, B., & Whiting, J. W. M. (1975). *Children of six cultures.* Cambridge, MA: Harvard University Press.

Whitman, W. (1950). *Leaves of grass.* New York: Modern Library.

Whyte, M. K. (1978). *The status of women in preindustrial societies.* Princeton, NJ: Princeton University Press.

Zorpette, G. (1994, Summer). Dynamic duos. *ARTnews,* pp. 167.

Zuckerman, H. (1977). *Scientific elite: Nobel laureates in the United States.* New York: Free Press.

Zukow-Goldring, P. (1995). Sibling caregiving: Being and becoming and giving and getting. In M. H. Bornstein (Ed.), *Handbook of parenting* (Vol. 3). Mahwah, NJ: Lawrence Erlbaum Associates

CREDITS

Introduction quote reprinted with the permission of Cambridge University Press from *Cognition and Communication at Work*, edited by Yrjo Engestrom and David Middleton. Copyright © 1998.

Chapter 1 quote reprinted with the permission of Simon & Schuster from *Dual Autobiography* by Will and Ariel Durant. Copyright © 1977 by Will and Ariel Durant.

Chapter 2 quote reprinted with the permission of Oxford University Press from *Subtle Is the Lord: The Science and Life of Albert Einstein* by Abraham Pais. Copyright © 1982.

Chapter 3 quote from *The Life of Picasso (Volume 1)* by J. Richardson. Copyright © 1991 by J. Richardson. Reprinted by permission of Random House, Inc.

Chapter 4 quote from *Women's Ways of Knowing* by Mary Field Belenky et al. Copyright © 1986 by Basic Books, Inc. Reprinted by permission of Basic Books, a member of Perseus Books, LLC.

Chapter 5 quotes reproduced by permission of Penguin Books Ltd. from *Bitter Fame: A Life of Sylvia Plath* by Anne Stevenson (Viking, 1989). Copyright © Anne Stevenson, 1989. Appendix I copyright © Lucas Myers, 1989; excerpts from "The Blue Flannel Suit" and "The Shot" from *Birthday Letters* by Ted Hughes. Copyright © 1998 by Ted Hughes. Reprinted by permission of Farrar, Straus and Giroux, LLC; excerpts from "Daddy" from *Ariel* by Sylvia Plath. Copyright © 1963 by Ted Hughes. Reprinted by permission of HarperCollins Publishers, Inc.

Chapter 6 quotes reprinted by permission of St. Martin's Press, LLC from *Copland: 1900–1942* by Aaron Copland and Vivian Perlis. Copyright © 1984 by Aaron Copland; and from *With a Daughter's Eye* by Mary Catherine Bateson. Copyright © 1984 by Mary Catherine Bateson. Reprinted by permission of HarperCollins Publishers, Inc.

INDEX OF SUBJECTS

conflict
  artistic collaboration and, 84
  conceptual, 44
  intimate partners and, 18–19, 21,
    36, 133, 139–142
  in mentor/apprenticeships, 164, 170,
    172, 177–179
  negotiation of, 6–8, 133, 202
  in science partnerships, 44, 49–54, 52
  in sibling partnerships, 30–32
  women's collaboration and, 100,
    115–116, 118, 121
conflict resolution, 6–8, 44, 133, 202
connected knowledge, 6, 101
connectedness
  across generations (*See* inter-
    generational collaboration)
  artistic collaboration and, 64, 70,
    73, 75, 85–86, 89, 91–92, 94
  gender differences in, 99, 101–103,
    106–107
  intimate partnerships and, 128–129,
    132–133
  mutual appropriation and, 199
  in professor/student collaborations,
    164–165, 169
  women's collaboration and, 112–114,
    120–121
consensus, in professor/student
    collaborations, 171
constructed knowledge, 6, 100–101.
    See also knowledge construction
continuity, as natural phenomena,
    47–48, 52
contradictions, of self, 126
conversational communities. *See*
    discourse communities
cooperative activities, 12, 15, 180
Creating Minds (Gardner), 65
creative activities
  in artistic collaboration, 70–74
  complementarity in, 7–8
  as emotional, 123–124
  intergenerational collaboration and,
    179–181
  knowledge co-construction by, 3, 7,
    73, 189, 203
  as social, 3–5, 35, 37

creative cognition, 56, 165, 171, 192,
    200
Creative Couples in the Sciences (Pycior,
    Slack and Abir-Am), 5, 142–143
creative growth
  in artistic collaboration, 78–87
  intimate partners and, 19, 33–34, 127
  professor/student collaborations and,
    167–168, 171
  in science collaboration, 48, 50
  in thought communities, 188–192
  women's collaboration and, 118
Creative People at Work (Gruber and
    Wallace), 17, 144, 159
Creative Vision (Csikszentmihalyi and
    Getzels), 167
creativity
  artistic fields of, 71
  of childhood, 30, 32, 37, 40, 45–50
  cultural-historical context of, 5–6,
    8–9, 123
  emotional dynamics of, 123–124, 126
  intimate partners and, 16–17, 20,
    127
  mentoring impact on, 154–159, 167,
    171, 179
  relational-cultural context of, 6, 8,
    16, 123
critical mind, 99, 101
criticism
  artistic collaboration and, 67, 71, 74,
    77–78, 81, 86–87
  family partnerships and, 28–29
  intergenerational collaboration and,
    181
  intimate partners and, 13, 15–16,
    18, 23, 34, 127–128, 131
  science partnerships and, 44, 49–56
  women's collaboration and, 102,
    117–118
cross-cultural perspectives. *See* ethnicity
Crown of Columbus (Durant and
    Durant), 33
Cubism
  analytical period of, 69, 85
  interaction focus of, 64–65, 67,
    69–70
  synthetic period of, 69–70, 142

cultural-historical theory
    of artistic collaboration, 88, 90–91
    of collaborative learning, 91,
        175–176, 188, 191–194, 199,
        203–204
    of creativity, 5–6, 8–9, 35, 76, 123,
        191
    of gender differences, 98, 101–103
    of intergenerational collaboration,
        169–170, 172, 181–185
    of joint thinking, 191–192, 194
    of mutuality and interdependence,
        103–109, 123–124
    of science partnerships, 50–55, 56
    of women's collaboration, 98,
        101–103, 118–119
cultural organism, 88, 191

dance, collaboration in, 35, 81–82, 87
debate, women's collaboration and,
    99–101
decision making, in partnerships, 25, 29
dependence
    intimate partnerships and, 133, 137
    professor/student collaborations and,
        165, 169
    thought communities and, 193
depression, 82, 136, 138, 140
Descartes' Error (Damasio), 55
development. *See* creative growth;
        growth and development
dialogue. *See* discourse
dialogical thinking, 45–50
Diaries (Nin), 78
differences. *See* conflict; diversity
disciplinary complementarity, 40–52,
    126
disciplinary training
    artistic collaboration and, 70–71
    complementarity dimensions of, 126
    science partnerships and, 7, 40
discipline, creativity and, 80, 126
discontinuity, in physical phenomena,
    47–48
discourse
    academic, 99–101, 170–171,
        173–174
    artistic collaboration and, 68, 77, 86

distributed collaboration and,
        197–198
    electronic, 176, 197–198
    intimate partners and, 15–16, 29,
        34–35, 136–137
    as mentoring: families, 29, 153–154,
        156; peers, 179, 183;
        universities, 170–174
    women's collaboration and, 98–101,
        116
discourse communities, 3, 15, 17, 22,
    57, 56, 197
discovery
    in artistic collaboration, 83, 85–86
    in scientific collaboration, 197
    in women's collaboration, 120
discreteness, in nature, 52
dissociation, psychological, of women,
    105, 120
distributed collaboration
    characteristics of, 197–198
    cognitive dynamics of, 192–195
diversity
    artistic collaboration and, 80–81
    emotional dynamics of, 128, 131
    in intimate partners, 12, 14, 17–20,
        33, 39
    professor/student collaborations and,
        170
    in science partnerships, 52–58
    in sibling partnerships, 30–31
    thought communities and, 188,
        191–192
    women's collaboration and, 104–105,
        107, 111
division of labor
    artistic collaboration and, 70–71,
        73–75, 86–87
    as collaboration component, 6,
        197–204
    family partnerships and, 31, 126
    gender differences in, 101, 103–104,
        107–108, 122
    intimate partners and, 12–15, 17, 19,
        24, 32, 87
    mutual appropriation and, 3–4, 79,
        90, 92–96, 199
    domains, disciplinary, 202–203

dominator societies, 108
A Double Singleness (Aaron), 26
Dual Autobiography (Durant and
    Durant), 12
dualism, 55, 100, 102

e-mail discussion groups, 176, 197–198
editing. *See* criticism
educational transformations
    community collaboratives for,
        174–178
    innovative, 165, 173
    professor/student collaborations in,
        164–174
egalitarianism, 84, 89, 107, 144, 173.
        See also equality
electrons, conceptualization of, 43–48
emotional dynamics
    of artistic collaboration, 65, 68,
        74–78, 81–85; in acting,
        88–90
    of collaboration, 6, 8–9, 55,
        123–124
    complementarity of, 124–126,
        130–134
    confidence from, 126–129
    inequality issues in, 142–146
    of intellectual ownership, 142–146
    intimate partners and, 14, 26, 35;
        challenges of, 134–142
    rationality and, 55
    of sibling partnerships, 28, 30, 32
    temperament and, 124–126, 130
    trust issues of, 130–134
emotional growth, 123, 128, 130, 133,
        145–146
emotional scaffolding, 128
emotional zone of proximal
        development, 127–128
empowerment, through collaboration,
        65, 93, 200
enculturation, 152
English-as-a-Second-Language Project,
        183
enhancement. *See* creative growth
enterprise, network of, 66, 88
environmentalism, 102
equality. *See also* egalitarianism
    in collaboration, 7–8
    complementarity and, 40, 132

intellectual ownership and,
        142–146
intimate partners and, 13–15, 18,
        23–24, 35–36
in professor/student collaborations,
        163, 169, 174
*Essays Inspired by "Women's Ways of
        Knowing"* (Belenky, Clinchy,
        Goldberger, Tarule), 118
essentialism, 102, 105
ethics
    in collaboration, 6, 16, 193
    gender differences in, 101, 111, 182
ethnicity
    artistic collaboration and, 82–83
    intergenerational collaboration and,
        169–170, 172–173, 181–185
    intimate partners and, 33–36, 201
    scientific collaboration and, 50–56
    women's collaboration and, 101, 105,
        107–108
exhaustion, artistic collaboration and,
        90
expansion. *See* creative growth
expectations. *See* gender roles
experiences. *See also* childhood
        experiences
    artistic collaboration and, 65–66,
        74
    empowerment through, 200
    gender differences in, 101–104
    in science constructs, 41–46, 46–52
    women's collaboration and, 101–104,
        121
expert/novice interactions, 163, 169,
        174, 180, 201

family collaboration. *See also* intimate
        partnerships
    as apprenticeships, 151–158, 183
    in art, 80–82, 85–92
    characteristic patterns of, 7–8, 36,
        123, 200–203
    emotional dynamics of, 124–126,
        128–129
    in writing careers: sibling, 25–32;
        spousal, 11–25, 32–37
feelings, rationality and, 55
felt knowledge, 55. *See also* emotional
        dynamics

marginality
  adversarial thought and, 99–100
  emotional dynamics of, 126, 128, 144
  intergenerational collaboration on,
    181–184
Martha (Mille), 82
The Mathematical Experience (Davis and
    Hersh), 49
mathematics
  collaboration in, 5–6, 29, 33
  complementarity in, 49–54
  intergenerational collaboration in,
    178–179
  in science constructs, 42–47, 45–51,
    189
maturational theory, of self, 188–189
media, impact of, 104–105
mediation, in collaboration, 56, 72,
    192, 194
Meeting at the Crossroads (Brown), 114
Memories Cast in Stone (Sutton), 157
mental health, gender differences in,
    104–109
mentors and mentoring
  artistic collaboration and, 74, 79, 95
  conflict in, 164, 170, 172, 177–179
  within educational community,
    174–178
  future of, 184–185
  parents as, 151–158
  peer friendships as, 178–184
  professors as, 163–174
  revival of purpose by, 9, 142,
    158–163
  shift to collegial relationships, 152,
    154–161
  single *vs.* multiple, 151, 165–166
  successful components of, 151, 158,
    166, 174, 177
  women as, 119, 128, 134
metaphors
  in artistic collaboration, 92
  in mentor/apprenticeships, 154–155,
    179
  in science constructs, 45–50, 179
  of successful collaboration, 189–191,
    198, 201
  in women's collaboration, 117, 133
Metaphors We Live By (Johnson and
    Lakoff), 179

Mind, Culture and Activity (journal),
    171
Mind over Machine (Dreyfus and
    Dreyfus), 28–29, 127
mindfulness, of actions, 92
modernists, 67, 77, 84
molecular phenomena, 42–48
motivation
  in collaboration, 8, 23, 81, 199
  felt knowledge and, 124, 128
Movements (ballet), 94
Mrs. Leicester's School (Lamb and Lamb),
    26
music
  collaboration in, 4, 35, 87, 95
  mentoring relationships in, 159–163,
    165
  thought communities and, 189–191
mutual appropriation
  in collaboration, 3–4, 79, 90, 199
  interdependence and, 92–96
mutual confirmation, 51, 77
mutuality
  artistic collaboration and, 73, 75, 77,
    83, 85, 90
  dynamics of, 3–5, 8, 132, 191, 196
  interdependence and gender in,
    97–98, 103–109, 122
  intimate partners and, 13–14, 16,
    24–25, 131
  in professor/student collaborations,
    164
  in science partnerships, 48, 50–55,
    61, 73
  in sibling partnerships, 30–32
  women's collaboration and, 97–98,
    109–118

nativist theories, of language, 53–58
naturalistic environments, 171–177
nature/nurture debate, 56, 102
negotiation
  by children, 171
  of conflict, 6–8, 133, 202
  of differences, 6–8
  intimate partners and, 18–19, 131
network of enterprises, 66, 88
novice/expert interactions, 163, 169,
    174, 180, 201
nuclear phenomena, 42–47, 45

nurturance
  artistic collaboration and, 83
  gender roles and, 56, 102–106, 109,
    128
  intimate partners and, 26–27,
    29–30, 37

objectivity, in women's collaboration,
    99–101, 107, 121
oppositional complementarity, 52–59
organizational work
  artistic collaboration and, 90
  intimate partners and, 12, 20, 23–24,
    43
Organizing Genius (Bennis and
    Biederman), 71, 83, 126, 187,
    201
Our Heritage (Durant), 12
Our Own Metaphor (Bateson), 154–155
ownership. *See* intellectual ownership

painting, collaboration in, 64–70, 127,
    151
paradigm shift
  in art, 64–65
  in learning, 170–172
  in physical sciences, 45–50, 51
parent/children relationships
  collegial form of mentoring, 152,
    154–155, 157
  felt knowledge in, 128, 134
  as mentor/apprenticeships,
    151–158
  in writing careers, 25–26, 30
parental loss, sibling partnerships and,
    26–28
participation, transformation of,
    171–172
partnership societies, 108
partnerships. *See also specific type*
  creative, 4–5, 7
  knowledge co-construction by, 3, 7,
    73–74, 189, 203
  patterns of, 196–204
passion
  artistic collaboration and, 80, 82–84
  as collaboration success, 189–190
  intergenerational collaboration and,
    158–163, 183–184
patience, intimate partners and, 35

peer collaboration
  artistic, 70–74
  intergenerational, 178–184
Perestroika (Kushner), 4, 63–64
personal agency, cognition and, 190, 193
personality
  artistic collaboration and, 63, 68, 70,
    79, 90
  intimate partners and, 19–20
  science partnerships and, 7, 40
  as system *vs.* traits, 130, 132
Philosophy in the Flesh (Lakoff and
    Johnson), 179
phonology, 54
physical forces, in science constructs,
    45–46, 55
physical relationships, in science
    constructs, 41–46, 47, 55
physical sciences
  collaboration importance of, 3–4, 6
  complementarity in, 40–52, 52–58,
    125
  intimate partners and, 32–33
  objective thought in, 99–101
play, mentoring through, 30,
    175–177
playfulness, creativity and, 80, 117,
    126
playwriting, collaboration in, 4, 63–64,
    80
  intense patterns of, 87–92
poetry, emotional collaboration and,
    135–143
political climate, of collaboration, 81,
    90, 180, 202
possessiveness, 133
power relations
  artistic collaboration and, 84–85
  intimate partners and, 12–14, 16,
    20, 23, 25, 37
  in professor/student collaborations,
    165–166, 169, 172–173
  social construction of, 6, 128
  women's collaboration and, 100, 108,
    114
Principles of Geology (Lyell), 159
privacy, 133
problem solving, 25
  artistic collaboration and, 80
  as collaborative process, 192–193

problem solving (*continued*)
  intimate partners and, 25
  mentoring programs for, 175
  in physical sciences, 42, 44–50
professional collaborations,
      intergenerational, 178–184
professor/student collaborations
  educational transformation through,
      163–174
  knowledge transmission through,
      163–174
  large-scale projects, 164–165, 170
  as mentor/apprenticeships, 9,
      163–164, 167–168
Project Zero, 165
psychic costs, of intimate partnerships,
      141–142
psychology
  historical basis of, 107
  mentoring relationships in, 164–167,
      172–174
  of women, 105, 109, 112, 120
purpose
  revival through mentoring, 158–163
  thought communities and, 189–190,
      192

Q-sort collaboration tool
  applications of, 23–24, 172, 179, 196
  items of, 7, 205–208
quantum mechanics, 4, 43–48, 46–51,
      56–57, 55

rational thought and behavior
  collaboration and, 92, 99, 101
  emotions and, 55
reality, in artistic collaboration, 80
reciprocity, in mentoring, 166
Reclaiming Cognition (Freeman and
      Nuñez), 179
recognition
  artistic collaboration and, 75, 77, 79
  inequality issues and, 142–146
  intergenerational collaboration and,
      180–181
  intimate partners and, 20, 77, 136,
      139–140, 201
  in professor/student collaborations,
      168–169
  women's collaboration and, 118–119

reconciliation, in sibling partnerships,
      31–32
reductionism, 55, 68
The Reformation (Durant and Durant),
      14
relational-cultural context
  of creativity, 6, 8, 16, 123
  of women's collaboration, 101–103,
      113, 118–119
relativity theory, 41–46
reliance, gender differences in, 101–104,
      106
Renaissance, 13–14, 67, 73, 107
The Renaissance (Durant and Durant),
      13
representational activity
  in artistic collaboration, 64, 67, 72
  cognition and, 5, 193
  in physical sciences, 42, 44–50, 56,
      189
*Rescuers: Portraits of Moral Courage in
      the Holocaust* (Block and
      Drucker), 20–21
resentment, artistic collaboration
      and, 83
respect
  artistic collaboration and, 85, 127
  intimate partners and, 13–14, 16,
      23–25, 127
  science partnerships and, 50
responsibility. *See* division of labor
rewards, artistic collaboration and, 80
rights, gender differences in, 101
risk taking, creativity and, 79, 124
Rodeo (Copland), 162
role expectations. *See* gender roles
role fluidity and flexibility
  in apprenticeships, 152, 154–157,
      175
  artistic collaboration and, 87, 126
  cognitive development and, 171, 175
  as collaboration component,
      197–204
  emotional dynamics of, 87, 126, 145
  women's collaboration and, 114,
      122
role models. *See* mentors and
  mentoring
roles, as collaboration component,
      197–204

scaffolding, 39, 128, 176
Schoolhouse Politics (Bow), 165
science collaboration
    complementarity and, 7–8, 39–44,
        48
    disciplinary training and, 40–52
    family mentoring and, 154–156
    importance of, 3–4
    intimate partners and, 32–33
    models for, 4–6, 40, 54–61
    opposing perspectives and, 52–58
    thought and analysis in, 54–61
    working styles and, 48–56
Scout groups, intergenerational
    collaboration in, 171
self
    contradictions of, 126
    maturational theory of, 188–189
self-assertion
    in apprenticeships, 154–156, 158, 163
    in professor/student collaborations,
        165–166, 169
self-boundaries, thought communities
    and, 190, 193
self-confidence, 200
    artistic collaboration and, 66, 77–79
    intimate partners and, 15–16, 21
self-doubt, 128, 200
self-expansion. *See* creative growth
self-identity
    in artistic collaboration, 73
    intimate partners and, 16, 37
    social construction of, 6, 72, 128, 188
    women's collaboration and, 105,
        120–121
self-in-relation, 79, 105–106
self-knowledge
    role models for, 128, 151, 156
    thought communities and, 188–192
self-presentation, adversarial mode of,
    100
self-reliance
    artistic collaboration and, 83–84
    gender differences in, 104
self-sacrifice, family partnerships and, 26
sensual imagery, in science constructs,
    46–47, 47
sentence completion
    by partners, 48, 180
    by siblings, 29–30

separate knowledge, 6, 101
separation
    in apprenticeships, 155, 157–158
    artistic collaboration and, 68, 78, 82,
        84–85
    family partnerships and, 27–28
    healthy individuation through,
        105–106
    intimate partners and, 14, 21, 24–25,
        129, 140–141
    professor/student collaborations and,
        164, 169
service communities, 100
sexual partners. *See* intimate
    partnerships
shared knowledge, 151, 192–195
Shared Minds (Schrage), 194–195
shared vision
    as collaboration component, 64, 73,
        124, 197–204
    in thought communities, 188–192,
        197
sibling bonds, 26, 31–32, 36
sibling partnerships
    in painting, 74–75, 83
    in writing careers, 25–32, 36
sibling rivalry, 30, 32
*Significant Others: Creativity and
    Intimate Partnerships* (Chadwick
    and de Courtivron), 4, 92, 127
simplification, 55, 82
situated knowledge, 6, 101
skills and skill level
    after-school programs for, 174–178
    in artistic collaboration, 70–71, 74,
        93
    intimate partners and, 19–20, 23–24,
        36
    learning through mentoring, 151–152
    in science collaboration, 48
Snow White and the Seven Dwarfs
    (Disney), 71
social context
    of academic discourse, 99–100,
        170–171
    of artistic collaboration, 70–74
    of growth and development, 6, 37,
        60, 103–105, 128, 187
    of knowledge, 3–6, 35, 37, 99,
        187–188, 192, 203

INDEX OF NAMES

Courtivron, Isabelle de, 4, 15, 92
Craft, Robert, 94
Crawford, Cheryl, 88
Crawford, Ruth, 161
Crick, 4
Csikszentmihalyi, Mihaly
    artistic collaboration and, 71–72, 91
    felt knowledge and, 126, 130, 132
    intergenerational collaboration and,
        164, 166–169, 173
Curie, Irene. *See* Joliot-Curie, Irene
Curie, Jacques, 39
Curie, Marie
    felt knowledge and, 124–125, 130,
        144
    intergenerational collaboration and,
        155, 158, 198
    intimate collaboration and, 32–33,
        36, 39
Curie, Pierre
    felt knowledge and, 124–125, 130,
        144
    intergenerational collaboration and,
        155, 158, 198
    intimate collaboration and, 32–33,
        36, 39

Damasio, Antonio, 55
Damon, William, 13
Dann, Sophie, 26
Dante, Alighieri, 79
Darwin, Charles, 159
Daughaday, William, 48
Davis, Philip J., 49–56, 127, 132, 190
Dean, Christopher, 95
Degas, Edgar, 67, 73
Descartes, René, 99
Dewey, John, 175
DeWitt-Morette, Cecile, 98, 101
Dlugoszewski, Lucia, 83
Dorris, Michael, 33–35, 8236
Drabble, Margaret, 25
Dreyfus, Hubert, 28–32, 36, 126, 132
Dreyfus, Stuart, 28–32, 36, 126
Drucker, Malka, 19–20
Dufy, Raoul, 67
Durant, Ariel, 11–15, 17, 25, 36, 132,
    201

Durant, Will, 11–15, 17, 25, 36, 132,
    201
Dyson, Ann, 47, 70
Dyson, Freeman, 47, 70, 131

Einstein, Albert, 20–21, 131, 143
    scientific collaboration by, 40, 42,
        49–50, 52–58, 196
Eisler, Riane, 108
Elbow, Peter, 98
El Greco, 66
Eliot, T. S., 79–80
Engestrom, Yrjo, 175, 193, 202
Erdrich, Louise, 33–36, 82
Erikson, Erik, 187
Ervin-Tripp, Susan, 181–184
Eustis, Oskar, 64

Feldman, David, 88, 103, 164, 191
Feynman, Richard, 46–51, 70, 154
Fillmore, Lily Wong, 181–184
Fine, Michelle, 81, 110, 114–117,
    131–132, 174
Fischer, Ernst, 72
Fleck, Ludwik, 9, 119, 195–196, 203
Fleisher, Julian, 156
Flynn, Kimberly T., 64
Fokine, Michel, 93
Foote, Daisy, 156
Foote, Hallie, 156
Foote, Horton, 156
Foucault, Michel, 6
Freeman, Walter, 179
Freud, Anna, 26
Freud, Sigmund, 102, 123, 166, 187
Friedrichs, Kurt, 52

Gallimore, Ronald, 158, 185
Gardner, Howard
    artistic collaboration and, 65–66,
        94
    felt knowledge and, 123, 127,
        130–131
    intergenerational collaboration and,
        164–165, 173
Gary, Barbara, 192
Gauguin, Paul, 67
Gerhardt, Julie, 184